D0271145

GOING GLOBAL: IDENTIFYING TRENDS AND DRIVERS OF INTERNATIONAL EDUCATION

GOING GLOBAL: IDENTIFYING TRENDS AND DRIVERS OF INTERNATIONAL EDUCATION

EDITED BY

MARY STIASNY
Institute of Education, University of London, London, UK

TIM GORE
University of London International Programmes, London, UK

United Kingdom – North America – Japan
India – Malaysia – China

Emerald Group Publishing Limited
Howard House, Wagon Lane, Bingley BD16 1WA, UK

First edition 2013

Copyright © 2013 Emerald Group Publishing Limited

Reprints and permission service
Contact: permissions@emeraldinsight.com

No part of this book may be reproduced, stored in a retrieval system, transmitted in any form or by any means electronic, mechanical, photocopying, recording or otherwise without either the prior written permission of the publisher or a licence permitting restricted copying issued in the UK by The Copyright Licensing Agency and in the USA by The Copyright Clearance Center. Any opinions expressed in the chapters are those of the authors. Whilst Emerald makes every effort to ensure the quality and accuracy of its content, Emerald makes no representation implied or otherwise, as to the chapters' suitability and application and disclaims any warranties, express or implied, to their use.

British Library Cataloguing in Publication Data
A catalogue record for this book is available from the British Library

ISBN: 978-1-78190-575-3

ISOQAR certified
Management System,
awarded to Emerald
for adherence to
Environmental
standard
ISO 14001:2004.

ISOQAR
REGISTERED

Certificate Number 1985
ISO 14001

INVESTOR IN PEOPLE

Contents

List of Contributors   ix

Foreword   xiii

Introduction   xv

View from Sir Patrick Stewart   xix

SECTION 1. REGIONAL POLICY TOWARDS INTERNATIONALISATION

1.1. Editors' Introduction to Section 1   3

1.2. New Landmarks in Building Qualitative Education in Kazakhstan   5
Kulyanda Nurasheva and Vera Bondarenko

1.3. Internationalisation of Higher Education in Central Asia:
The Case of Kazakhstan   17
Aida Sagintayeva and Kairat Kurakbayev

1.4. Australian International Education in 2012 — A Focus on
Quality and a Long-Term Strategy   29
Colin Walters

1.5. Higher Education and Building Winning Formulas for the
Knowledge Economy in Pakistan   41
Javaid R. Laghari

1.6. Transnational Higher Education Partnerships: Overcoming
Higher Education Access Barriers and 'Brain Drain' in Greece   55
Vangelis Tsiligiris

1.7. Quality Assurance of Higher Education through Referential
Standards: A Challenge for the Science Council of Japan   69
Kazuo Kitahara

1.8. Internationalisation in Africa: Where to Focus Funding
for Real Impact   75
James Otieno Jowi and Milton Odhiambo Obamba

SECTION 2. INSTITUTIONS AND INTERNATIONALISATION

2.1. Editors' Introduction to Section 2   87

2.2. Perspectives on Internationalisation: Creating an
International Masters of Design   89
Gareth Barham

2.3. Collaborative Reach: A Model for International
Collaborations through Engaging Different Levels
within Partner Institutions   99
Ian Willis

2.4. Malaysia's Twinning Programmes and the Challenge of
Achieving (More) Reciprocal 'International Partnerships'
in the Emerging Global Higher Education System   109
Cameron Richards and Mohd Ismail Abd Aziz

2.5. Going Agile — Agile Methodologies in the Education of
Global Citizens   119
Jasmina Nikolic and Jelena Gledic

2.6. Setting up an Entrepreneurial University — Lessons from
Sri Lanka   129
Chandra J. Embuldeniya

2.7. Do Networks Work?   139
*Tim Gore, Dinos Arcoumanis, Colin B. Grant, Julia Haes,
John Hearn, Alex Hughes and Maurits van Rooijen*

SECTION 3. STUDENTS AND INTERNATIONALISATION

3.1. Editors' Introduction to Section 3   149

3.2. Growing Global Citizens: A Personal Perspective on the Future
      of Transnational Higher Education   151
      Joan K. Stringer

3.3. Transnational Education: Examining and Improving the Student
      Experience   157
      Christine Humfrey

3.4. The Education of Global Citizens in Mexico through
      International Programmes: The Tecnológico De Monterrey Case   167
      Alejandra Ma. Vilalta y Perdomo

3.5. Shaping the Internationalisation of Higher Education through
      Student Mobility: Focus on Malaysia   175
      Mohd Ismail Abd Aziz and Doria Abdullah

3.6. Assessing Student Exchange Programmes: Putting Students
      at the Centre of Internationalisation Efforts   183
      David X. Cheng

3.7. Breaking Down the Borders? Widening Access to Higher
      Education and International Student Mobility   193
      Graeme Atherton

3.8. Internationalisation of African Higher Education:
      Case Studies of Student-Led Initiatives from the
      University of Zambia   201
      Jayasree Anitha Menon

SECTION 4. TRENDS AND INTERNATIONALISATION

4.1. Editors' Introduction to Section 4   211

4.2. Rethinking the Concept of Internationalisation   213
      Hans de Wit

4.3. Rethinking the Internationalisation of Higher Education:
Sharing the Benefits, Avoiding the Adverse Impacts   219
Eva Egron-Polak

4.4. The Future of English in International Higher Education   231
Michael Carrier

4.5. Success in a Post-Disruption Marketplace: Lessons from
Other Sectors   241
Wendy Purcell

4.6. Strategic Implications of the New Economy in Regard to Higher
Education   249
Abe Harraf

4.7. Building Bricks of a New Knowledge World Order?
Implications of the Knowledge Revolution for Building
Winning Strategies in Higher Education   255
Ingo Rollwagen

4.8. Responses to the British Council's *The Shape of
Things to Come: Higher Education Global Trends and
Emerging Opportunities to 2020*   267
Chiao-Ling Chien

4.9. International Trends in Women's Leadership in Higher
Education   279
Louise Morley

What is Changing in Higher Education   299
Janet Ilieva, Michael Peak and Kevin Van-Cauter

About the Authors   309

List of Contributors

Doria Abdullah	Doctoral candidate, Office of International Affairs, University of Technology, Malaysia
Dinos Arcoumanis	Deputy Vice-Chancellor, Research and International, City University London, UK
Graeme Atherton	Head, Access HE, London Higher, UK
Mohd Ismail Abd Aziz	Director, Office of International Affairs, University of Technology, Malaysia
Gareth Barham	Principal Lecturer, Product Design and Director, International Development, Cardiff School of Art and Design, UK
Jo Beall	Director, Education and Society, British Council, UK
Vera Bondarenko	Director of Research, Institute of Education Issues, M. Auzov South Kazakhstan State University, Kazakhstan
Michael Carrier	Head, English Language Innovation, British Council, UK
David X. Cheng	Associate Vice-President, Mainland and External Affairs, City University of Hong Kong, Hong Kong SAR, China
Chiao-Ling Chien	Researcher and Data Analyst, UNESCO Institute for Statistics, Canada
Hans de Wit	Director, Centre for Applied Research in Economics and Management, Amsterdam University of the Sciences, Netherlands

Eva Egron-Polak	Secretary-General, International Association of Universities, France
Chandra J. Embuldeniya	Vice Chancellor, Uva-Wellassa University of Sri Lanka, Sri Lanka
Jelena Gledic	Assistant Professor, University of Belgrade, Serbia
Tim Gore	Director, Global Networks and Communities, University of London International Programmes, UK
Colin B. Grant	Pro-Vice-Chancellor, University of Bath, UK
Julia Haes	Senior Programme Manager, Centre for International Cooperation, Freie Universität Berlin, Germany
Abe Harraf	Professor of Management, Montfort College of Business, University of Colorado, USA
John Hearn	Chief Executive, Worldwide Universities Network, Australia
Alex Hughes	Pro-Vice-Chancellor External, University of Kent, UK
Christine Humfrey	Special Professor, University of Nottingham, UK
Janet Ilieva	Senior Education Advisor, British Council, Hong Kong
James Otieno Jowi	Executive Director and Secretary-General, African Network for Internationalization of Education, Kenya
Kazuo Kitahara	Professor Emeritus, Graduate School of Science Education, Tokyo University of Science, Japan
Kairat Kurakbayev	Educational Manager, Centre for Educational Policy, Nazarbayev University, Kazakhstan
Javaid R. Laghari	Chairperson, Higher Education Commission, Pakistan
Jayasree Anitha Menon	Senior Lecturer, Department of Psychology, University of Zambia, Zambia
Louise Morley	Director, Centre for Higher Education and Equity Research, University of Sussex, UK

Jasmina Nikolic	Higher Education Reform Expert, University of Belgrade, Serbia
Kulyanda Nurasheva	Director, Monitoring and Quality Management Centre, M. Auzov South Kazakhstan State University
Milton Odhiambo Obamba	Research Fellow, Centre for Higher Education Research, Leeds Metropolitan University, UK
Michael Peak	Education Research Manager, British Council, UK
Wendy Purcell	Vice-Chancellor and Chief Executive, Plymouth University
Cameron Richards	Professor of Policy Studies, Perdana School of Science, Technology and Innovation Policy, University of Technology, Malaysia
Ingo Rollwagen	Senior Analyst, Deutsche Bank Research, Germany
Aida Sagintayeva	Director, Centre for Educational Policy, Nazarbayev University, Kazakhstan
Sir Patrick Stewart	Chancellor, University of Huddersfield, UK
Mary Stiasny	Pro-Director, Learning and International, Institute of Education, London, UK
Joan K. Stringer	Principal and Vice-Chancellor, Edinburgh Napier University, UK
Vangelis Tsiligiris	College Principal, MBS College, Greece
Kevin Van-Cauter	Education Adviser, British Council, UK
Maurits van Rooijen	Rector Magnificus and Chief Executive, Nyenrode Business University, Netherlands
Alejandra Ma. Vilalta y Perdomo	Director of Human Capital, Internationalisation and Student Affairs, Tecnologico de Monterrey, Mexico
Colin Walters	Chief Executive Officer, Australian Education National, Canberra, Australia
Ian Willis	Director of Studies, Postgraduate Certificate in Learning and Teaching in Higher Education, University of Liverpool, UK

Foreword

I am delighted to introduce *Going Global: Identifying Trends and Drivers of International Education*. This publication brings together the thinking of global leaders in the field of international tertiary education, each offering unique perspectives and experiences of internationalisation.

The papers included in this publication were presented at Going Global 2012 under the theme 'Changing Education for a Changing World'. Going Global 2012 attracted more than 1000 leaders of international education to discuss and debate current trends and issues.

The British Council is the United Kingdom's cultural relations organisation, working in 110 countries and promoting dialogue and co-operation in a variety of ways. Tertiary education is one such area and Going Global is one such forum. Through it, the British Council offers a platform and convening space for the world's leaders in international education to discuss ideas, debate policy, and share knowledge, research and best practice. Going Global builds on the British Council's network, which includes leaders from governments, national agencies, universities, colleges and industry, and explores how international and cross-border collaboration in the field of tertiary education can shape a better world.

This publication is the second in a series and follows on from the first volume entitled *Going Global: The Landscape for Policy Makers and Practitioners in Tertiary Education*, published in 2012 to bring together papers presented by speakers who contributed to Going Global 2010 in London and Going Global 2011 in Hong Kong.

Information about Going Global conferences is available on our website at http://www.ihe.britishcouncil.org/going-global.

We would like to sincerely thank all of the authors who have contributed to the publication. We would also like to thank our International Steering Committee for their continuous support in developing and delivering our conferences. Lastly, we would like to express our gratitude to the editors, Tim Gore and Dr Mary Stiasny, for their time and dedication in delivering a publication of genuine value and interest to the international education community.

Dr Jo Beall
Director, Education and Society (Executive Board)
British Council

Introduction

The first Going Global conference was held in 2004. The intention was to explore the systems and structures that support and drive global education, and to facilitate the discussion of the role of the private sector in the international delivery of post-secondary education. There was also a wish to enable participants to understand how quality might be maintained — and what role the growth of global English might be playing in this increasingly internationalised sector. A key focus was on the ways institutions internationalise — and the part played by international students. And underpinning the whole was the fundamental commitment to ensure that the needs of developing countries were represented and recognised in the course of aiming to achieve the Millennium Development Goals.

Going Global pulled together practitioners, policy makers and theorists for the first time in the United Kingdom for a hard look at the current state of international education — and to develop a vision for the future. Eight years on, and six Going Global conferences later, there is still a need and a drive to explore these same issues, yet over the years there have been shifts of emphasis and of the awareness of the policy and economic influences.

In 2006, at the second Going Global conference, there was an increased focus on the internationalisation of institutions, with a closer exploration of internationalisation policies, the changing needs and patterns of both demand and funding, and marketing and branding. A second major theme was the international students themselves, and what is considered good practice in meeting their needs — with some thought to the future possible pattern of international mobility.

The changing roles of international professionals was a further key theme, with a sharing of experiences, while the rise of the private sector led this time to a focus on public–private partnerships.

In 2008, the third Going Global conference explored the international flow of knowledge — vitally important to sustain developed knowledge economies and advancing the education systems of emerging economies. The major themes of the conference were: international collaboration and partnership; student mobility and international student recruitment; the role of international education in promoting entrepreneurship; and employability. Clearly, this conference was moving beyond the 'traditional' themes, to look at the purposes served by and the impact of this phenomenon that is internationalised education.

By 2010 Going Global was to become an annual event, and this, the fourth conference, explored the role international education can and does play in a world which is 'increasingly volatile and interconnected'. The world that year had faced major changes in the global economy — and in the global balance of power, and the conference provided a platform for participants to explore how these changes would impact on staff and students, on knowledge exchange and on collaboration over ideas. Those by now familiar themes of: staff and student mobility; global partnership; global citizenship and policy leadership became the focus of the conference, providing opportunities for participants to share and understand the impact of the global changes, and the global context on the individual and the institution.

The next year, in 2011, the world economic situation continued to provide the backdrop for Going Global, and conference delegates were invited to consider 'World Education: The New Powerhouse'. The recognition that 'higher and tertiary education is under huge pressure from world governments to drive economic growth and play a key role in securing their global position' led the conference to explore the 'challenge this presents to the traditional roles of universities and colleges' with the main themes: investing for return, returning the investment; regional education hubs, global aspirations; new purposes, new partnerships; universities and colleges, challenge and change. In other words, the conference was evolving into a dynamic exploration of the close relationship between the economic, political and social structures and education. The recognition of this tightly interwoven interrelationship has been central to the way Going Global has developed, to the role it can play in providing a platform for discussion and opinion formation — and for deeper and more lasting international partnership and dialogue. In other words, this conference has evolved from its role as an observer to a role as a major influencer.

And in 2012 the sixth conference took as its driver the proposition that 'education can change the future of the world'. Participants were challenged to critically appraise and reconsider universities and colleges, their shape, structure and the role they play.

Repeatedly participants were challenged to examine and explore presuppositions and assumptions and to 'get under the skin' of the institutions we so often take for granted because they have strong traditions which are largely unquestioned. Participants were asked to consider the future world, the connected world and the potential winners and losers in a changing global picture. In considering these orientations, participants were asked to look at the ways institutions might wish to reconstruct themselves in order to move beyond their traditional boundaries and the roles they ought to play to contribute to a future connected world. And who might be the key players and partnerships for this future, connected world? And how can these be innovative? Again participants were asked to remember and recognise the vital role public–private partnerships might play, as well as the vital importance of internationalisation and mobility.

Clearly, the underlying themes and concerns remain the same throughout the lifetime of Going Global — internationalisation, staff and student mobility, institutional partnerships and collaborations, public–private partnerships, innovation, knowledge exchange and knowledge economies, development, and the role of global citizens. And the fundamental question about the nature of the relationship between education and its role in an international world has evolved over the eight years. This is a key, if not *the* key relationship. At times the emphasis has been on the way the international context shapes education and its institutions; by 2012 Going Global the emphasis was on the role education must play to shape the future world — and in order to do that, the emphasis was soundly on the vision we must have in order to have such a dynamic impact. Speakers and participants at Going Global in 2012 were challenged to hold a radical vision for the future in order to create this new reality.

This book represents a selection of papers from participants at Going Global 2012. The authors present their thoughts as they shared them at the conference; some papers are views of what the vision might look like; others are practical proposals capable of turning the vision into reality. All of them celebrate the importance of 'challenging education for a challenging world'.

We invite you to share the thoughts and visions of participants of Going Global 2012.

Mary Stiasny and Tim Gore

View from Sir Patrick Stewart ☆

As Chancellor of the University of Huddersfield I was delighted to be involved in the 2012 Going Global conference. You might ask what is my connection to Huddersfield? Well, it is, effectively, my home town university, for I was born and raised just a few miles away. I accepted the position on the proviso that I could be a hands-on Chancellor, spending time at the University, and meeting the students. The global nature of the University has made a deep impression on me and I enjoy meeting young people from all over the world who are determined to fulfil their full potential.

Whatever one thinks about the globalisation of business — and there are persuasive arguments both for and against — it is hard to see the free movement of students around the world as anything other than a positive development. What better way can there be to break down barriers that have been erected by generations of mutual misunderstanding? This can only be good for future world relations, both politically and economically.

I am also astonished at the global collaboration now practised in pushing back the frontiers of knowledge. There is no doubt that the world faces enormous challenges: the balancing of economic growth and environmental concerns, of fairness and equity in life chances and access to resources, of understanding the human condition. And there is no doubt that changes on this scale can only be met if the very best brains and brightest minds are recruited to the task from every nation. More than half of the world's research is now conducted in partnership across national boundaries and the whole process of globalisation supports and powers this.

In order to compete on the global stage universities across the world must ensure that higher education is of the highest possible standard everywhere. To operate in the world, we must all be world class and we must offer all our students exceptional experiences wherever they are studying.

All of our universities are playing a key role in ensuring the future of our higher education systems and our societies. And they are fostering a global outlook among our students whether from home or from overseas. When international students return home, they will retain understanding of their host countries, and they will have left something of themselves and their culture behind. We are truly 'Going Global'.

☆ Edited transcript of Sir Patrick Stewart's speech at the final plenary session of Going Global 2012, London.

SECTION 1
REGIONAL POLICY TOWARDS INTERNATIONALISATION

Chapter 1.1

Editors' Introduction to Section 1

At Going Global 5, held in Hong Kong in 2011, there was a strong focus on the way regional policy and collaboration builds a strength and confidence in response to opportunity and challenge (Stiasny & Gore, 2011[1]). This emphasis has continued, and at Going Global 2012 the theme continued to underpin much of the discussion. It is through regional developments and the building of regional policy that internationalisation is strengthened and, in some cases, encouraged, enabled and supported. We include in this section a selection of papers which explore some outward-looking, regionally focused practice, as well as the rather more isolated practices in other cases. The spread presents the reader with the opportunity for interesting comparisons and gives a picture of the worldwide shifts and developments.

There are two papers from Kazakhstan. Kulyanda Nurasheva and Vera Bondarenko explore the way that Kazakhstan's understanding of the relationship between social values, education and competition between countries has, they claim, given it the edge in Central Asia in implementing education reforms — and the processes necessary in order to build quality in higher education. Aida Sagintayeva and Kairat Kurakbayev look at the changes and stages the education system of Kazakhstan is going through as it emerges from the Soviet era — and internationalises. With one eye on the region of Central Asia and the other on the global context, higher education in Kazakhstan has become an international player.

---

1. Stiasny, M., & Gore, T., (Eds.). (2012). *Going global: The landscape for policy makers and practitioners in tertiary education.* Bingley, UK: Emerald.

Going Global: Identifying Trends and Drivers of International Education
Copyright © 2013 by Emerald Group Publishing Limited
All rights of reproduction in any form reserved
ISBN: 978-1-78190-575-3

The paper by Colin Walters on Australia's international education is an interesting comparison, as it highlights the very singular role Australia plays in the global higher education context. Australia has played a central role in the Regional Convention on the Recognition of Studies, Diplomas and Degrees in Asia and the Pacific, and at the same time has further engaged in co-operation and collaboration internationally.

The role higher education has played in Pakistan has been vital in helping to build and drive a knowledge economy. Javaid R. Laghari makes interesting comparisons with the growth achieved in other countries in the region, concentrating chiefly on Sri Lanka and India.

In Europe, Greece is an interesting case study, having traditionally seen its young people leaving to study in other countries. Vangelis Tsiligiris, with a particular knowledge from Crete, highlights the significance of EU legislation for student mobility, and the importance of the development of transnational higher education in Greece, which has provided an alternative to outbound student mobility.

In Japan there has been an 'universalisation of higher education' says Kazuo Kitahara, and he highlights the global influences (rather than regional ones) and their impact on higher education in Japan.

Finally, James Otieno Jowi and Milton Odhiambo Obamba talk about the way that higher education has expanded in recent years, with internationalisation as one of the strongest influences on Africa's higher education. While each country has its own drivers to build capacity across their knowledge-production infrastructures, there is a clear set of regional collaborative practices which will generate growth in regional capacity and co-operation.

All our authors highlight the clear link between higher education and social, political and economic development, and while some explore the explicit regional links, others maintain the individualism of single contexts. It remains for us to ask whether regional policy is essential to international growth and impact?

Chapter 1.2

New Landmarks in Building Qualitative Education in Kazakhstan

Kulyanda Nurasheva and Vera Bondarenko

Higher Education: Conditions, Problems and Government Regulation

Education is a key indicator of the level of development in all civilised countries of the world. It plays the most important role in the processes determining the basic parameters of society. Countries compete not only in goods and services but also in systems of social values and education. It is the understanding of this that allowed Kazakhstan to be among the first countries in Central Asia to implement reforms in the education system.

A national model of education was developed which included: the creation of a network of innovation and research universities; the formation of a corporate structure; the introduction of wide-ranging autonomy in universities with boards of trustees and supervisory boards; institutional pass procedures and specialised accreditation.

The government increased funding, and measures were taken to raise the competitiveness of higher education. State programmes such as 'Path to Europe' and 'Intellectual Nation' are in operation; human resources training is taking place under a programme of accelerated industrial innovative development in Kazakhstan (RK PAIID) for 2010–2014. The laws 'On Education' and 'On Science' have been adopted. The focus is on the quality of human capital and the enhancement of the instructor's role.

The country's president, Nursultan Nazarbayev, has called for the creation of 100 absolute innovations in the framework within which

Going Global: Identifying Trends and Drivers of International Education
Copyright © 2013 by Emerald Group Publishing Limited
All rights of reproduction in any form reserved
ISBN: 978-1-78190-575-3

scientists and specialists make suggestions for dual-use technology that can be used both for civil and military purposes. Thus education is a catalyst for innovative technology development in various fields of knowledge (Zhumagulov, 2011).

The desire for a radical reform of the education system is reflected in the aims set out in the State Programme of Education Development for 2011–2020 (Ministry of Education and Science of the Republic of Kazakhstan, 2010). The mechanism of state regulation of education is shown in Figure 1. The current global economic crisis has shown that regardless of forms of ownership there must be government regulation of the education system. This provides social protection to a wide proportion of the population and stabilises society.

The fact that higher education is widespread throughout the world is undeniable. However, at this moment Kazakhstan is experiencing difficulties related to the over-saturation of the market by educational institutions. In Kazakhstan, with a population of 16.7 million, there are 143 HEIs, only 51 of which are public. In 2005 the United Kingdom, with a population of 60.2 million there were 115 universities; in Finland per 5.2 million there were 20 HEIs (Korol, 2011; Project EUA, 2005).

There is a 'brain drain', not so much out of the country, but into different businesses. There is a shortage of personnel not only in faculty members, but also in potential teachers and scientists coming from the number of talented students and graduates. The number of students studying scientific

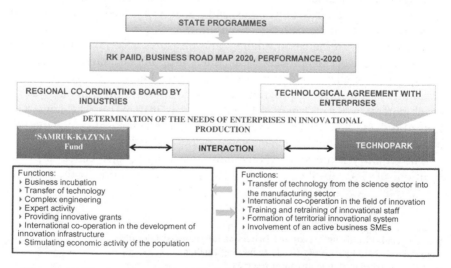

Figure 1: Mechanism of implementation of government programmes.

research and engineering majors is decreasing. This is leading to a slowdown of the scientific and technological development of the economy.

In a move to improve the situation the government has provided substantial financial support for the research and development of innovative universities. They are becoming self-sufficient research centres with a developed infrastructure. Western standards of education, based on the system of academic credits, training of professional personnel in the Bachelor–Master–Doctorate system, with emphasis on the number of masters and doctoral students over the number of students, have been introduced. A national independent system of quality assessment of higher education has been established, and a number of specialties in large universities have been internationally accredited (Figure 2). In short, the success is provided by a concentration of talent, an abundance of resources and effective management.

What is Innovational HEI?

Aligning with the universities that have made scientific and technological breakthroughs in development (High quality higher education — One of the main priorities in the development of the country's competitiveness), M. Auezov South Kazakhstan State University (SKSU) is making efforts to take its place in the global educational sphere.

SKSU is a classic multi-profile university, which in Soviet times prepared engineers for the whole of Central Asia. Scientific schools were therefore developed and it offered studies in unconventional and renewable sources of energy; chemical and metallurgical processing methods of natural and

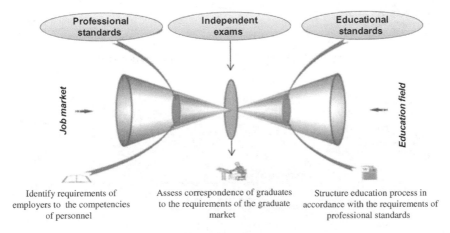

Figure 2: National qualification system.

man-made materials; geo-ecology; health and safety; technology for production of mineral-polymer materials based on natural raw materials; technology for production biological products, dietary supplements, food products; methods of uranium leaching and electrochemical processing of radioactive wastes; manufacturing of potassium, nitrogen and phosphorus-containing fertilisers and salines on the basis of domestic deposits, and more. Research in these areas and implementation of developments today have changed the face of the various industries in the country.

The regional technopark, with the participation of the university, proved to be a positive experience. To promote ideas SKSU created the Office of Commercialization, the Innovation Centre, the Technology Incubator, the Laboratory of Physical-Chemical Methods of Analysis, the Laboratory of Structural and Biochemical Materials (Figure 3). They provide a full cycle of support and the commercialisation of scientific developments.

In these laboratories students, under the guidance of professors, develop new products, technologies, and bring them up to a test sample. Thus the students get acquainted with the full cycle — from idea to product sales. For example, for over 60 years, at the Department of Silicate Technology of the university, there has been a laboratory in which students perform tests and even make samples of ceramic and glass products.

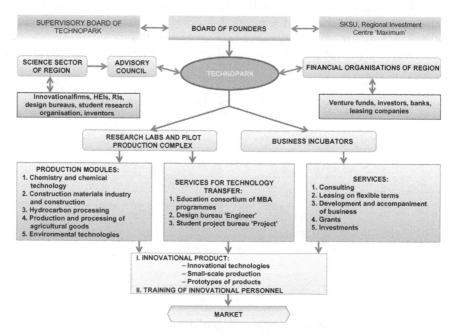

Figure 3: Innovation infrastructure of the university.

This has allowed us to achieve results recognised by the academic environment and all groups of consumers. The quality of the educational programmes is confirmed by the international accreditation agency in Germany, ASIIN. The position of the university has considerably improved in national and global rankings. In the QS ranking SKSU is in 601st place among 2000 universities. In the ranking of the National Agency for Quality Assurance of Education the university is in the top four.

It is clear that a specialist of new formation must possess not only professional knowledge but also be able to freely navigate modern technologies and world market trends, which is why the training programmes are designed to take into account professional and socio-cultural competences (Figure 4).

Since 2004 SKSU has implemented a quality management system based on ISO 9001. After reviewing several models of self-assessment — the model of the European Foundation for Quality Management (EFQM), the Malcolm Baldrige Award, the model of self-assessment according to Herbert Kells, the model of Tito Conti, President of the RK Award 'Altyn Sapa' (Kalanova & Bishimbayev, 2006, p. 476) — we have developed an integrated model of quality of education processes.

This integrated model includes the following framework standards: policy and procedures of quality assurance of work; monitoring and periodic evaluation of educational programmes and qualifications; assessment of students' level of knowledge; quality assurance of teaching staff; material and financial resources; social protection of students; a system of informing the public.

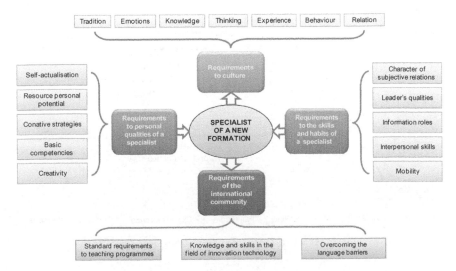

Figure 4: Model of a specialist of new formation.

Quality Management System — Guarantee of Success

This was our first step. Later SKSU realised the dynamics of our development rate and felt the need for institutional changes. Using the criteria of EFQM we saw our strengths and weaknesses and have developed a strategic plan for the university's development for 2011–2015, and revised the mission and quality policy of SKSU.

Modern life prompted the need to create a corporate culture of the university. To do this we used the criteria for a 'successful organisation', of which the most important are development of partnerships with key leaders in the region, and the management of the university as a business.

The ideas of the Bologna Process influenced the development of mechanisms of internal and external evaluation of the HEI activity (Baydenko, 2010).

We developed our own view of the quality assurance system of education. The following key indicators that reflect the quality of work were determined (Figure 5):

- K1: The quality of educational programmes
- K2: The quality of applicants and students
- K3: The quality of science and innovation
- K4: The quality of the methodological and logistical support
- K5: The quality of the staff
- K6: The quality of motivation of the staff

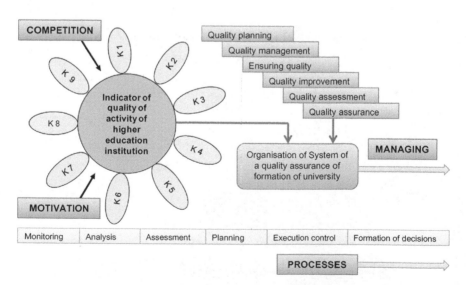

Figure 5: Key indicators of the quality of the university.

- K7: The quality of learning technologies
- K8: The quality of international co-operation and mobility
- K9: The quality of management and growth of the prestige of the university

At SKSU, we have developed education quality assessment criteria that are transparent and objective and which can comprehensively evaluate the whole activity of the HEI. Each criterion is evaluated on 10-point scale and has five levels of excellence. Table 1 shows an example of evaluation of the

Table 1: Criterion 'The leading role of university management'.

Name of criteria	Points
Personal participation of the management of HEI in formation of mission, vision, core values, policy, goals and tasks in the field of quality	10

Levels	Description of levels of excellence of criteria	
1	The management has its own vision of the quality of the working processes and makes necessary decisions. This vision is not widely discussed with personnel. Mission, vision, core values and policy in quality area are not clearly formulated and documented.	1–2
2	The management extends its vision to the personnel of the HEI. Questions of mission, vision, core values and policy in the field of quality are discussed with the personnel.	3–4
3	The management is the initiator of an extensive discussion with the personnel of mission, vision, core values and policy in the field of quality. Information for policy and strategy correction is systematically collected.	5–6
4	For development and updating of strategy and policy all interested parties are involved by the management. Strategy and policy in the field of quality are analysed and improved constantly.	7–8
5	In the HEI functions the complex system of collecting and analysing information about the research and educational activity. Measurable indicators and monitoring methods are determined. Received results are used for amendment of policy and strategy.	9–10

criterion, 'The leading role of university management'. If the university management has its own vision of the quality of the working processes, but the mission, core values and the quality policy are not clearly stated and not documented, this can be the first level of excellence — therefore, 1–2 points. However, if the measurable indicators and monitoring methods of the management system are clearly identified and stated, this can be the fifth level of excellence — therefore, 10 points. The results of this kind of assessment are documented and further used for the correction of SKSU policy and strategy.

It was not easy to achieve significant results. The management system of the university has been continuously improved, following extensive discussions at meetings of the Academic Council, the Co-ordinating Council for Quality and many valuable ideas were put forward. Our success was highlighted in the media; constant monitoring and assessment of the quality of processes were carried out.

Internationalisation: Experience, Further Development

Since Kazakhstan is a multi-religious, multi-cultural country, with over 120 ethnic groups, graduates of HEIs should possess at least three languages, should have good communication skills and should be able to work in a team. Therefore, a multi-language policy has been introduced into the educational process in the Republic. Not many countries of the CIS have developed a multi-language policy at state level. The majority of the post-Soviet republics with a strong bilingualism turned their language policy towards mono-lingualism. In Kazakhstan, the Head of State's initiative — the project 'Unity of Three Languages' has been introduced.

Internationalisation and globalisation give rise to new challenges. Today, more and more international students come to Kazakhstan to study — from Russia, China, Turkey, Afghanistan, Pakistan, Uzbekistan and other Central Asian countries. There are problems of validating foreign certificates of secondary education, which is dealt with by a special department in the Ministry of Education and Science.

In addition, to attend classes with our students, international students need a certain level of knowledge. Our educational programmes are adapted as an extension of secondary education after high school and special vocational education after college, while international students come with various level of knowledge. Therefore, the SKSU aligns the learning trajectory for one to two semesters from the State budget.

Some international students are returned migrants, whose ancestors left the country after the 1917 revolution and lived in other countries during the period of the Soviet Union. They have a good command of the Kazakh literary language, but living for almost a century in another culture, where economics, politics, lifestyle and moral values were markedly different, requires us to provide an individual approach. Some of them, while studying, apply for citizenship of Kazakhstan. The Department of Foreign Students helps them with this matter.

Internationalisation significantly contributes to the social life of the country. Interests of various ethnic groups are expressed by the Assembly of Peoples of Kazakhstan. Congresses of world and traditional religions are held every year. Students keep in touch with their national cultural centres, and most holidays are international. As a result, we not only know about the history and culture of other nations, but also borrow the best practices when conducting research, working in a creative workshop or to solve social problems.

Agreements and memorandums of co-operation are being implemented with 80 universities and research institutes from countries both near and far. For example, the scientists of four countries are involved in a project with a grant from NATO: 'Assessment of pollution of trans-boundary waters in Central Asia'.

Research is being conducted, with a grant of the European Economic Community, into waste utilisation in the phosphoric acid industry through the development of ecologically sustainable and environmentally friendly processes for a wide class of phosphorus.

A joint graduate programme with the Hamburg Graduate School of Applied Sciences (HAW) in Renewable Energy Systems and the Science of Food is being implemented. The SKSU has the right to assign students as ECTNA (European Chemistry Thematic Network Association) — 'Euro undergraduates' — in chemistry and chemical technology. SKSU is a member of European Association of Institutions in Higher Education (EURASHE) and a signatory of the Great Charter of Universities.

In recent years, large-scale funding for a double degree and foreign academic mobility have been launched. The students study abroad for a specific academic period. Many instructors are trained abroad. They absorb best practice and bring to the educational process an element of innovation and creativity.

Higher education is one of those areas that did not create problems when Kazakhstan joined the Customs Union, the Common Economic Space (CES), indicating its internationalism and integration into the global community. However, today there are already differences in the education system. For example, in Russia, there is still a system of training candidates and doctors of science, while our country completely switched to a multi-level system of Bachelor–Master–Doctor (PhD).

It is expected that the accession of Kazakhstan to the WTO will create some problems, because our specialists are low competitive. A closed circle appears: if specialists are low competitive, they generate a low competitive economy. On the other hand, an economy based on raw materials, which the Kazakhstan economy is now, cannot generate high technology or innovation, and it does not need high-order specialists (scientists, engineers, computer programmers, financial analysts). It should be noted that the CIS countries have for many years faced a quiet emigration of young people with higher, engineering or technical education, and they are replaced by immigrants with a low level of education or education that is different from ours and unable to meet demand.

Universities in the countries that have developed in similar socio-political conditions, where there are common problems (e.g. environmental, social), could create associations to research common problems and jointly train specialists. Unfortunately, there are no attempts of even minimal integration in this issue, for example in Central Asia, where in addition to Kazakhstan, there are four more republics. The population of this region is more than 62 million, which provides a big educational market. Currently, contacts are formal in nature; at the level of participation in conferences and publishing papers there is a flow of people entering the educational institutions from the diaspora.

HEIs of different countries should establish close contacts in the academic field in order to seek to align to a worldwide level of education, to accumulate intellectual potential of all world citizens, which could prevent the outbreak of wars, and mass migration. Ultimately, it will create conditions for sustainable development of national economies, improving the welfare of people, and the interpenetration of cultures.

References

Baydenko, V. I. (2010). *The Bologna Process: 2007–2009 between London and Leuven* (Vol. 5, p. 302). Astana, Kazakhstan: Ministry of Education and Science of the Republic of Kazakhstan.

International Institute of Modern Politics. *High quality higher education — One of the main priorities in the development of the country's competitiveness.* Analytical Report, International Institute of Modern Politics, Almaty. Retrieved from http://www.iimp.kz. Accessed on 10 April 2012.

Kalanova, S. M., & Bishimbayev, V. K. (2006). *Quality management in higher education* (p. 476). Astana, Kazakhstan: Foliant.

Korol, D. Y. (2011). *Education system in the republic of Kazakhstan.* Belorussian State University, Minsk, Belarus, Retrieved from http://www.charko.narod.ru. Accessed on 5 April 2012.

Ministry of Education and Science of the Republic of Kazakhstan. (2010, 7 December). *State programme of education development in the Republic of Kazakhstan for 2011–2020.* Astana, Kazakhstan: Ministry of Education and Science of the Republic of Kazakhstan.

Project EUA. (2005). *Developing an internal quality culture in European universities.* Report on the quality culture. Project EUA, Brussels, Belgium.

Zhumagulov, B. T. (2011). Innovation — Into education. *The Country and the World Magazine,* p. 7, 7 November, Almaty, Kazakhstan.

Chapter 1.3

Internationalisation of Higher Education in Central Asia: The Case of Kazakhstan

Aida Sagintayeva and Kairat Kurakbayev

Education in general and higher education in particular has been increasingly understood as a prerequisite for national development and global economic competitiveness. This shared meaning about the role of education can be traced in official documents, speeches and policy briefs in countries across the globe. Both developing and developed countries seem to be in accord about the importance of education for maintaining growth, development and ultimately progress (Moutsious, 2010, p. 121). However, the idea of progress and development, and the sets of policy responses that have been conceptualised to implement this idea in practice, continue to vary across the globe.

This paper discusses the case of Kazakhstan as an emergent post-Soviet country which actively engages with education policies primarily developed in the West (Ball, 1998). The case of gearing the country's higher education internationalisation plans, on both national and institutional levels through legitimating, translating and recontextualising policies, is indeed an interesting case to review as it provides insights into a new array of policy dynamics and transformations of the higher education system at the beginning of the third post-independence decade of a transition economy.

In the regional context of Kazakhstan, the rationales for internationalising higher education are at the same time social, political, economic and academic, as these rationales for driving internationalisation are not mutually exclusive and indeed cross-cutting (Knight, 2004, p. 22). In the case of Kazakhstan, the rationales are based on the idea of nation-building,

Going Global: Identifying Trends and Drivers of International Education
Copyright © 2013 by Emerald Group Publishing Limited
All rights of reproduction in any form reserved
ISBN: 978-1-78190-575-3

national identity of citizens, knowledge production, economic growth and competitiveness, enhancement of quality and international recognition of academic institutions.

From Global to Local: Setting out the Agenda

Over the last 20 years the Central Asian countries of the former Soviet Union have not kept up with the global policy agenda and have each developed their own sets of policy responses and national policy priorities. These policies, which at first shared some common strategies and rhetoric (Silova, 2005) in the last few years have evolved in a rather distinct and separate manner, not yet captured by academic literature.

What is particularly interesting is that all of the five Central Asia republics — Kazakhstan, Kyrgyzstan, Tajikistan, Turkmenistan and Uzbekistan — have faced common issues originating from the same, previously highly standardised and state-controlled education system and each of these countries has come up with different development strategies. As Chapman, Weidman, Cohen, and Mercer (2005) note, 'this created a naturally occurring experiment that allows for an examination of the efficacy of differing policies and implementation strategies' (p. 515). The common element of radical educational reforms in post-Soviet Central Asia is that these countries have embarked on the task of enhancing their education structures where the international dimension of higher education has been part and parcel of the reforms.

We believe that internationalisation not only encompasses opening up study abroad, student mobility programmes and establishing branch campuses but also refers to the institutions' policies receptive to the challenges of modern society. As Knight (2004) points out, 'internationalization is the process of integrating an international, intercultural or global dimension into the purpose, functions or delivery of post-secondary education'.

In this paper we want to outline briefly the government's responses towards academic globalisation and the influence of internationalisation trends on tertiary education policies and structures in Kazakhstan with a special focus on the following developments:

- the impact of the Bologna Process on academic mobility development;
- academic mobility opportunities for students;
- academic mobility opportunities for faculty;
- the Presidential International Scholarship 'Bolashak' and its impact on the human capital development;

- 'Board of Trustees' as a new managerial unit in the higher education structures;
- the role of international faculty in building a research university in the case of Nazarbayev University.

Though internationalisation in higher education is not a new concept on the global scale, as it has been firmly embedded in institutional mission statements, policies, strategies and national policy frameworks (Knight, 2011, p. 14), little research has been done on the impact of internationalisation on the human capital development of fledgling countries, including post-Soviet transition economies such as Kazakhstan.

The Higher Education System of Kazakhstan: Some Key Numbers and Features

The country, one of the fastest-growing economies, has become a leader of educational reforms in Central Asia. Getting independence from the former Soviet Union in 1991, Kazakhstan has made great efforts to gear its higher education system towards the Western academic model over a relatively short period. In 2010 the country officially became part of the European Higher Education Area (EHEA) as a signatory of the Bologna Process. The recent large-scale developments include the privatisation of the higher education sector, strengthening quality assurance mechanisms, implementing a European three-tiered system of Bachelors, Masters and PhD degrees, developing institutional autonomy and academic freedom, introducing initiatives for integrating academia, research and industry, and developing a national qualifications system.

Figure 1 represents the dynamics of academic institutions, which have been fluctuating since independence. During the early post-Soviet period, market relations and the private sector of educational services started to expand dynamically. In 2005, of 181 higher education institutions 130 were private.

The number of private institutions started to diminish as the Ministry implemented tight quality control mechanisms. Currently there are 146 higher education institutions including 73 private, 33 public, 16 institutions with the legal status of joint-stock company, 13 specialised military academic institutions, 9 national academic institutions, 1 international university and Nazarbayev University, the autonomous academic institution which has its own legally independent status enabling it to enjoy institutional, academic and financial autonomy.

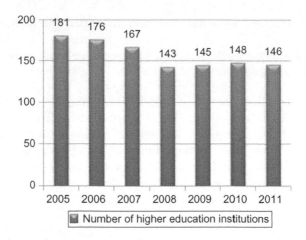

Figure 1: Dynamics of higher education institutions in Kazakhstan.

Over the last two decades, the Ministry of Education and Science has built a firm legislative framework in order to align the education system with internationally recognised trends and reforms. Apart from new laws on education and research development — seven of them having been ratified in 2011 — the State Programme of Education Development for 2011–2020 sets a long-term development strategy for all higher education institutions. One of the ambitious goals of the programme is to diversify higher education structures and grant autonomy to all the institutions by 2018 (State Programme of Education Development for 2011–2020, Astana, 2010).

The State Programme of Education Development for 2011–2020 has introduced a new system of classification for academic institutions:

1. national higher education institutions
2. national research universities
3. research universities
4. universities
5. academies
6. institutes

The concept of 'research university' is a new phenomenon in the Central Asian educational discourse, as the higher education sector has always been expected to train and educate specialists rather than generating research output. The Ministry of Education and Science will examine the R&D strategies of established institutions in order to decide which should be granted research university status and thus receive governmental funding for R&D.

At present the tertiary education population includes 360,894 full-time students (57.3 per cent), 259,531 part-time students (41.2 per cent), 9082 students (1.4 per cent) attending evening schools. The total number of undergraduate students is 629,507 (360,894 full-time students, 259,531 part-time students and 9082 evening-school students). There are 40,531 academic staff (Electronic Government of the Republic of Kazakhstan, 2012).

Figure 2 shows the reduction in undergraduate enrolment in the higher education sector since 2007, due to the demographic situation.

Currently there are about 10,000 Masters candidates, which is only 2.3 per cent of the whole tertiary education population (Woodword, 2011, p. 14). The launch of PhD pilot programmes at two national universities in 2005 resulted in 184 PhD graduates between 2008 and 2010. To date the number of university teachers with Masters degrees is 6057 or 14.9 per cent of the faculty; 473 of academic faculty have PhD degrees or just 1.2 per cent of the teaching staff (Electronic Government of the Republic of Kazakhstan, 2012). As the government strives to increase the academic mobility rate, there is good reason to expand postgraduate education across the nation.

The Impact of the Bologna Process on Academic Mobility Development

One of the milestones of the national policy appropriation towards global trends of internationalisation is the ratification of the Concept of Academic

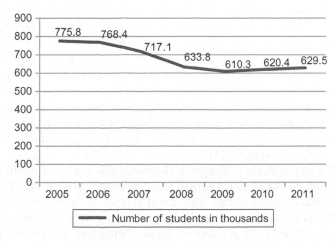

Figure 2: Yearly undergraduate enrolment in higher education institutions.

Mobility, approved by institutional rectors under the supervision of the Ministry of Education and Science in 2011. According to the Concept, the key aim of the policy enactment is integrating the higher education system into the international education area. The key indicator of the Concept is to provide 20 per cent of students with study-abroad experiences between 2011 and 2020. As Kazakhstani academic institutions embark on their way to EHEA, the Concept of Academic Mobility states that all the compulsory terms and conditions of the Bologna Process for academic mobility development will be met by 2020. The structural development of the higher education system over the last 10 years has enabled academic institutions to initiate academic mobility and student exchange.

The official document reflects the educational leaders' understanding of academic mobility as 'the mobility of students, faculty and researchers over a certain period of time within and outside the country intending to study or carry out research with the mandatory transfer of credits according to the established regulations of academic programmes at their home universities' (Ministry of Education and Science of the Republic of Kazakhstan, 2011). Along with the development of legislative frameworks for the policy enactment of the academic mobility, the government is providing financial support to increase the number of incoming students and expanding opportunities for outgoing students.

To establish an effective legislative framework for meeting international standards of academic mobility, the Ministry is about to restructure the National Accreditation Centre into the Centre for the Bologna Process and Academic Mobility. This policy enactment is intended to ensure that the internationalisation and transnational policy-making is on the right track in Kazakhstan (Knight, 2011; Moutsious, 2010). Established in 2005, the current National Accreditation Centre pursues international academic standards and adapts best practices of the European Union and the United States. The Centre is in charge of external evaluation of academic institutions such as licensing, attestation, accreditation, rankings and centralised testing. It is a member of the International Network for Quality Assurance Agencies in Higher Education, the Asia-Pacific Quality Network and the European Association for Quality Assurance in Higher Education (Ministry of Education and Science of the Republic of Kazakhstan, 2011, p. 48; National report on the status and development of education of the Republic of Kazakhstan, 2011).

The Ministry intends to design a Kazakhstani model of credit transfer based on the model of European Credit Transfer System (ECTS). Most institutions have gone ahead and created special units responsible for maintaining alignment of academic programmes with the Bologna Process conventions. By 2011, 28 per cent of higher education institutions adopted the credit transfer process in accordance with the ECTS. It is envisaged that this policy enactment will be fully completed by 2015. Academic mobility has served as a good basis for launching international joint programmes especially at postgraduate level. At present 38 academic institutions implement joint/double-degree programmes.

Academic Mobility Opportunities for Students

To date the Ministry has signed 113 international scholarship agreements with other countries. In order to facilitate the outgoing students' academic mobility, the government has recently signed eight intergovernmental agreements. Within the framework of these agreements, foreign governments grant academic scholarships to Kazakhstani outgoing students, while the Kazakhstani government, in its turn, grants scholarships to foreign nationals. In 2011 according to the intergovernmental agreements, the distribution of outgoing students by country was as follows: 100 scholarships were offered by academic institutions of Russia, 85 scholarships were offered by higher education institutions of Turkey, 47 scholarships for outgoing students were offered by universities of the Arab Republic of Egypt, 27 scholarships were offered by the institutions of the People's Republic of China.

The development of incoming students' mobility has been also taken into account. In 2011, the international scholarship distribution by country was as follows: 5 academic scholarships for incoming students from Kyrgyzstan, 6 scholarships for students from Belorussia, 152 scholarships for students from Afghanistan and 98 scholarships for students from the People's Republic of China.

In 2011, in order to facilitate academic mobility on the postgraduate level, the Ministry allocated US$200 million to send Masters students to foreign universities for short-term study (one term). In order to adopt the Bologna Process more actively, the Ministry has prompted the institutions to send their postgraduate students to study principally at the countries of the European Union. The Ministry is planning to collaborate closely with academic institutions of the European Union as it is expected to allocate around 600 Bachelors and Masters students in 26 European universities. This is likely to be a key step of the Ministry's Eurocentric transnational policy-making in the near future.

In line with the Masters programmes, the development of doctoral education in 2005 fostered academic mobility at a significant pace. The system of doctoral education is based on the Western PhD model. In order to internationalise doctoral education, the Ministry sets dual supervision of doctoral theses by local professor and their international counterpart as a mandatory requirement of the doctoral programme. Enrolling in a PhD programme, a candidate should naturally find their international adviser with shared research interests. The doctoral student's English language competence is crucial as doctoral candidates are requested to publish scholarly papers in English-medium journals. International internships at hosting foreign universities are also a must on the doctoral programmes. At present 29 academic institutions run doctoral programmes. Currently the total number of PhD students is around 200.

The role of international PhD supervisors is hard to overestimate. In 2011 the government allocated US$2.5 billion for foreign PhD faculty recruitment. To date 1647 international PhDs were recruited to Kazakhstani academic institutions. In 2011 the international faculty recruitment plan was approved, which suggested 1493 foreign professors visiting 27 institutions.

Beside the need of international faculty recruitment, universities need international academic expertise in administering and managing PhD programmes so that they can meet international academic standards. Kazakhstan's PhD programmes could be viewed as a policy instrument of national and global competition as doctoral education opens a way to developing research-intensive universities (Marginson, 2006).

Academic Mobility Opportunities for Faculty

Faculty and staff development has always been part of national education development programmes in Kazakhstan. According to the British Council in Kazakhstan, up to 20 per cent of faculty has taken part in professional development internships abroad. More than 25 per cent of academic staff have taken part in research internships and 18 per cent of faculty has been engaged in joint international research projects (Woodword, 2011, p. 14).

At the same time, some challenges remain. International faculty collaboration has been somewhat fragmentary on the institutional level. It is in the interest of senior leaders to systematise institutional internationalisation strategies on the faculty exchange level. English language competence has always been an issue. English language improvement programmes are implemented as the academic globalisation prompts the faculty to engage in international research projects, publish scholarly papers in reputed journals and use English as a medium of instruction in international classrooms. According to the British Council, only 4 per cent of university faculty based in Almaty have a fully operational command of English (Woodword, 2011, p. 14).

Presidential International Scholarship 'Bolashak' and Its Impact on the Human Capital Development

The Presidential International Scholarship 'Bolashak' (meaning 'future' in Kazakh) Programme is worth discussing as it has been developed with the rationale for nation-building and human resources development for Kazakhstani citizens, predominantly the young population. The Programme allows thousands of students to study abroad every year.

According to the statistics data of the Centre for International Programs responsible for supervising the Programme, within the period of 2005–2011, the Bolashak has granted 3379 Bachelors degree scholarships, 3411 Masters degree scholarships and 136 PhD scholarships. The selection of hosting foreign universities is based on the institution's position in global rankings. Among universities of more than 30 countries, 3031 students have chosen British universities, 2287 students US universities, 741 students Russian academic institutions, 323 students German universities and 283 students Canada (Centre for International Programs, 2011).

Apart from the degree programmes, the Bolashak also invests in faculty professional development. Around 300 of academic staff have been offered international non-degree scholarships enabling them to study and engage in joint research at hosting universities.

'Board of Trustees' as a New Managerial Unit in Higher Education Structures

The internationalisation processes have had an impact on institutional structures. In the context of institutional autonomy, the Ministry has decided to adopt the notion of the 'Board of Trustees' and apply it to national-status universities for experimenting and to follow by implementing this policy across all the academic institutions.

The Board of Trustees will be expected to maintain a culture of accountability, creating sound long-term public–private partnership in education management and fund raising. Some institutions attract international experts to sit on their boards, which is also a sign of the senior leaders' need for international advice in the field of higher education management (Altbach & Salmi, 2012). The practice of recruiting international advisers to the rectors is highly likely to become common in the near future.

The Role of International Faculty in Building a Research University: The Case of Nazarbayev University

Officially opened on 28 June 2010, Nazarbayev University is the government's initiative to build a 'world-class' university. It is intended to be a flagship university in Kazakhstan, internationally competitive on the global scale. It was envisioned by the Ministry of Education and Science that the newly built Nazarbayev University would serve as a model of a research university whose management experience could be then adapted by other established local institutions.

Pursuing the idea of developing international community of practice, the University has signed partnership contracts with prestigious foreign universities including University College London, the University of Cambridge, the University of Pennsylvania, Wisconsin-Madison University, Duke University, Harvard Medical School and the National University of Singapore. The partnership schemes have a compartmentalised view of collaboration as each school of the University has its own partner. It is envisaged that the international faculty collaborating with the local faculty as well as local young scholars, predominantly holders of the Bolashak Scholarship, will form an academic community of practice which in its turn will facilitate a research-active environment at the University.

Summary

This paper has briefly outlined the sets of internationalisation policies implemented at national and institutional levels of Kazakhstan. The internationalisation of higher education in Kazakhstan has just started to gain momentum. The rationales for internationalisation processes vary. Economic growth and predominantly nation-building and national social identity development are highly likely to be important. The government's resources allocation and financial support have been instrumental. Kazakhstan will actively pursue transnational policy-making with Eurocentric perspectives. The universities will continue to seek qualified international faculty and develop scholarship programmes for incoming and outgoing students. We believe there is great scope to further research on the economic, social, cultural and political consequences of the internationalisation of higher education in Central Asia. In the case of Kazakhstan, the long-term processes of aligning academic programmes with the EHEA, clear internationalisation strategies on the institutional level, development of the faculty's English language competence, increasing the number of inbound

English-speaking students on campus and internationalising the postgraduate education sector are yet to be developed further.

References

Altbach, P., & Salmi, J. (2012). What international advice do universities need? *International Higher Education, 67,* 11–12.

Ball, S. (1998). Big policies/Small World: An introduction to international perspectives in educational policy. *Comparative Education, 34*(2), 119–130.

Centre for International Programs, Bolashak Programme. (2011). *Statistics report on 1994–2011.* Retrieved from http://www.edu-cip.kz/Media/Default/HtmlWidget/Articles/statistika2012new.pdf. Accessed on 7 June 2012.

Chapman, D., Weidman, J., Cohen, M., & Mercer, M. (2005). The search for quality: A five country study of national strategies to improve educational quality in Central Asia. *International Journal of Educational Development, 25,* 514–530.

Electronic Government of the Republic of Kazakhstan. (2012). *Higher education institutions of the Republic of Kazakhstan in the 2011/2012 academic year.* Retrieved from http://egov.kz/wps/portal/Content?contentPath=/library2/obrazovanie/obrazovanie/article/post_heis1112&lang=en. Accessed on 25 September 2012.

Knight, J. (2004). Internationalization remodeled: Definitions, approaches and rationales. *Journal of Studies in International Education, 8*(1), 5–31.

Knight, J. (2011). Five myths about internationalization. *International Higher Education, 62,* 14–15.

Marginson, S. (2006). Dynamics of national and global competition in higher education. *Higher Education, 52,* 1–39.

Ministry of Education and Science of the Republic of Kazakhstan. (2010). *State programme of education development for 2011–2020.* Astana: Ministry of Education and Science of the Republic of Kazakhstan.

Ministry of Education and Science of the Republic of Kazakhstan. (2011). *Concept of academic mobility of students at higher education institutions of the Republic of Kazakhstan.* Astana: Board of University Rectors.

Moutsious, S. (2010). Power, politics and transnational policy-making in education. *Globalisation, Societies and Education, 8*(1), 121–141.

National report on the status and development of education of the Republic of Kazakhstan. (2011). Astana: Ministry of Education and Science of the Republic of Kazakhstan.

Silova, I. (2005). Traveling policies: Hijacked in Central Asia. *European Educational Research Journal, 4*(1), 50–59.

Woodword, D. (2011). *Collaboration between Kazakhstan and the United Kingdom in higher education — Inspire project.* Almaty: Luxe Media Group.

Chapter 1.4

Australian International Education in 2012 — A Focus on Quality and a Long-Term Strategy

Colin Walters

By the middle of 2012 the Australian Government will have completed the development and implementation of a three-year reform programme in support of the quality, integrity and sustainability of Australian international education.

The Government's reform programme was initiated in response to the record growth in student enrolments in the second half of the last decade and a number of resulting issues that directly and indirectly impacted on the sustainability of the Australian international education sector. In 2009 Australia recorded 630,663 international student enrolments — an effective doubling of the numbers recorded in 2004. While there has been a fall in overseas student enrolments since 2009, the 557,425 enrolments recorded in 2011 are still among the highest on record (Figure 1).

The last three decades have seen Australia develop into one of the world's most prominent international education destinations. Australian institutions deliver onshore education services to half a million international students annually. Seven per cent of the world's tertiary students who study away from their home countries study in Australia (Organisation for Economic Cooperation and Development [OECD], 2011). The international student population at our 39 universities currently stands at 21.5 per cent, which is the highest proportion of international students in any higher education system (Organisation for Economic Cooperation and Development

Going Global: Identifying Trends and Drivers of International Education
Copyright © 2013 by Emerald Group Publishing Limited
All rights of reproduction in any form reserved
ISBN: 978-1-78190-575-3

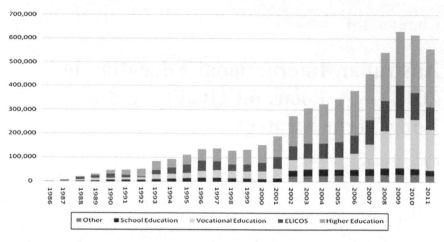

Figure 1: International student enrolments by sector: 1986–2011.

[OECD], 2011). In the financial year 2010–2011 international education contributed more than A\$16 billion to the Australian economy and was estimated to support more than 100,000 jobs (Australian Education International [AEI], 2011a).

With its important reform programme bedded down, the Government will re-focus its efforts onto the development of a long-term strategy for Australian international education. To help inform the Government's development of the strategy, an International Education Advisory Council has been set up, chaired by Michael Chaney AO, Chairman of the National Australia Bank and Chancellor of the University of Western Australia, comprising eminent people from Australia's education and business sectors.

Supporting and Protecting Students

In hindsight, much of the growth between 2006 and 2009 can be attributed to the expansion of the private vocational education and training (VET) sector and a perception that a VET course would lead to a successful migration outcome. Annual growth rates in VET student enrolments reached 45 per cent annually in 2007 and 2008, which was clearly unsustainable. While Australia has a well-regarded VET sector with many international students coming to Australia to learn advanced practical skills, unfortunately, at that time, some providers encouraged students to enrol in vocational courses as an easy route to seeking Australian permanent residency.

As a first step in lifting the bar for the delivery of education services, the Australian Government made it a requirement that all providers of international education in Australia undergo a rigorous re-registration process by 31 December 2010.

Each institution delivering education to international students was required to demonstrate that education was their principal purpose for operating and that they had the capacity to deliver education services to the required standard. At the completion of this process, 1100 providers met the criteria, while some 200 providers left the system.

In 1991 the Australian Government introduced protections for international students into law. A pioneering development of its time, the Education Services for Overseas Students Act 1991 (the ESOS Act) underpinned the growth of the emerging international student sector over the following years.

The ESOS legislation protects the interests of overseas students by setting minimum standards for the delivery of education services, providing tuition and financial assurance and protecting Australia's reputation for delivering quality education services. In light of the rapid growth in student numbers, the ESOS Act was the subject of a major review in 2009. The review conducted by the Hon. Bruce Baird AM investigated the currency and suitability of the legislation to support a sector delivering education services to half a million students annually.

The Baird Review Report was delivered to the Government in February 2010 and considered the need for enhancements to the ESOS Act's legal framework in four key areas:

- supporting the interests of students
- delivering quality as the cornerstone of Australian education
- effective regulation
- ensuring the sustainability of the international education sector.

In response to the review, the Australian Government has introduced two major sets of legislative amendments into Parliament. The first round of legislative change was enacted in April 2011 with a focus on strengthening registration, risk management, enforcement options and complaints handling. A particularly important outcome for students was the creation of the Overseas Students Ombudsman. The Overseas Students Ombudsman is a free, independent and impartial service that investigates complaints that current or intending students may have with private education and training providers in Australia.

A second set of legislative amendments was passed by the Parliament on 1 March 2012. The legislation will be implemented from 1 July 2012. The centrepiece of the changes is the Tuition Protection Service (TPS). The TPS will assist students who have been affected by the closure of an education provider to transfer to a new provider of their choice in a timely way or, as a last resort, refund students the unused portion of their prepaid tuition fees. The TPS will be a single point of contact for students using the latest technology. It will offer students greater choice and control in the placement process. In addition, the legislation introduces limits on the amount of upfront fees a provider can collect from students and further protects tuition fees paid before the student starts a course (Australian Education International [AEI], 2012).

Ensuring Visa Integrity and Streamlining Entry Requirements

In 2009 the Australian Government implemented wide-ranging changes to visa arrangements that explicitly decoupled the linkages between permanent migration and student visas. Australia's skilled migration programme is solely focused on attracting the people and skills most in demand in Australia's expanding economy. The skills in demand change over time and are independent of the subjects and courses international students study in Australia. The reforms included measures aimed at strengthening and protecting the integrity of the student visa system against people seeking to exploit the student visa pathway.

Building on the 2009 measures, a major review of the student visa programme was commissioned in December 2010 to consider the integrity of the student visa programme and to review the requirements for student visa applicants. The Hon. Michael Knight AO reported the findings of his strategic review of the student visa programme to the Government in June 2011. The Australian Government responded in September 2011, supporting in principle all 41 of the report's recommendations (Department of Immigration and Citizenship [DIAC], 2011).

Streamlined visa processing is a key measure of the Government's response and was made available on 24 March 2012. It treats all student visa applicants for study at bachelor or higher level courses at universities, irrespective of their country of origin, as a low migration risk. This means a less onerous process for these applicants. This measure recognises that the Australian university sector has a track record of providing high-quality international education with low levels of risk. The Government has also taken steps to support the competitiveness of the VET sector by reducing the financial requirements for students based in countries assessed as higher risk for migration purposes.

Students undertaking a higher degree by research will especially benefit from these measures as it will become more attractive for these students to study in Australia through streamlined processing of their visas, access to a three-year or four-year post-study work visa, unlimited work rights during study and the prospect of a six-month visa extension for the purpose of interactive marking of their thesis.

A Sustainable Future

The reforms outlined above are evidence of Australia's commitment to a high-quality positive international education experience. The reputation and integrity of Australia's education system can only be enhanced by the way governments, systems and institutions have embraced these reforms.

The Australian Government has a tradition of working with international partners in education, science and research, bi-laterally and in multilateral forums such as Asia-Pacific Economic Cooperation (APEC), the OECD, United Nations Educational Scientific and Cultural Organisation (UNESCO), and the European Union.

The benefits of participation in these forums include increased cross-border investment, regional economic integration, greater quality and diversity of education provisions, the transfer of ideas, technologies and cultural understandings and people to people business, research and cultural links that help to keep Australia at the forefront internationally.

International Co-operation and Collaboration

The Australian Government became a party to the 1997 UNESCO Convention on the Recognition of Qualifications concerning Higher Education in the European Region (Lisbon Recognition Convention) in 2002. An obligation of the Lisbon Recognition Convention is the establishment of an Australian Government National Information Centre (NIC). The NIC supports international co-operation and mobility through the provision of expert advice on the recognition of qualifications, including information about the Australian higher education system and the educational level of overseas qualifications against the Australian Qualifications Framework.

In recognition of the key role the Lisbon Convention has played in supporting mobility and linkages across and beyond Europe, Australia has played a lead role in the revision of the 1983 UNESCO Regional Convention on the Recognition of Studies, Diplomas and Degrees in Higher Education in Asia and the Pacific (Regional Convention).

Australia became a party to the Regional Convention in 1985. The Regional Convention has been revised to take account of developments in the higher education sector since its inception and to support current and future international mobility needs across the Asia-Pacific region. Clear articulation of qualifications recognition principles will be supported by the development and maintenance of government-authorised NICs across the region, as well as advocating the use of good practice recognition tools such as the UNESCO Diploma Supplement and UNESCO/OECD Guidelines for Quality Provision in Cross-Border Higher Education. The Australian Government has already implemented key measures advocated by the revised Regional Convention, specifically the establishment of an NIC and adoption of the UNESCO Diploma Supplement, which is issued across the Australian higher education sector. The Australian Government will commence the process for ratifying the revised Regional Convention upon UNESCO's release of the final text.

Australia has played a very active role in an international roundtable forum to discuss and progress solutions around policies and arrangements that support the integrity of international education, including the effectiveness of regulatory systems, student visa arrangements, student welfare and the overall student experience. This roundtable comprises representatives from six English-speaking countries that collectively host more than 42 per cent of the world's international higher education students[1] (Organisation for Economic Cooperation and Development [OECD], 2011). A statement of principles for the ethical recruitment of international students by education consultants and agents has been completed and released this year.

Bilateral Engagement

Australia also engages bilaterally, most notably in the Asia-Pacific region, by entering into partnerships and agreements with other countries, bringing together governments, industry, institutions and students. These partnerships go beyond student numbers leading to strategic and strong collaborative relationships.

This builds on the reforms and experience to date and represents the third wave of international education engagement. Examples of successful educational engagement in India and China demonstrate the strength of these relationships.

---

1. The members are Australia, Canada, Ireland, New Zealand, the United Kingdom and the United States.

Australia–India Collaboration

The Australia India Education Council

The Australia India Education Council (AIEC), established in 2010 to expand bi-lateral collaboration in education, training and research, provides a forum for senior representatives from academia, industry and government to jointly develop strategic advice and shape collaborative efforts. The AIEC will focus on institutional collaboration, student mobility, skills, quality assurance and research.[2] The August 2011 inaugural meeting in New Delhi was co-chaired by the Australian Minister for Tertiary Education, Skills, Science and Research, Senator the Hon. Chris Evans and the Indian Minister for Human Resource Development, the Hon. Kapil Sibal. The AIEC will meet annually in conjunction with the annual India–Australia Ministerial Dialogue on Education Cooperation.

GMR Group — customising training courses for industry

GMR Group (GMR) is one of the fastest growing infrastructure enterprises in India with interests in the airports, energy, highways and urban infrastructure sectors. In 2009 GMR partnered with Holmesglen Institute of Technical and Further Education (TAFE) to establish a commercial project to increase the skills of GMR's construction workers. The project brings together one of India's foremost infrastructure conglomerates and one of Australia's leading technical and further education institutions to establish a unique workforce development initiative. A Skills Development Institute (SDI) has been established at GMR's Hyderabad Airport with Holmesglen consulting on learning resource development, design of classroom and practical learning environments, procurement of consumables, tools and equipment and administrative systems. Together they have trained over 120 of GMR's site supervisors. These 'master trainers' are working across GMR's infrastructure projects delivering skills training and coaching to onsite workers in carpentry, formwork and brick and block laying.

The project has resulted in increased workforce productivity and provided excellent professional development opportunities for Holmesglen staff. High levels of camaraderie have been established between teaching and management staff in both organisations. The mutual

---

2. For further information about the AIEC please visit www.australiaindiaeducation.com

benefits of collaboration have established a solid foundation for future development projects. It is anticipated that a new Master Trainer programme in civil construction will be designed and a potential study tour to Holmesglen for existing master trainers will extend their capacities to develop a skilled workforce at GMR.

Australia–China Collaboration

The Australia–China University Leaders Forum

To celebrate 40 years of diplomatic relations between Australia and China, and building on the strong history of institutional collaboration, Universities Australia, the Department of Industry, Innovation, Science, Research and Tertiary Education, and the Chinese Ministry of Education are partnering to host the Australia–China University Leaders Forum in Canberra, Australia, 26–27 November 2012. Entitled 'Celebrating 40 years of engagement — The future of Australia–China education collaboration', the two-day forum will showcase the history of successful education collaboration between Australia and China and explore possibilities for future collaboration.

Case Study — The China–Australia Executive Leadership Program

Established in 1999, the China–Australia Executive Leadership Program (CAELP) has seen almost 100 university leaders from Australia and China travel to universities in each other's countries to understand the management practices of the host university. The Australian Government provided funding for the first three cohorts of the programme, which is managed by Universities Australia (UA) and their counterpart agency the China Education Association for International Exchange (CEAIE).

A hugely successful programme, the CAELP has contributed towards significant linkages between Australian and Chinese universities, and has produced a number of prominent alumni. It has formed a cornerstone of the strong relationship between UA and CEAIE, generating ongoing institutional linkages and associated collaboration.

The Future — A New Advisory and Strategic Framework

In October 2011, the Minister for Tertiary Education, Skills, Science and Research, Senator the Hon. Chris Evans, announced the establishment of the International Education Advisory Council. The Advisory Council will provide high-level advice about how the Government can, in partnership with stakeholders, encourage quality and sustainability in the international education sector.

The Advisory Council will initially provide feedback on trends in international education and on current and proposed policies affecting the sector. In the longer term, the deliberations of the Council will help inform the Government's development of a five-year national strategy to support the sustainability and quality of the international education sector.

Complementing the current programme to reform Australian international education was the strategic redirection in late 2011 by the Australian Government which brought together international education and higher education with innovation, science and research through the creation of the Department of Industry, Innovation, Science, Research and Tertiary Education. In addition, 2011 saw the creation of two new regulatory bodies that on 1 July 2012 took full control of the responsibility for the registration, compliance monitoring and enforcement of international education providers. The Australian Skills Quality Authority (ASQA) is the national regulator for Australia's VET sector while the Tertiary Education Quality and Standards Agency (TEQSA) has become Australia's regulatory and quality agency for higher education.[3] The establishment of the two national regulators will play a vital role in strengthening regulatory activities in relation to international education across Australia.

The Student in Focus

International students expect that the quality of their education will be high and that it will form the basis of a successful career. International students' non-academic needs also have to be supported including by local government, cultural, community and professional networks.

In 2010 all Australian states and territories and the Australian Government launched a range of initiatives aimed at supporting these needs under the auspices of the International Students Strategy for Australia (ISSA). The ISSA focuses on four action areas: student wellbeing; quality of education; consumer protection; and better information. An annual report on progress has recently been prepared for the Council of Australian Governments (COAG) and substantial progress has been made in all four action areas.[4]

---

3. For more information, please visit www.asqa.gov.au and www.teqsa.gov.au
4. For more information about the ISSA, please visit www.coag.gov.au

Australia is committed to monitoring the views of international students about their experiences. The results of the 2010 Australian International Student Survey of 50,000 international students were published in December 2010. The survey showed that 84 per cent of international university students were satisfied with their study experience and 86 per cent were satisfied with their living experience. More than 85 per cent were satisfied with the level of support they received on arrival, confirming Australia's reputation as a country that welcomes international students.

The top four factors that influenced tertiary students' decisions to study in Australia were the quality of teaching (94 per cent), the reputation of the qualification (93 per cent), personal safety (92 per cent) and the reputation of the institution (91 per cent). The 2012 Australian International Student Survey will be conducted later this year and will help us better understand the challenges and demands international students currently face.

Students' high rating of Australia as a destination for international education was supported by a recent study that saw Australia's two biggest cities, Melbourne and Sydney, ranked in the top six of the world's best student cities. Overall, five Australian student cities were ranked in the top 30 (Quacquarelli Symonds, 2012).

The Government also learns about how international students are faring through the annual international student roundtable, where international student representatives meet with legislators and regulators to discuss the challenges and opportunities that impact on their study and living experience.

The second International Student Roundtable, convened in Canberra in August 2011, brought together 30 international students from 18 countries. The roundtable presented a communiqué to the Government with recommendations in five key areas: the education experience; social inclusion; cost of living pressures; safety and welfare; and visa related matters. The communiqué was presented to COAG in the context of its annual review of the International Students Strategy for Australia (Australian Education International [AEI], 2011b).

In Conclusion

International education is an important part of the Australian economy and acts as an enabler for Australia's extensive co-operation and collaboration with the world's leading knowledge nations, institutions, academics and students. International education builds links and relationships with leaders in politics, industry, trade and education.

The Australian international education sector saw its reputation for quality and integrity challenged by the period of rapid expansion in enrolments at the end of the last decade. The passage of legislation on 1 March 2012 to implement the final set of legislative amendments in response to the Baird Review marks the end of a period of intensive reform. In the words of Mr Baird himself, we now have a 'stronger, simpler and smarter' framework to support the sector.

The reform package, now in place, demonstrates Australia's commitment to a high-quality international education sector. We believe it is important to remain focused on quality and sustainability and to pursue these goals with other like-minded governments and agencies. To this end Australia is working through its strategic partnerships with the British Council, the European Commission, and through European and regional networks, to promote and ensure that the reputation and integrity of international education continues to be held in high regard.

International education has an important and strategic role to play in our economies, our societies and our relationships and it is important that we maintain and sustain the health, the quality and integrity of the sector.

With the reform programme having laid down the basis for a sustainable sector and the appointment of the International Education Advisory Council, the development and implementation of a new strategic plan will guide the future direction of Australian international education.

We believe Australia is well placed for the third wave of international education engagement.

References

Australian Education International (AEI). (2011a). *Research snapshots: Export income to Australia from education services in 2010-11* (Table of statistics). Canberra. Retrieved from http://www.aei.gov.au/research/Research-Snapshots/Documents/Export%20Income%202010-11.pdf

Australian Education International (AEI). (2011b). 2011 International Student Roundtable Communiqué released. Canberra. Retrieved from http://www.aei.gov.au/News/Latest-News/Pages/Article-Releaseofthesecondinternationalstudentroundtablecommuniqu%C3%A9.aspx

Australian Education International (AEI). (2012). *ESOS legislative framework*. Canberra. Retrieved from http://www.aei.gov.au/REGULATORY-INFORMATION/Pages/Regulatoryinformation.aspx

Department of Immigration and Citizenship (DIAC). (2011). *Implementation of the government response to the knight review of the student visa program*. Canberra. Retrieved from http://www.immi.gov.au/students/knight/

Organisation of Economic Cooperation and Development (OECD). (2011). *Education at a glance 2011* (pp. 322–333).

Quacquarelli Symonds. (2012). *Best studies cities in the world 2012 ranking* (web page). Retrieved from http://www.topuniversities.com/student-life/best-student-cities/2012/

Chapter 1.5

Higher Education and Building Winning Formulas for the Knowledge Economy in Pakistan

Javaid R. Laghari

The World Bank has identified education and skilled workforce, information and communication technologies, and innovation as three of the four pillars of the knowledge economy (World Bank, 2011). Similarly, the World Economic Forum Global Competitiveness Report (2011–2012) has identified 12 pillars for the development of a knowledge economy. These pillars include higher education and training, technology readiness, and innovation. Innovation covers research, creativity, inventing new technologies and processes; however, in developing countries it can also mean adopting technologies and processes that have already been developed elsewhere but are new to the local industry.

Universities are the most important producers of knowledge and research that can lead to innovation and entrepreneurship, and can be prime builders of a knowledge economy. In developing countries, there has been a slow and gradual shift in the role of higher education institutions in building up knowledge economies. Socio-economic transformation is led by a change from the traditional role of universities from imparting and creating knowledge to their new role of innovation and entrepreneurship as depicted in Figure 1.

Going Global: Identifying Trends and Drivers of International Education
Copyright © 2013 by Emerald Group Publishing Limited
All rights of reproduction in any form reserved
ISBN: 978-1-78190-575-3

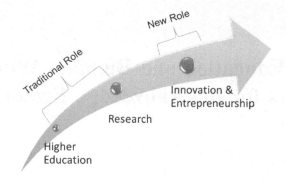

Figure 1: Shifting role of higher education institutions.

Developing societies should bridge the missing gap from higher education and research to innovation and entrepreneurship. Building this bridge is therefore among the key winning formulas in creating a knowledge economy in developing countries.

In Pakistan, the Higher Education Commission (HEC) is currently focusing on building a knowledge economy. The mission of the HEC is to 'serve as an engine for the socio-economic development of Pakistan'. The strategic thrusts of the HEC towards building this knowledge economy include the following: excellence in higher education, technology readiness, focus on research and innovation, spirit of entrepreneurship, global perspective, and socio-economic impact (HEC, 2011–2015).

Higher education is clearly linked to knowledge economy, and the relationship is demonstrated in Figure 2. It can be seen that the economic prosperity of a country, or its GDP per capita, is directly related to the higher education enrolment per capita. As evident from the figure, countries which have the highest enrolment densities in higher education enjoy the highest GDP per capita, and therefore are prosperous and developed. Visible examples of knowledge economies are Finland, Denmark, Ireland, Iceland and Switzerland. On the other hand, countries that have the lowest higher education enrolment per capita are the least economically prosperous and the least developed. These include countries in sub-Saharan Africa and South Asia. It is therefore evident, as indicated by the World Bank and the World Economic Forum, that to increase prosperity, there is a definite need to increase accessibility to quality higher education, for it is initially this increase that forms the basis to innovation and research, to entrepreneurship and therefore to an upward economic mobility. Higher education and skills development therefore essentially form the first and key pillar of a knowledge economy.

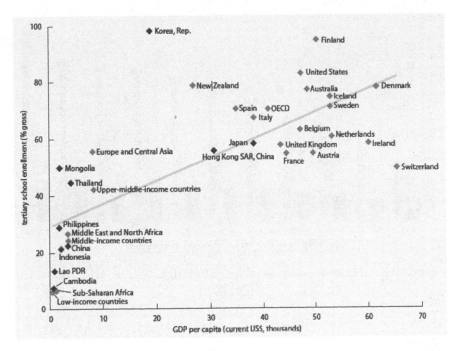

Figure 2: Higher education enrolment and GDP. *Source*: World Bank (2010).

First Pillar: Higher Education and Training

There has been a considerable growth in accessibility to higher education, and in the number of higher education institutes (HEIs) in Pakistan, under the HEC. In the last 11 years, the number of universities in Pakistan has increased from 59 to 134. If the campuses and sub-campuses of these universities are included, then the growth is from 116 to 295, as can be seen in Figure 3. As a consequence, there has been phenomenal increase in the enrolment at HEIs. Since 2001, there has been a fourfold increase in enrolment from 276,000 to over one million, as shown in Figure 4. If two-year colleges are also included, then the enrolment is around 1.5 million.

The enrolment trends in three South Asian countries: Pakistan, India and Sri Lanka, are shown in Figure 5. It can be seen that higher education enrolment in Pakistan has increased at a much faster pace over the last eight years as compared to its two neighbours. However, this growth is not enough, and Pakistan needs to further increase its accessibility to higher education by at least twice by 2020 as per its National Education Policy, 2009.

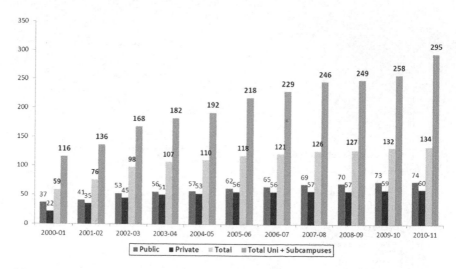

Figure 3: Establishment of universities in Pakistan. *Source*: HEC, Statistics (2012).

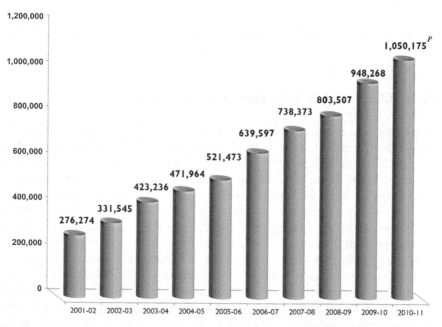

Figure 4: University enrolment in Pakistan. *Source*: HEC, Statistics (2012).

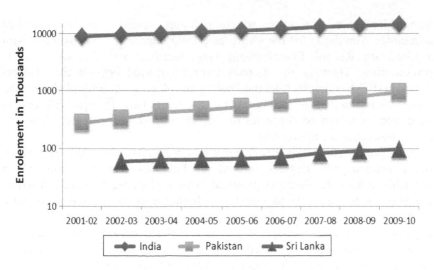

Figure 5: Enrolment trends in HEIs. *Source*: Annual Reports of UGC, India, Sri Lanka and HEC, Pakistan (2011).

However, an increase in accessibility alone is not sufficient and does not make up the first pillar for knowledge economy unless it is on a solid foundation, and this foundation is quality. Also, producing more graduates will only create unemployment unless the other parameters of knowledge economy relating to higher education, such as creating employment through innovation and entrepreneurship, or reforms carried out at the government level to facilitate business development models, etc., are also accomplished.

It is therefore essential to ensure quality in all academic programmes so that the graduates excel in the skills that they are imparted training in. To do that, a number of quality assurance reforms have been introduced in Pakistan, and there has been considerable progress. The reforms include among others, bringing about an awareness in academia on the importance of quality culture, development of quality criteria and standards, development of quality assurance processes and capacity building of universities, and monitoring and evaluation for quality assurance.

To improve quality, a large number of reforms have been undertaken at Pakistani HEIs. Minimum standards of Bachelors, Masters and PhD degrees have been established as per global standards. All Bachelors degrees are now four years, after 12 years of schooling in accordance with international global standards. A new two-year skills-based Associate Degree Programme has been introduced. The Masters degree is another two years beyond the four-year Bachelors. Curriculums of over 120 programmes are reviewed every three years and upgraded in accordance with world standards by a committee which includes senior and distinguished academics. Standards for the award of a PhD degree are even stricter, with a Graduate Record Examinations type entrance test for all graduate programmes. There is an 18-credit course required beyond the Masters degree. HEC has a zero tolerance policy on plagiarism, and all theses and dissertations must be evaluated by at least two foreign referees in academically advanced countries in the relevant area of research. There is also a publication requirement.

A Degree Qualification Framework has been introduced through which the equivalency of degrees offered in Pakistan can be evaluated in accordance with the Bologna protocol. This is depicted in Figure 6 where the years of education from primary to higher education are equated with level and award type. The Qualification Framework will enable Pakistani degrees to be internationally recognised and the graduates employable.

With an increase in universities and enrolment, there is a simultaneous need to train and recruit high-quality faculty to accommodate this growth. Therefore, faculty development programmes are the mainstay of HEC. About 7500 scholars are currently pursuing their PhD degrees on HEC scholarships both within and outside the country, and they are all being placed at universities upon graduation. It is estimated that with the projected growth in universities, at least an additional 10,000 PhD faculty will be required by 2020. Starting in 2014, all lecturer appointments will

	Years	Levels	Award Type	Award Example
Higher Education Levels	21 20 19	8	Doctoral	PhD
	18 17	7	Masters	M.Phil./MS/MBA, M.Sc. (Eng.), M.E, MArch etc
	16 15	6	Bachelor	BS, B.E, B.Arch., BSc (Eng.), BSc (Agri), MA/MSc (16 year), LLB, B.Com (Hons, MBBA, DVM, PharmD, etc
	14 13	5	Associate Ordinary Bachelor	BA/BSc (Pass), ADE, Associate Degrees etc
Intermediate Level	12 11	4	Higher Secondary School Certificate (HSSC)	F.A, F.Sc, ICS, I.Com, DBA, D.Com etc
Matriculation Level	10 9	3	Secondary School Certificate (SSC)	Matric
		2	Middle (3 Years)	
		1	Primary (1-5 Years) Pre-Primary (1-2 Years)	

Figure 6: Degree Qualification Framework in Pakistan.

require an MPhil/MS degree, and from 2016, all assistant professors and above will require a PhD degree. The tenure track programme for faculty has already been introduced, and all appointments are based on performance. Research journals that are published out of Pakistan are evaluated for quality and impact, and are given a weightage for publication. Knowledge transfer through teaching, research, entrepreneurship, and community service, and not just experience, will become mandatory for faculty promotion.

Pakistan has acquired full membership in a number of international QA bodies. Thirteen Accreditation Councils have been established (nine through autonomous act, four under HEC), while Quality Enhancement Cells (QEC) have been introduced and established in 85 public and private universities in the last four years. The role of these cells is to monitor and own quality at the local universities through a self-evaluation process, and report results to both the vice-chancellor and the QA Division at HEC, so improvements in education can take place with proper and relevant feedback. The outcome of those QECs has turned out to be promising and there is a marked improvement in the quality of teaching at the universities.

There is continued emphasis on good governance, as there can be no maintenance in quality without good leadership. Very recently, Institutional Performance Evaluation (IPE) has been developed by the HEC with seven indicators, and a pilot test run has been made across five universities. Based on the feedback received, the evaluation will be extended across all universities by the end of the year. This will assist the university leaders in ensuring good governance. Better selection of vice-chancellors is also being ensured by the HEC policy of appointing vice-chancellors through search committees, and evaluating their performance. Challenges for new vice-chancellors include leadership skills, academic leadership, financial management, strategic planning, fundraising and building economies, communities and leadership. HEC has since the last one year introduced a two-day leadership workshop for all newly appointed vice-chancellors to prepare the next generation of university leaders to face these challenges. As the jury is still out, it is too early to evaluate the impact of this training. If the results are meaningful in terms of better performance of university leaders, then there are plans to offer this orientation workshop to other countries in the region as well.

Ranking of all universities was carried out for the first time this year, and universities have been ranked in seven categories: general, medical, business education, engineering and technology, computer science and information technology, agriculture and veterinary sciences, and arts and design. This is enabling the universities to identify their weaknesses, as well as building on their strengths, so as to compete, and be ranked, globally. All private universities are being monitored for infrastructure and quality, and are awarded a rating based on a number of factors which include, faculty — student ratio, the number of PhD faculty, library books and computers, bandwidth, teachers' evaluation. The universities performing below standard are being asked to refrain from offering new admissions. This measure has drastically improved the quality of education at private universities.

Second Pillar: Technology Readiness

Universities have also enhanced their technology readiness, which is the second pillar of knowledge economy, both at the operational and at the research level. Pakistan Education & Research Networks (PERN) provides a 10Gbps bandwidth over a fibre-optic backbone that connects over 250 institutes. All universities now have access to a digital library which includes a database of over 45,000 e-books and 25,000 e-journals available to over one million students across the country. The latest digital video-conferencing (DVC) facilities have been established at each university, and as a result, conferences, meetings and lectures through DVC have become the norm. New knowledge is now being transferred between campuses and from across the world. All universities have been equipped with a campus management solution, and online registrations have been introduced. HEC has an alliance with Microsoft in which licensed software is made available to all universities, faculty and students at no cost. State-of-the-art research facilities are now available at top research universities and programmes, as a result of which the quality of operation and research has considerably improved. Some of the technology drivers in support of higher education and research are shown in Figure 7.

Third Pillar: Innovation

There has been a strong focus on research and innovation, which constitutes the third pillar of the knowledge economy. In particular, there has been a significant growth in the number of PhDs awarded by Pakistan universities. In the first 55 years since Pakistan's independence in 1947, a total of 3281 PhDs were awarded at Pakistani universities. However, since the establishment of HEC in 2002, 4850 PhDs have been awarded, more than the total of the previous 55 years. This is shown in Figure 8. The number of PhDs awarded per year has now increased to over 850 in the year 2011, and it is expected that over 1000 PhDs will be awarded in 2012. There has been a focus on engineering and technology, agriculture, biological sciences,

Figure 7: Technology drivers for knowledge exchange.

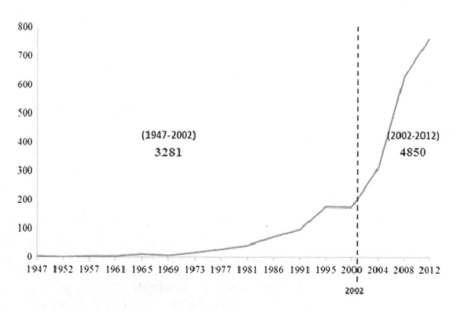

Figure 8: PhD graduates in Pakistan. *Source*: HEC, Statistics (2012).

business education and social sciences, all vital subjects for the socio-economic development of Pakistan.

The PhD production trends in Pakistan, India and Sri Lanka are shown in Figure 9. It can be clearly seen that Pakistan has made the most significant gain in producing PhD graduates of the countries in the region. While there is a gain in the number of PhD graduates in Pakistan, India shows a decline while Sri Lanka shows a steady performance.

As a result of the new flourishing research culture at HEIs, the number of research publications in international journals with impact factor has increased drastically by a factor of eight in the last 10 years. While 816 papers were published in 2002, the total has now increased to over 6200 in 2011 as shown in Figure 10. As for the subjects of PhDs awarded, the largest number of publications is now in areas of relevance to economic development. It is estimated that these numbers will continue to rise through future years. Scimago (2012), an independent database, forecast how the world will perform in research by 2018, based on their past performance. Pakistan has been shown to have the second-highest growth in the Asiatic region, as shown in Figure 11.

As a result of this phenomenal increase in research publications, Pakistan's share of world research has gone up by 300 per cent in the last five years.

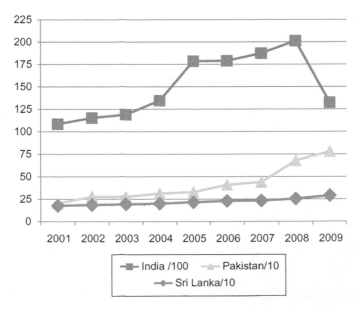

Figure 9: PhD graduation trends. *Source*: Annual Reports of UGC, India, Sri Lanka and HEC, Pakistan (2011).

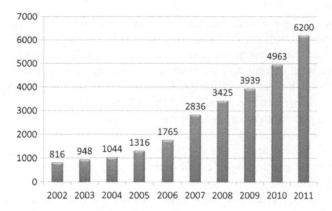

Figure 10: Research publications from Pakistan. *Source*: HEC, Statistics (2012).

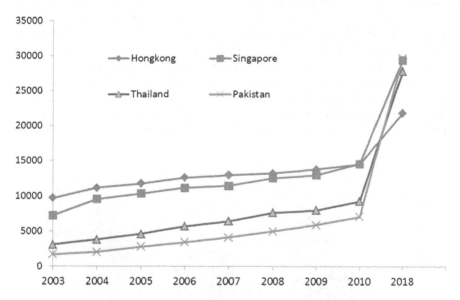

Figure 11: Research output forecast to 2018: Select Asiatic countries. *Source*: Scimago (2012).

Once quality in teaching and education, and technology readiness was enforced at the universities, the higher education sector focused on research relevant to economic development. A number of research centres, which are performing adoptive research relevant to national economic and regional needs, were set up across Pakistan., The Date Palm Research Center at Shah Abdul Latif University, Khairpur; The Food Technology Center at the

University of Agriculture, Faisalabad; The Gemstone Training Center at UET Peshawar; and the Institute of Sustainable Halophyte Utilization at the University of Karachi are just a few examples of these centres that are serving the local community by assisting in setting up new enterprises with the farmers or the local community. A similar centre at the Arid Agriculture University, Rawalpindi is a state-of-the-art hydroponic facility, which is focusing on producing local crops, local seeds and nutrients to the benefit of the farming community. The centre is now expanding to increase hydroponic agriculture in the local communities by developing skills, as well as through continuing education and extension programmes across all regions of Pakistan.

As a result of these major reforms, Pakistan's higher education sector is finally beginning to appear on the world scene. According to the most recent *QS Asian Universities Rankings* (2012), there are now six Pakistani universities ranked among the top 300 universities. Similarly, according to *QS World Universities Ranking* (2011), two Pakistani universities are ranked among the top 300 technology universities in the world. It is only a few years since no Pakistani universities appeared in world rankings. This is an achievement and recognition that has been widely acknowledged.

The selected indicators on the *World Economic Forum Global Competitiveness Report* on higher education and training, technology readiness and innovation are showing a significant improvement for Pakistan, as shown in Figure 12. This is clear proof that the higher education sector in Pakistan

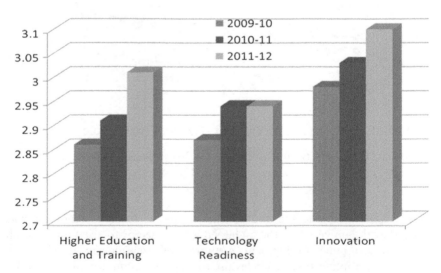

Figure 12: Pakistan's score on selected indicators on Global Competitiveness Index. *Source*: World Economic Forum Global Competitiveness Report (2011–2012).

has considerably improved in both quantity and quality of higher education and research, and is on the winning track towards building a knowledge economy.

Now that Pakistan has successfully increased its accessibility to quality higher education, research and innovation, it has reached a crucial point where the gap between education and research, and innovation and entrepreneurship must be efficiently bridged for it to become a knowledge economy power.

With this focus in mind, the way forward, and the new challenges, for Pakistan require a paradigm shift: to realise the importance of innovation and entrepreneurship; to establish offices of innovation, research and commercialisation (ORICs) at its universities; to link university with industry; market research and focus towards industry problems; transformation from lab-scale to commercial projects; transfer of knowledge, research and innovation; and to establish incubators, centres for innovation and entrepreneurship, and technology and science parks at the campuses.

Continuing in its transformation to building winning formulas to boost the knowledge economy, recent developments in Pakistan have included the following:

Five business and technology incubators have been established, while six more are in approval phase.
Small Business Innovation and Research (SBIR) Grants have been introduced.
Ten ORICs have been established, while twenty more are to be established in the next two years.
Three advanced study and research centres in the priority areas of energy, agriculture, and water are in the design stage, to be launched by March 2013.
One technology park is in development.

While the higher education sector has shown considerable performance, it is important to realise that higher education and research, technology readiness, and innovation leading to entrepreneurship do not work by themselves in isolation from each other. There are other institutional pillars, as identified by the World Bank and the *World Economic Forum Global Competiveness Report*, which include good governance and institution building, infrastructure, macroeconomic environment, health, primary education, market efficiency, labour market efficiency, financial market development, market size and business sophistication, that must also be focused on and improved upon by the government and the private sector before all can work together in unison for building up a knowledge economy and make the country a knowledge power. Discussion of other pillars is beyond the scope of this paper.

References

Annual reports of UGC, India, Sri Lanka and HEC, Pakistan of various years. (2011). Retrieved from http://www.ugc.ac.in/page/Annual-Report.aspx, http://www.ugc.ac.lk/en/university-statistics-2010.html, http://www.hec.gov.pk/MediaPublication/Pages/AnnualReports.aspx. Higher Education Commission, Medium Term Development Framework-II (2011–15). Retrieved from http://hec.gov.pk/InsideHEC/Documents/MTDF%202011-15%20FINAL.pdf

Higher Education Commission, Statistics. (2012). Retrieved from http://www.hec.gov.pk/Stats/Pages/Default.aspx

QS Asian Universities Ranking. (2012). Retrieved from http://www.topuniversities.com/university-rankings/world-university-rankings/2012. Accessed on October 9, 2012.

QS World Universities Ranking. (2011). Retrieved from http://www.topuniversities.com/university-rankings/world-university-rankings/2011. Accessed on October 9, 2012.

Scimago. (2012). *World's top 50 countries by scientific knowledge output, a scientometric characterization.* Retrieved from http://www.scimagolab.com/blog/wp-content/uploads/2012/06/TOP-100-Companies-by-Output.pdf. Accessed on October 9, 2012.

World Bank. (2010). Education statistics database. Retrieved from http://go.worldbank.org/WBYFTX6CM0

World Bank. (2011). *The four pillars of the knowledge economy.* Retrieved from http://go.worldbank.org/5WOSIRFA70

World economic forum global competitiveness report. (2011–2012). Retrieved from http://www.weforum.org/reports

Chapter 1.6

Transnational Higher Education Partnerships: Overcoming Higher Education Access Barriers and 'Brain Drain' in Greece

Vangelis Tsiligiris

Despite the growth of TNE, there is limited research about the benefits for the receiving countries. This study considers the role of transnational higher education partnerships (TNEPs) in helping receiving countries to overcome problems of access to higher education and reduce outbound student mobility which relates to brain drain. The case of Greece is used to achieve the aim of this study, as it poses some interesting characteristics. First, Greece is a major exporter of students to other countries; second, it has a large number of TNEPs, and third, in such a highly protectionist country, TNE is not a recognised form of education.

Greece as a Major Exporter of Students to Other Countries: Implications and Developments

As shown in Table 1, in the 1980s and 1990s Greece was the major exporter of students among European countries and in the top ten globally. According to relevant literature (Saiti & Prokopiadou, 2008; Wächter & Ferencz, 2012) in the period from 1970 to 1995, Greek student outbound mobility is driven mainly by factors such as the limited access, low quality

Going Global: Identifying Trends and Drivers of International Education
Copyright © 2013 by Emerald Group Publishing Limited
All rights of reproduction in any form reserved
ISBN: 978-1-78190-575-3

Table 1: Top ten source countries for international students.

1968	1980	1985	2002	2004
China	Iran	China	China	China
US	Malaysia	Malaysia	US	US
Canada	**Greece**	Iran	India	India
Syria	China	**Greece**	Korea	Korea
UK	Nigeria	Morocco	Japan	Germany
Germany	Morocco	Korea	Germany	Japan
Greece	US	Jordan	Morocco	France
Korea	Hong Kong	Hong Kong	**Greece**	Turkey
Italy	Germany	Germany	France	Morocco
Malaysia	Jordan	US	Turkey	**Greece**

Source: Gürüz (2008, p. 170).

Figure 1: Greek students abroad as a percentage of the total tertiary population. *Source*: UNESCO Institute for Statistics (2012).

and low employment prospects of the domestic higher education system. As shown in Figure 1, the period from 1994 to 1999 shows a significant increase in Greek student outbound mobility due to the leveraging of EU legislation for student mobility, which meant low or even no fees for Greek students studying abroad in countries like the United Kingdom and Netherlands. This explains why Greek students chose the United Kingdom as their prime study-abroad destination (Findlay, 2011).

The impact of the persistent increased outflow of young Greeks to other countries relates to problems in the balance of payments and brain drain. On the latter, it has been observed that a great number of young Greeks who complete their higher studies abroad are reluctant to return to Greece. A study by OECD (2002) shows that more than 60 per cent of the Greek PhD students in United States have plans to stay abroad. Also, the same study argues that 35 per cent of Greek PhD students in United States already have a job offer.

Greek graduates of foreign universities appear to have very little motive to return to Greece, something which relates to the significantly lower pay in Greece in comparison with countries which usually host Greek students (i.e. the United Kingdom and United States) (Psacharopoulos, 2003). Also, their reluctance to return to Greece relates to the lack of private sector jobs and the meritocratic recruitment system in the public sector (Tsiligiris, 2012).

As shown in Figure 1, Greek student outbound mobility has fallen dramatically during the past ten years or so, from 66,919 students (8 per cent of the total tertiary population) in 1999 to 28,825 students (4.7 per cent of the total tertiary population) in 2010. Popular opinion ascribes this decline in the number of Greeks studying abroad to the increase in the number of places offered in the domestic HE system. For example, Wächter and Ferencz (2012) explain the drop as an outcome of the 'removal of earlier "push factors" in the guise of insufficient higher education provision in Greece' (p. 401).

Nevertheless, Findlay (2011) explains this significant drop in outbound mobility as a consequence of: the increase in the number and range of transnational partnerships established between UK/US universities and private institutions in Greece; the expansion of distance learning; the rise of other study destinations, such as Central European countries; and the expansion of places offered at Greek public universities.

This paper explores further the role of TNEPs operating in Greece as an alternative to outbound student mobility.

TNEPs in Greece

TNE activities began in Greece in the mid-1980s as a result of the structural problems and inefficiencies of the domestic education system (McBurnie & Ziguras, 2007). Specifically, the development of TNE activities in Greece was geared by the failure of the domestic education system to meet, in terms of available places and standards of quality, the increasing demand for HE.

Greece has not considered TNE as a recognised form of education and has imposed extreme barriers to its development. However, despite the

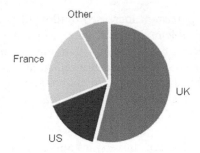

Figure 2: Countries of origin of TNE programmes in Greece.

hostile environment, TNE was developed in Greece in line with the argument by McBurnie and Ziguras (in Stella & Bhushan, 2011) that TNE slips between the regulatory cracks in the national systems and develops in spite of the existing restrictions.

In 2008, in an effort to combat the uncontrolled development and operation of TNE in Greece, the Greek government introduced a new legal framework[1] to regulate the establishment and operation of Greek private institutions engaging in TNE activities in collaboration with foreign universities.

In 2012 there were 30 licensed TNEPs in Greece which, as shown in Figure 2, offer programmes in collaboration[2] with universities from the United Kingdom (53 per cent), France (23 per cent) and United States (15 per cent) (Drew et al., 2008; McBurnie & Ziguras, 2007; Baskerville, MacLeod, & Saunders, 2011).

As shown in Figure 3, the number of students in TNEPs in Greece has grown from approximately 10,000 in 2000 to nearly 25,000 in 2011, a 150 per cent increase.[3] It is worth noting that this significant growth in the number of students is despite the existing structural problems in TNE in Greece, which are primarily about the lack of professional or academic recognition of the degrees awarded via TNEPs. According to the Hellenic College Association, as Greeks are particularly sensitive about the issue of academic and professional recognition, if the Greek government had fully and properly

---

1. (law 3696/2008 & 3848/2010) www.minedu.gov.gr/publications/docs/n3848___arthro_45_kentra_metalykeiakhs_ekpaideyshs_100607.pdf
2. Most of the partnerships are in the form of franchise collaboration.
3. The data presented in this section is gathered from a range of different sources. There appears to be confusion about the total number of students who study in Greek TNEPs: for example McBurnie and Ziguras argue that the total number is 65,000 in 2007. However, this study has adopted the numbers reported by ICAP as appear to be more realistic. The numbers where verified with the Hellenic College Association (www.hca.gr) which is the representative body of TNEPs in Greece.

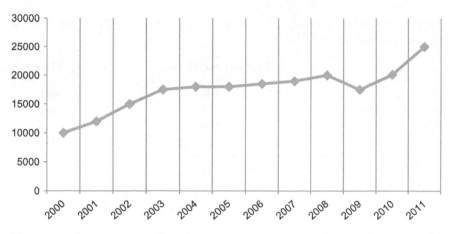

Figure 3: Students enrolled in Greek colleges. *Sources:* ICAP (2010), Hellenic Colleges Association (2012).

adopted the EU legislation and granted professional rights to TNEPs' graduates, the total number of students would have been much greater.

TNEPs as an Alternative to Outbound Student Mobility

To consider the role of TNEPs in the trajectory of Greek student outbound mobility a range of data was combined and statistically tested, including: the number of Greek students abroad; the number of places offered in the domestic HE; and the number of Greek students enrolled in TNEPs in Greece. Three phases of Greek student outbound mobility are identified and discussed below.

Phase 1. 1974–1993: Quantity-Led Outbound Mobility

The period prior to 1982 is marked by a significant correlation (0.85), shown in Table 2, between the number of places offered in the Greek HEIs and the number of students abroad. As shown in Figure 4, during that period, the lower the number places offered in Greek HEIs the higher the number of students abroad. This is in line with the argument by Psacharopoulos (2003) and others (McBurnie & Ziguras, 2007) that the emergence of Greece as a major exporter of students is attributable to its highly protectionist HE system. This extreme protectionism has led to insufficient student places in universities, leading in turn to extreme rationing of entry, which acted as a push factor for outbound student mobility. In support of this, during the

Table 2: Correlation of places offered in Greek Public HEIs v. number of Greek students abroad.

	Pearson correlation	Sig. (1-tailed)
Period 1975–1982	.849[a]	.008
Period 1983–1993	.489	.076
Period 1994–1999	.850[b]	.016
Period 1999–2010	−.352	.144

[a]Correlation is significant at the 0.01 level (1-tailed).
[b]Correlation is significant at the 0.05 level (1-tailed).

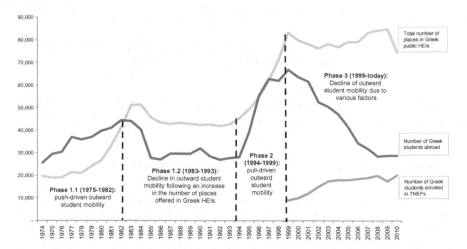

Figure 4: Greek student outbound mobility, places offered in the domestic system and Greek students in TNEPs.

period from 1983 to 1993 the mobility of Greek students slows down as a result of the increase of the number of available places in the Greek HEIs. There is positive correlation (0.48), however less strong, between the number of available places in the domestic HE system and the number of students abroad.

Phase 2. 1994–1999: Upsurge in 'Pull-Driven' Outbound Student Mobility, Facilitated by EU Policies

The period from 1994 to 1999 represents a huge increase in Greek student outbound mobility, in spite of the concurrent significant increase in the number of places offered in the Greek HEIs, which is shown by the significant correlation (0.85) shown in Table 2. This marks a change in the factors which drive Greek student outbound mobility. It is argued that both high protectionism which led to a lack of competition and accountability, and political opportunism which was responsible for the significant increase in the number of places offered in Greek HEIs that could not be properly supported, resulted in the degradation of quality of Greek HEIs (Tsiligiris, 2012). Additionally, graduates of Greek HEIs had low employability prospects as an outcome of the inappropriate planning of the content and the range of programmes offered (Hellenic Quality Assurance Agency, 2011; Livanos, 2010).

Greek students in the period 1994–1999 pursued studies abroad in an effort to overcome the quality and employability problems of the domestic HE system (Kyriazis & Asderaki, 2008). This was facilitated by the EU legislation which allowed Greek students to pay 'home' fees in European countries. This resulted in an upsurge in the number of Greek outbound students to EU countries, primarily the United Kingdom, pursuing HE studies in anticipation of higher employability prospects (Saiti & Prokopiadou, 2008). Therefore, the period from 1994 to 2000 is characterised by a 'pull' rather than 'push' for the outbound mobility of Greek students.

1999–2010: Decline in Greek Student Outbound Mobility and the Role of TNE

As shown in Figure 4 and Table 3, in the period from 1999 to 2010 the number of Greek students abroad declined sharply (− 57 per cent). In Table 2, the period 1999–2010 is marked by a negative correlation (− .352)

Table 3: Greek student outbound mobility 1999–2010: factors and trends.

	1999	**2010**	**% Change (1999–2010)**
Greek students abroad	66.918	28.825	− 57%
Greek students in TNEPs in Greece	9.000	20.125	124%
Total population in tertiary education	831.980	608.096	− 27%
Number of places in Greek public HEIs	83.235	84.690	1,7%

which shows that while the number of places offered in Greek public HEIs remains high the number of Greek students abroad declines. As Table 3 presents, this decline could be attributed to three factors: (1) the demographic effect from the decline by −27 per cent of tertiary student population in Greece; (2) the consistently high number of places in the public HEIs; and (3) the significant increase (124 per cent) in the number of students enrolled in TNEPs operating in Greece.

In Figure 5, the number of students studying in TNEPs in Greece, the available places in the domestic HE system, and the outbound student mobility are combined and presented as a percentage of the total tertiary domestic population for the period from 2000 to 2010. This allows the observation of the effect of TNEPs on the trajectory of Greek student outbound mobility taking into consideration the demographic factor as well as the capacity increase of the domestic system. There seems to be a relationship between the increase in the number of students in TNEPs and the decrease in outbound student mobility.

To further examine the role of TNEPs as an alternative to Greek student outbound mobility the case of the United Kingdom was considered.[4] As Figure 6 shows, considering the data by HESA about the number of Greek

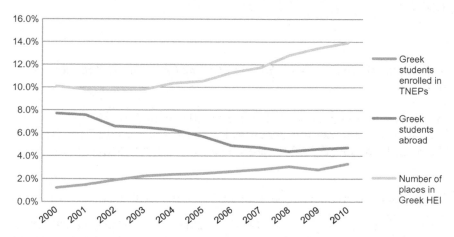

Figure 5: Students in TNEPs in comparison to places offered in domestic HE system and student outbound mobility (as percentage of domestic tertiary population). *Sources:* UNESCO Institute of Statistics (2012), ICAP (2010).

---

4. This is because UK has been the major destination of Greeks. Also, Greece has been among the top source countries of foreign students to UK for a number of years.

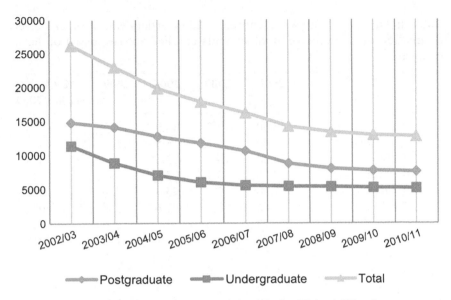

Figure 6: Greek students studying in the United Kingdom.

students studying in the United Kingdom for the period 2002–2011, a decrease of 51.3 per cent (from 26.175 students in 2002 to 12.760 students in 2011) is observed in the total number of Greek students studying in the United Kingdom.

Similarly, Table 4 summarises the data from UNESCO Institute for Statistics about the percentage of Greek students abroad per country of destination for the period 2006–2009. It is observed that the percentage of students who choose to study in the United Kingdom has decreased significantly from 43.5 per cent to 34.7 per cent as a share of the total number of Greek students abroad. This could be associated with the fact that, as shown in Figure 3 earlier, most of TNEPs in Greece involve UK universities. It is arguable, therefore, that Greek students who in the past would have gone to the United Kingdom for undergraduate or postgraduate studies now stay in Greece in one of the many TNEPs offering programmes in collaboration with UK universities. Also, the data below shows an increase in the percentage of students who choose Central European countries for study because of lower costs: a notable example is the increase by 700 per cent in the number of Greeks who choose to study in the Slovak Republic. These findings are in line with Findlay's argument (2011) discussed earlier, about Greeks turning to more economical alternatives.

It is expected that Greek students will continue to choose TNEPs for undergraduate and postgraduate studies as a more economical alternative to

Table 4: Number of Greek students enrolled in tertiary education in a given destination as a percentage of all students enrolled abroad, based on head counts.

		2006	2007	2008	2009	% Change (2006/2009)
1	United Kingdom	43.50	42.2	36.9	34.7	− 20%
2	Germany	15.40	16	16.5	16.6	8%
3	Italy	13.50	13.3	13.3	12.4	− 8%
4	France	5.00	5.1	5.6	5.4	8%
5	United States	5.30	5.3	5.8	5.4	2%
6	Turkey	2.40	2.3	2.6	2.4	0%
7	Netherlands	1.10	1.6	2	2.1	91%
8	Slovak Republic	0.20	0.5	1.1	1.6	700%
9	Belgium	1.20	1.1	1.3	1.4	17%
10	Switzerland	0.70	0.8	1	1.2	71%
11	Spain	0.50	0.5	0.5	1.1	120%
12	Austria	0.60	0.6	0.9	0.9	50%
13	Sweden	0.70	0.8	0.7	0.9	29%
14	Czech Republic	0.30	0.3	0.4	0.7	133%

Source: UNESCO Institute of Statistics (2012).

outbound mobility. This is primarily driven by the significant reduction in the Greek GDP resulting from the ongoing debt crisis and the introduction of fees in major outbound student destination countries like the United Kingdom.

However, despite the increase in the number of students staying at home to study in a TNEP, the brain-drain trend is not reversed — quite the opposite. Since the beginning of the Greek debt crisis in 2010 the number of young Greek graduates who seek employment abroad has increased significantly (*The Economist*, 2012). Also, Malkoutzis (2011) cites evidence claiming that 84 per cent of Greeks graduating from foreign universities reject the opportunity to return and that since the beginning of the crisis in 2010 the brain drain of young Greek graduates has intensified.

It is clear that TNE does not reverse the brain-drain dynamics in Greece, which are primarily caused by the poor domestic macroeconomic and employment conditions. In fact, TNE is attractive to those who want to obtain a degree from a reputable European university without moving abroad and at much lower cost — they then use this degree to pursue employment abroad. TNE is facilitating a process of 'staying at home to prepare to move abroad' for students in countries with a high level of unemployment and unfavourable future economic prospects.[5]

Conclusions

Greece has been a major exporter of students to other countries in the past and an extreme protectionist case of TNE receiving country. Over the years there has been a change in the type of factors which fuelled Greek student outbound mobility. From the early 1970s up until the 1980s Greek student mobility was primarily due to the shortage of available places in Greek HEIs, along with significant barriers to entry. In the mid-1990s, following the degradation of quality in Greek HEIs and the low employability prospects of their graduates, Greek student outbound mobility increased significantly towards EU countries.

Despite the extreme protectionism against the development and recognition of TNEPs, the number of students enrolled in these provisions has risen dramatically (+124 per cent) during the period 2000–2010. TNEPs, along with other factors such as the demographic decline in the Greek tertiary population, seem to act as a means to reverse the expanding Greek student outbound mobility. TNEPs seem to capture student demand for high-quality standards along with aspirations for higher employability prospects after graduation, which in the period prior to 2000 was taking the form of outbound student mobility to countries like the United Kingdom.

Based on the findings from the Greek case, it is arguable that TNE plays an important role in building capacity of domestic systems to bridge demand for HE, while also helping host countries to capture student demand for higher quality standards and higher employability prospects.

Finally, brain-drain effects of TNE are subject to wider factors, like macroeconomic stability and domestic unemployment in host countries. The example of Greece reveals that despite the dramatic reduction in outbound student mobility, the brain drain has risen due to the negative prospects of the Greek economy following the ongoing debt crisis which started in 2010. TNE, under certain conditions, seems to worsen the brain drain, as students can obtain a degree from a foreign university without moving abroad and at a lower cost, which then they use to find employment in other countries.

---

5. This seems to contradict with the role of TNE in countries where employment and economic prospects are favourable. In these countries, like India and Malaysia, Choudaha (2012) comments that students pursue studies in TNEPs with the prospect of staying at home, and he calls these students 'glocals'.

As it appears from this and other studies, short-term benefits from TNE are primarily quantitative and relate to the capacity of domestic HE systems to meet domestic demand, however the longer term benefits of TNE are subject to employment and macroeconomic factors in host countries.

References

Baskerville, S., MacLeod, F., & Saunders, N. (2011). *A guide to UK higher education partnerships for overseas universities*. London: Higher Education International and Europe Unit.

Choudaha, R. (2012). The rise of 'glocal' students and transnational education. *The Guardian*. [Online]. 21 June. Retrieved from http://www.guardian.co.uk/higher-education-network/blog/2012/jun/21/opportunities-in-transnational-education. Accessed on June 27, 2012.

Drew, S., McCaig, C., Marsden, D., Haughton, P., McBride, J., McBride, D., ... Wolstenholme, C. (2008). *Trans-national education and higher education institutions: Exploring patterns of HE institutional activity*. Sheffield: Sheffield Hallam University.

Findlay, A. M. (2011). An assessment of supply and demand-side theorizations of international student mobility. *International Migration, 49*(2), 162–190.

Gürüz, K. (2008). *Higher education and international student mobility in the global knowledge economy*. Albany, NY: State University of New York Press.

Hellenic Colleges Association. (2012). *Interviews*. Retrieved from: http://hca.gr/%CE%BD%CE%AD%CE%B1/%CF%83%CF%85%CE%BD%CE%B5%CE%BD%CF%84%CE%B5%CF%8D%CE%BE%CE%B5%CE%B9%CF%82/. Accessed on 27 December 2012.

Hellenic Quality Assurance Agency. (2011). *Εκθεση για την ποιότητα στην Ανωτατη Εκπαίδευση 2010–11* [Report on quality of higher education 2010–11]. Athens.

ICAP. (2010). *Τριτοβάθμια Ιδιωτικη Εκπαίδευση* [Private Tertiary Education]. Athens.

Kyriazis, A., & Asderaki, F. (2008). *Higher Education in Greece*. Monographs on Higher Education. Bucharest: CEPES European Centre for Higher Education.

Livanos, I. (2010). The relationship between higher education and labour market in Greece: The weakest link? *Higher Education, 60*(5), 473–489.

Malkoutzis, N. (2011). Young Greeks and the crisis: The danger of losing a generation. Friedrich Ebert Stiftung. Retrieved from http://library.fes.de/pdf-files/id/ipa/08465.pdf. Accessed on June 26, 2012.

McBurnie, G., & Ziguras, C. (2007). *Transnational education: Issues and trends in offshore higher education*. New York, NY: Routledge.

OECD. (2002). *International mobility of the highly skilled*. Paris: OECD.

Psacharopoulos, G. (2003). The social cost of an outdated law: Article 16 of the Greek constitution. *European Journal of Law and Economics, 16*(2), 123–137.

Saiti, A., & Prokopiadou, G. (2008). The demand for higher education in Greece. *Journal of Further and Higher Education, 32*(3), 285–296.

Stella, A., & Bhushan, S. (2011). *Quality assurance of transnational higher education: The experiences of Australia and India* (1st ed.). Melbourne: National University of Educational Planning and Administration (India), Australian Universities Quality Agency.

The Economist. (2012). Greek woes: The Mediterranean blues. [Online]. Retrieved from http://www.economist.com/node/21542815. Accessed on February 16, 2012.

Tsiligiris, V. (2012). The debt crisis and higher education reforms in Greece: A catalyst for change. *Anglohigher*, *4*(1), 15–16.

UNESCO Institute of Statistics. (2012). Data centre: Education (Online). Retrieved from http://stats.uis.unesco.org/unesco/tableviewer/document.aspx?ReportId=143. Accessed on February 16, 2012.

Wächter, B., & Ferencz, I. (2012). Student mobility in Europe: Recent trends and implications of data collection. In A. Curaj, P. Scott, L. Vlasceanu & L. Wilson (Eds.), *European higher education at the crossroads*. Dordrecht: Springer Science + Business Media.

Chapter 1.7

Quality Assurance of Higher Education through Referential Standards: A Challenge for the Science Council of Japan

Kazuo Kitahara

In Japan, more than 55 per cent of young people aged from 18 to 22 attend higher education. This is known as the 'universalisation of higher education' and implies that most graduates do not remain working in academia. Therefore, we have to clarify the relevance of learning in higher education in the context of professional life and citizenship in society, against an international backdrop. In other words, the production of adaptable professionals is not the whole purpose of higher education, but rather that higher education should produce professionals who are responsible to our present and future society. This may lead to a substantial change of the direction of higher education: from one based upon the traditional concept of inheriting academic knowledge within academia, to the 'socialisation' of knowledge (Bijker & d'Andrea, 2009). In the present trend towards the diversification of universities, each university should carefully choose its stakeholders to collaborate in its own purpose to society. Thus, quality assurance should be based on the balance between the autonomy of individual universities and dividing society's goals among universities.

Society itself is not the same as it was in the last century. We live in a global world wherein any local change might affect anywhere else in the world, thanks to developments in transport, communication tools or the widespread growth of industry. Students therefore should be equipped with

Going Global: Identifying Trends and Drivers of International Education
Copyright © 2013 by Emerald Group Publishing Limited
All rights of reproduction in any form reserved
ISBN: 978-1-78190-575-3

knowledge and skills relative to such international and global changes. Thus, a university education may not offer exactly the same as that taught in the past: rather it should include and deal with international and global issues.

Discussion about quality assurance at the Science Council of Japan (SCJ) — the representative body of academic communities — was initiated at the request of the Ministry of Education, Culture, Science, Sports and Technology (MEXT) in 2008. The Central Council of Education of MEXT published 'Towards the Construction of Undergraduate Education' (2008), stating that Japanese universities today are unable to provide a clear answer to the question of what skills are assured by degrees, and that priority has not been given to maintaining a minimum requirement of undergraduate programmes for each subject within all the universities. Such issues become more important in the case of international student exchange, which requires equivalence of degrees.

MEXT considered that SCJ would be the appropriate institution for consultation on these issues, because most of members of SCJ are academics in higher education institutions. SCJ inaugurated the Committee for Subject-Specific Quality Assurance in September 2008 and in January 2009 the committee organised three sub-committees: one for the framework for assuring quality of subject-specific education; one for linking liberal arts/general education and subject-specific education; and one for bridging the gap between university education and the workplace. After conducting a survey and holding discussions with various sectors, including university associations, university accreditation organisations, staff of the Quality Assurance Agency (QAA) in the United Kingdom, and area-specific academic committees of SCJ, the report Subject-Specific Quality Assurance: Answer to MEXT (SCJ, 2010) was published in August 2010. The report recommends that referential standards for each subject should be formulated or verbalised to provide basic concepts of each subject to be studied in higher education. From September 2010, SCJ formed sub-committees for subject-specific referential standards. Here 'referential' implies that the standard is not a collection of learning items in a curriculum but is for the clarification of core concepts of the subject learning to be shared by all universities despite the differences in resources and back-ground conditions of universities. The idea of referential standards was stimulated by QAA's 'Subject benchmark statements', which have already been published for various subjects.

In the next section, the referential standards will be described in detail. In the final section, the proposal of SCJ towards the link between university education and the workplace is described together with reactions from the society.

Referential Standards

The main aims of our referential standards (RS) are not for detailed assessment issues of universities but for the support of education programmes of each university by giving core concepts of subjects. The basic contents of RS are: (1) characterisation of the subject area, by giving a definition of the subject and by showing how it is meaningful in the present world; (2) basic knowledge, concepts, subject-specific skills and general skills for students to become good professionals as well as good citizens; (3) the basic concept of assessment of the learning process and outcomes, which result in the ability of relating acquired knowledge to reasonable actions; and (4) the co-ordination of general education and subject-specific education resulting in good citizenship.

Besides the main aim of RS as support for university programmes, they serve to promote university education to society and to secondary schools, so that the learning process may be meaningful from their primary and secondary education through to their career as professionals in society.

In 2010 SJC created Referential Standard Committees for management, laws, linguistics/letters, biological science, mechanical engineering, mathematical science, domestic science and civil engineering/architecture. In August 2012 RS for management were completed. These define management as learning for the understanding of 'going concerns', or sustainable enterprises, which may be profit and non-profit organisations, such as companies, governments, social welfare institutions, schools and homes. These are assemblies of individuals for the purpose of sustainable contribution to society in a variety of ways. The RS for management also emphasise learning management in a global world by introducing students to international internships. Actually the parameters of enterprises have changed drastically: they are now faced directly with international influences. Thus, it is important for enterprises to understand people of different cultures and to be able to communicate with them, thus extending the enterprises' dimension in the global world. These RS are appreciated not only by universities but also by society, especially by managers in industry who are faced with the global world in their business.

Link between University Education and the Workplace

In Japan, the tradition has been for most companies to hire graduates immediately after their graduation — on the first day of April. This causes many problems: the job-hunting process starts quite early, even while students are in the third year of university education. Students are forced to choose their future with an incomplete knowledge of their professions. It also means that students may often be absent from classes while they are job-hunting. SCJ has proposed that job-hunting should start at earliest in the latter half of the fourth year and the tradition of hiring new graduates immediately after the graduation should be modified. At least a few years after graduation should be reserved for job-hunting. This proposal has led to the government asking industry to modify traditional recruiting systems.

Conclusion

SCJ hopes our RS may serve as references for consideration of the educational content for each institution. The education of young people is the basis of innovation in the world. Universities should play an important and unique role for a better world through education, in collaboration with other education sectors — and society itself — using referential standards, which are regarded as common goods available to all, including secondary schools and industry, so that they know what should be taught in higher education.

Here we should mention the relevance of 'RS' to the internationalisation of Japanese higher education. Since our 'referential standards' are very much related to the 'Subject Benchmark Statements' (SBS) of QAA, further collaboration between the SCJ and QAA is desirable. In recent years we have been in contact with QAA at various stages of our development. Our RS put emphasis on the meaning of each discipline in the context of engaging in the sustainability of the globe. Therefore, learning should be associated with knowledge of the world's diversity of culture and environment: global problems cannot be solved from a domestic perspective. Thus, for the promotion of international collaboration, we need to co-ordinate the SCJ's referential standards with QAA's Subject Benchmark Statements. It is not necessary to have the same standards all over the world. The engagement of graduates in society will differ, depending on the culture and tradition of each nation. But it is necessary for us at least to understand each other's core concepts of subjects.

Since 2010 SCJ has also been considering the relevance of degree titles: since the relaxation of legal control, the names of degrees are now confusing. It is sometimes difficult to understand from the name of the degree what knowledge the graduate has gained. This situation is a barrier to international degree equivalence. We recently arrived at rather simple principles: (1) the name of the degree is to express what its graduates have learned and will bear the same meaning for their whole life; (2) the name should be rational and universal (i.e. valid worldwide) as a certificate of the graduate's ability; (3) If the graduate has made his/her study in interdisciplinary ways, the graduate's degree title need not bear the same name as the institution or programme. We hope that if these principles function among Japanese universities, the international degree equivalence process will be facilitated.

References

Bijker, W. E., & d'Andrea, L. (Eds.). (2009). *Handbook on the socialisation of scientific and technological research: Social science and European research capacities (SS-ERC) project.* Six Framework Programme. Rome, Italy: River Press Group srl.

Ministry of Education, Culture, Sports, Science and Technology. (2008, December). *Towards the construction of undergraduate education.* Retrieved from http://www.mext.go.jp/b_menu/shingi/chukyo/chukyo0/toushin/1217067.html (in Japanese).

Science Council of Japan. (August 2010). *Subject-specific quality assurance; answer to MEXT.* Retrieved from http://www.scj.go.jp/ja/info/kohyo/pdf/kohyo-21-k100-1.pdf (in Japanese, English translation is in preparation).

Chapter 1.8

Internationalisation in Africa: Where to Focus Funding for Real Impact

James Otieno Jowi and Milton Odhiambo Obamba

The higher education sector in Africa has expanded tremendously in the past few years — in the number and diversity of institutions, student numbers, in the emergence of new actors and the consequences of global dynamics. The sector has attracted attention from stakeholders, both internal and external, often due to the recognition of the important role of higher education in Africa's transformation (Bloom, Canning, & Chan, 2006). However, Africa's higher education still faces numerous challenges: funding, access, quality concerns, institutional capacities and governance.

The 2009 UNESCO World Conference on Higher Education marked an important turning point that affirmed the role of higher education and research in the future growth of Africa (UNESCO, 2009). Among other things, it identified priority areas and recommended strategies for mobilisation of resources to revitalise African universities (UNESCO, 2009). As a result, there have been a number of new initiatives involving different actors. Very importantly, university partnerships have been recognised as crucial, leading to new forms of collaboration shaping the sector (Jowi, 2009; Shabani, 2008).

The Rise of Internationalisation

Among the new developments in higher education globally is the growing impact of internationalisation on higher education activities, policies and

Going Global: Identifying Trends and Drivers of International Education
Copyright © 2013 by Emerald Group Publishing Limited
All rights of reproduction in any form reserved
ISBN: 978-1-78190-575-3

planning. Its diverse and unprecedented effects make it one of the major forces shaping Africa's higher education in the 21st century (Jowi, 2010). Its consequences include opportunities, challenges and attendant risks which demand closer analysis and understanding.

The new realities of internationalisation are compounding the challenges already facing the comparatively young African higher education sector. While other world regions have strategically realigned their higher education systems and activities to reap the enormous opportunities of internationalisation, African universities have generally approached internationalisation in a highly piecemeal and incoherent manner. This has meant that African universities have not benefited much from its opportunities and at the same time have borne the worst of its consequences. However, funding is one of the major challenges that prevent African countries and institutions from taking advantage of internationalisation opportunities or preparing adequately for its corresponding risks. The condition of scarcity requires that funding, alongside other critical resources, needs to be effectively and efficiently deployed, especially in the midst of competing demands and increasing limits on resources.

As a response to the growing importance of internationalisation, the African Network for Internationalization of Education (ANIE) was established in 2008 as a pan-African organisation with the main objectives of undertaking high-quality research, organising policy dialogues and fostering information-sharing on internationalisation in Africa. ANIE holds an annual conference on the different manifestations of internationalisation in Africa. The third ANIE conference was held in October 2011 in Abuja, Nigeria, in collaboration with the British Council and the National Universities Commission (NUC), Nigeria. The conference was organised as a policy dialogue which brought together university leaders, policy makers, and researchers to discuss the unfolding developments in internationalisation and recommend strategic areas needing priority support.

The theme of the conference was 'Internationalisation of Higher Education in Africa: Where to Focus Funding and Create Real Impact' — similar to the title of this paper. The main objective was to identify priority areas where support was needed to strengthen Africa's engagements with internationalisation. This was based on the outcomes of the previous conferences, which had raised awareness on the impact of internationalisation on Africa's higher education, including the challenges, risks and opportunities. This was therefore a call for African university leaders to prioritise internationalisation within their institutions and equally an opportunity to share with partners and stakeholders areas of priority in the agenda of African institutions with regard to internationalisation. It also discussed possibilities of using partnerships for enhanced internationalisation in Africa.

Determining Africa's Agenda for Internationalisation

What do African universities want from internationalisation and will the benefits override the risks? The stark reality is that African universities cannot afford to ignore internationalisation. They cannot evade engaging with the risks, challenges and opportunities it presents. The issue of whether to internationalise or not is no longer tenable, the question is how to internationalise most effectively. In essence then, African universities have to determine their agenda for internationalisation through clear conceptualisation, understanding and analysis.

Africa's higher education is part of the global higher education system. The absence of African voices in the conceptualisation and determination of key internationalisation processes and activities has resulted in internationalisation being largely externally driven. The need for more awareness by African university leaders, scholars and policy makers is therefore of utmost significance.

African scholarship continues to be shaped by Euro-American intellectual paradigms, preoccupations and perspectives, and remains largely overwhelmed by the dominant theoretical, epistemic, and methodological orientations of Western scholarship. It is therefore not grounded and nourished by African epistemic roots and is likely to reproduce and reinforce hegemonic Western knowledges which may carry little relevance to Africa (Zeleza, 2005). In a recent article, Akin Aina argued that 'universities in Africa will need to significantly change their current mode of organising knowledge production, the nature and content of knowledge, and the kinds of partnerships they seek and pursue' (Aina, 2010, p. 36). African universities' leaders and scholars therefore have to decide what knowledge and developmental interests they want to pursue through internationalisation.

Myriad Challenges and Risks

The agenda for internationalisation in Africa has to be pursued in cognisance of the several challenges and risks it presents to the continent. These need to be understood and addressed for positive and meaningful outcomes to be attained. These challenges and risks have been well documented (IAU, 2010; Jowi, 2009) and include funding, weak institutional capacities, quality of academic programmes, weak regulatory frameworks, institutional drawbacks, commercialisation, brain drain and unfair collaborations.

These need to be understood and addressed by governments and institutions with the involvement of local and international partners. New initiatives to promote internationalisation in Africa were viewed as crucial and needing support from all players. Responses to these drawbacks will elevate Africa's position to engage with internationalisation.

Identified Priority Areas

In the past few years, there have been more debates on internationalisation on the continent, seeking to address these challenges and opportunities and the role of Africa's higher education in the global knowledge society. The Abuja Conference identified some priority areas requiring concerted and immediate attention to make headway with internationalisation in Africa. Generally, they focus on the broader goal of building capacity for knowledge production and utilisation in African universities.

Symmetric Knowledge Partnerships

In the knowledge-based economic paradigm, the capacity to produce and disseminate knowledge is vital for sustainable socioeconomic development. Similarly, increasing global interdependence and the complexity of today's development challenges have clearly demonstrated that sustainable solutions cannot be found through the efforts and resources confined within a single discipline, institution or country (Koehn & Rosenau, 2010).The emerging knowledge partnership paradigm is widening the boundaries of international development, making it possible for universities to become increasingly strategic actors in development (King, 2008). African universities are expected to contribute to knowledge generation; but they also need to expand and strengthen their knowledge partnerships and networks across national and disciplinary boundaries in order to respond more adequately to the ever-more complex development challenges facing the continent. Increased collaboration with more developed countries can significantly contribute to research capacity strengthening in African universities.

However, the gap between rich and poor countries in terms of their capacity to access, generate, or utilise knowledge is growing and is likely to reinforce the hegemony of Western knowledge and intensify the marginalisation and dislocation of Africa from the global knowledge circuits (Jowi, 2009, p. 272; Zeleza, 2005). In many ways, the infrastructure of international academic mobility, knowledge partnerships, and cross-border provision remain deeply asymmetrical (Obamba & Mwema, 2009). The unequal division of labour indicates that the Northern partners dominate the setting of the overarching research agenda and scientific dissemination, whereas Southern partners are most involved in the more peripheral roles of project implementation and data collection. In most instances, the 'scientifically advanced' countries prefer to collaborate more intensely among themselves (Wagner, Brahmakulam, Jackson, Wong, & Yoda, 2001). In fact, the 2009 global survey (IAU, 2010) reported that most world regions did not prioritise Africa for future internationalisation activities — demonstrating the deepening marginalisation of Africa. These embedded material and power asymmetries associated with internationalisation need to be replaced with mutual and reciprocal partnerships which are also compatible with Africa's agendas and local development needs.

Strengthening Research Collaboration and Capacities

Inadequate funding for research and insufficient attention to professional development has hampered the development of research capacity in many African universities. Compared with other parts of the world, research capacities in African universities remain weak and fragmented. The African continent spends a paltry 0.3 per cent of its total GDP on research and development, whereas the industrialised countries spend approximately six times that amount and have ten times more research scientists (Oyewole, 2010). Africa has the lowest ratio of scientists in research and development in the world. African countries have an average of 35 research scientists per million inhabitants, whereas European countries and the United States have 2457 and 4103, respectively (AfDB, 2008, p. 3).

Unsurprisingly, Africa accounts for less than 1.5 per cent of the total global publications in scientific journals, with a large part supported through external funding and narrowly concentrated in a few disciplines and countries (Bloom et al., 2006; Wagner et al., 2001). A recent Thompson Reuters study shows that between 1999 and 2008 the entire African continent produced only 27,600 papers published in scientific journals, whereas the Netherlands alone published 27,000 papers during the same period (Adams, King, & Hook, 2010, p. 5). In fact, 80 per cent of research output in Africa comes from three countries — Egypt, South Africa and Nigeria.

These large and widening asymmetries between Africa and the developed countries illustrate the depth of Africa's marginalisation and the magnitude of the effort that is urgently required to revitalise Africa's battered knowledge-production infrastructure and its capacity to make any meaningful contribution in the global knowledge society. Research collaboration, both regionally and with international partners, is therefore a strategic priority for Africa in terms of generating internal capacity for rapid social and economic development. The partnerships should be aimed at contributing to knowledge production and exchange among universities and other stakeholders as well as building their capacity to respond to Africa's development challenges (Shabani, 2008; Teferra, 2008).

Since 2000, however, key African policy publications have demonstrated a unique focus on the importance of transnational knowledge partnerships at multiple levels (AfDB, 2008). North — South research collaboration can contribute to capacity building for knowledge production in African universities, but these partnerships must be structured in a manner that does not merely promote the vertical transfer of knowledge from the global North to the South. Instead, internationalisation initiatives should focus on localisation of knowledge production and prioritisation of local knowledge systems and infrastructure existing within Africa.

Developing the Next Generation of African Academics

African universities risk running out of high-quality academics. The scale of the crisis and reasons for it vary across countries and even institutions. The universities face the challenge of recruiting, training and retaining adequate levels of qualified academic staff. This is aggravated by the absence of sustainable staff development programmes (Hayward, 2010)

The brain drain has worsened the situation. African brain drain figures are astounding. Most African scientists and engineers work in developed countries. The declining numbers of postgraduate students in African universities is shrinking the pool of potential future academics. Enrolments of postgraduate students remain low, at an average of five per cent of the total student population (Tettey, 2009) and they attain their PhDs at comparatively advanced ages. At the same time, there is a very great need to replace the ageing academic staff, leading to an urgent need for African universities to invest in the development of the new generation group of scholars. African governments are increasingly supporting the idea of building diasporic knowledge networks to utilise the tremendous human capital accumulated within the global African diaspora.

The essence of continuous enhancement and upgrading of knowledge has been recognised as a priority area for comprehensive planning and investment in African universities. It is thus difficult for African universities to replace staff losses and enhance the capacity and quality of teaching and research at the same time (Hayward, 2010). These scenarios constitute an urgent wake-up call for African universities with regard to their staff requirements.

Strengthening ICT Capacities and Utilisation

African universities face significant barriers in their efforts to utilise ICTs for teaching, learning and research. Most of them have inadequate ICT infrastructure and at higher costs. The 2006 African Tertiary Institution Connectivity Survey summarised the state of ICT infrastructure in African higher education as 'too little, too expensive, and poorly managed' (Gakio, 2006). It further illustrated that an average African university had the same aggregate bandwidth as a single home user in North America or Europe but paid 50 times more for it (*ibid.*, iii), leading to more isolation of African universities from the global knowledge economy.

The situation is however quickly changing (Tusubira, Ndiwalana, Dindi, & Obbo, 2012) with new developments in ICT taking place in most African countries. The UbuntuNet Alliance, a Regional Research and Education Network for Eastern and Southern Africa, is one of the various landmark ICT initiatives. It utilizes advanced optic fibre technologies and other terrestrial infrastructure to establish a high-speed research and education backbone which interconnects all national research hubs across the two regions and provides high-speed connectivity to global research and knowledge collaboration (Tusubira et al., 2012). While there are positive developments in most parts of Africa, Northern and Southern African countries have produced some tremendous achievements. The use of open educational resources is also beginning to gain interest and with developments in distance education and e-learning, the opportunities are growing. These developments are tremendously important for the quality of teaching and learning, research, enhanced access to study opportunities and educational materials, governance and even strengthening of collaborations and Africa's position in the knowledge society.

Several initiatives are emerging to address Africa's disadvantaged position compared with the rest of the globe. One example is the East African Submarine Cable System, which has developed an undersea fibre-optic cable to link the countries of eastern Africa to the rest of the globe. Complementing this is the Africa Regional Communications Infrastructure Program (RCIP) which focuses on regional communication infrastructure. These would have a positive impact on Africa's higher education.

Fostering Intra-Africa Co-operation

Traditionally, African universities have developed partnerships and collaborations, mainly with Northern partners with little going on between African universities themselves. This was also exacerbated by linguistic balkanisation of Africa, with extensions to the colonial links associated with these languages. There are growing interests and initiatives in strengthening intra-Africa co-operation. This is spearheaded by the African Union Commission (AUC) and anchored on the Second Decade of the Education Plan of Action. It calls for revitalisation of higher education in Africa through partnerships in different areas.

An important development is that to strengthen Africa's Higher Education and Research Space (AHERS) to open up more opportunities for collaborations, mobility, harmonisation of degree programmes and establishment of cross-border quality assurance frameworks. Consequently, the Arusha Convention has attracted more attention in the recent past, in addition to establishment of new mobility schemes such as the Nyerere scholarship programme and the Pan Africa University.

African governments and international partners could contribute to this by supporting the emerging centres of excellence, the new mobility programmes and establishment of quality doctoral programmes within the continent. This will in the end strengthen Africa's higher education and contribute towards stemming some of the negative consequences of internationalisation and also help shape Africa's agenda for internationalisation.

Intra-Regional Co-operation

Africa is composed of five main geographical regions; Northern Africa, East Africa, West Africa, Central Africa and Southern Africa. Even with the developments in intra-Africa collaborations, it is already emerging that university collaborations in Africa are also taking a regional dimension. This is reflected in the activities of regional university organisations such as the Inter-University Council for East Africa (IUCEA) and the Southern Africa Regional Universities Association (SARUA). Regional mobility, research networks and harmonisation programmes are already taking root within these regions.

In both the Southern Africa Development Community (SADC) and East African Community (EAC) regions, students from partner states can now study in universities within the region and pay the same fees as local or home students. This is fostering mobility and exchanges within the regions and needs enhancement. Future programmes for undergraduate and graduate mobility, staff exchanges, sabbaticals as well as researcher mobility should consider this emerging regional dynamics. These are initiatives in which both local and international partners could concentrate their support.

Emphasis needs to be put on developing credit transfer systems, national and regional quality control mechanisms, regional research networks, mobilisation of industry and the philanthropic sector for funding support, increased investment in research and graduate programmes and improvement of facilities and working conditions for academics.

Institutional Governance and Management Capacities

Most African universities still suffer from weak internal governance and management, which also negates progress that could be made on internationalisation. Building institutional governance and management capacities is essential for fostering partnerships, collaborations and the implementation of internationalisation activities. Universities need to adapt best management practices to manage internationalisation.

Conclusion

That role of higher education in Africa's sustainable social, political and economic development is not contestable. Africa, through the various continental, regional and international bodies, is developing frameworks for enhanced internationalisation. This is in recognition of the growing importance and consequences of internationalisation and transnational co-operation.

In doing this, Africa has to reconceptualise and relate internationalisation to its context and priorities. Even though internationalisation is multilayered and presents many challenges, these can be surmounted through involvement of both local and international partners. It will be essential for African universities to develop internationalisation strategies and policies that are simultaneously realistic and ambitious in recognising and seizing opportunities.

Even though there are many areas of dissimilarity — in rationales, challenges and opportunities, internationalisation is a worldwide phenomenon that requires increased co-operation at all levels. Thus, the renewed commitment to the revitalisation of African higher education systems needs support. Africa's internationalisation strategies will have to be double-pronged, both focusing on intra-Africa co-operation and reaching out for strategic international partnerships. These, if well-structured, co-ordinated and supported, could promote the benefits and minimise the risks of internationalisation for Africa.

References

Adams, J., King, C., & Hook, D. (2010). *Global research report Africa*. Leeds, UK: Thompson Reuters.

AfDB. (2008). *Strategy for higher education science and technology.* Tunis: African Development Bank.

Aina, T. A. (2010). Beyond reforms: The politics of higher education transformation in Africa. *African Studies Review, 53*(1), 21–40.

Bloom, D., Canning, D., & Chan, K. (2006). *Higher education and economic development in Africa.* Washington, DC: World Bank.

Gakio, K. (2006). *The African tertiary institutions connectivity survey report.* Ottawa, Canada: International Development and Research Centre (IRDC).

Hayward, F. M. (2010). Graduate education in Sub-Saharan Africa. In D. Teferra & H. Greijn (Eds.), *Higher education and globalization: Challenges, threats and opportunities for Africa.* Maastricht: MUNDO.

IAU. (2010). *Internationalization of higher education: Global trends, regional perspectives.* Paris: IAU.

Jowi, J. O. (2009). Internationalization of higher education in Africa: Developments, emerging trends and policy implications. *Higher Education Policy, 22,* 259–261.

Jowi, J. O. (2010). Regional insights: Analysis of institutional findings - Africa. In E. Egron-Polak & R. Hudson (Eds.), *Internationalization of higher education: Global trends, regional perspectives: IAU 3RD global survey report* (pp. 159–165). Paris: International Association of Universities (IAU).

King, K. (2008). The promise and peril of partnership. *NORRAG News, 41,* 7–11.

Koehn, P., & Rosenau, J. (2010). *Transnational competence: Empowering professional curricula for horizon-rising challenges.* Boulder, MA: Paradigm Press.

Obamba, M. O., & Mwema, J. K. (2009). Symmetry and asymmetry: New contours, paradigms and politics in African academic partnerships. *Higher Education Policy, 22,* 349–371.

Oyewole, O. (2010). Africa and the global knowledge domain. In D. Teferra & H. Greijn (Eds.), *Higher education and globalization: Challenges, threats and opportunities for Africa.* Maastricht: MUNDO.

Shabani, J. (2008). The role of key regional actors and programs. In D. Teferra & J. Knight (Eds.), *Higher education in Africa: The international dimension* (pp. 464–489). Accra/Boston, MA: AAU/CIHE.

Teferra, D. (2008). The international dimension of higher education in Africa: Status, challenges and prospects. In D. Teferra & J. Knight (Eds.), *Higher education in Africa: The international dimension* (pp. 464–489). Accra/Boston: AAU/CIHE.

Tettey, J. W. (2009). Developing and retaining the next generation of academics in Africa: An analysis of issues and challenges. *AAU Newsletter, 15*(1), 1–7.

Tusubira, F. F., Ndiwalana, A., Dindi, S., & Obbo, H. (2012). *The impact of improved access and connectivity on intellectual property output: Baseline report for the UBUNTUNET alliance.* Lilongwe, Malawi: Ubuntunet Alliance.

UNESCO. (2009). *World conference on higher education: The new dynamics of higher education and research for societal change and development.* Paris: UNESCO.

Wagner, C., Brahmakulam, I., Jackson, B., Wong, A., & Yoda, T. (2001). *Science and technology collaboration: Building capacity in developing countries?* RAND MR-1357-WB. Santa Monica, CA: RAND.

Zeleza, P. T. (2005). Transnational education and African universities. *Journal of Higher Education in Africa, 3*(1), 1–28.

SECTION 2
INSTITUTIONS AND
INTERNATIONALISATION

Chapter 2.1

Editors' Introduction to Section 2

The many ways that institutions interact with internationalisation became a major theme of Going Global 6 and has been central to the conference since then. This section opens with two complementary papers on how cross-border partnerships work in reality and how such partnerships can be used as a transformative force within the institutions concerned. Gareth Barham looks in detail at a cross-border teaching collaboration between Wales and Seoul. He looks at Kitano's three levels of engagement with internationalisation from exclusive through 'inclusive' to 'transformed' and how the partnership is contributing to both the development of the institutional teaching and learning strategy as well as to the confidence, cultural fluency and employability of its students. Ian Willis uses the context of a Liverpool–Punjab collaborative arrangement to explore the concept of collaborative reach and the human and institutional gaps that need to be bridged in building an effective and sustainable cross-border collaboration.

The third paper, by Cameron Richards and Mohd Ismail Abd Aziz, examines the development of transnational education in Malaysia, using this context as an example of a wider phenomenon — contrasting varying rhetorical and philosophical bases for the activity and asymmetric goals does not imply that there cannot be an overlapping of aims and objectives, and indeed an integrative vision does seem to be possible. To achieve this, there needs to be a reconciliation of some of the dynamic contrasts between the aim for deep pedagogic enhancement and general capacity enhancement from the host country with the economic and competitive drivers of the provider countries.

The next two papers then move the focus on to individual institutions growing and developing within the context of internationalisation. Jasmina Nikolic and Jelena Gledic argue for an 'agile' approach as higher education faces an increasing speed of change in its operating environment. They offer a range of examples of the use of the basic Agile technologies. Perhaps

Going Global: Identifying Trends and Drivers of International Education
Copyright © 2013 by Emerald Group Publishing Limited
All rights of reproduction in any form reserved
ISBN: 978-1-78190-575-3

the most striking is the student parliament example where seemingly irreconcilable agendas were bridged and a joint declaration on the future challenges of the Bologna System was produced. Chandra J. Embuldeniya describes the creation of an entrepreneurially and internationally oriented university in Sri Lanka that would contribute to driving up employability within the local population.

The section closes with an overview of multi-institutional partnerships. Tim Gore et al. look at the growth of strategic university networks that offer ways for universities to expand their international engagement selectively and cost effectively. The authors present a number of such networks and use the examples to examine what makes such networks effective.

It seems likely that the context of institutions in internationalisation will continue to change and develop over the coming few years as increasing competitive forces and ongoing financial challenges beset the sector and we need to ask whether those that effectively embed internationalisation as part of their make-up are likely to spot and weather these changes more successfully.

Chapter 2.2

Perspectives on Internationalisation: Creating an International Masters of Design

Gareth Barham

This paper presents a case study of how two universities from opposite sides of the world have reached beyond traditional boundaries by collaborating in a jointly delivered Masters programme. It discusses the importance of internationalisation within the current economic educational context and explains how internationalisation theory has driven programme practice.

The financial challenges faced by the UK higher education sector provide the socio-economic context within which the collaborative programme developed. The temptation to develop internationalisation strategies aimed at increasing numbers of international students, regarding them only as a lucrative source of income, is likely to encounter resistance from staff and students who might have reason to perceive this as another example of the increasing commercialisation of higher education.

It is within this context that co-operation developed between the Cardiff School of Art & Design (CSAD) at Cardiff Metropolitan University and the Samsung Art & Design Institute (SADI) in Seoul, South Korea. Together the two institutions have developed a unique Masters of Design programme partly delivered in Cardiff and partly in Seoul. The principles and practices of an internationalised curriculum and student mobility are fundamental to the success of the programme and the programme responds to the needs of the global design employment market, preparing students to operate professionally and confidently in the international design arena by developing their international perspectives and capabilities.

Going Global: Identifying Trends and Drivers of International Education
Copyright © 2013 by Emerald Group Publishing Limited
All rights of reproduction in any form reserved
ISBN: 978-1-78190-575-3

CSAD/SADI MDes Programme Structure

The Master of Design (MDes) programme is part of a validated Integrated Masters Scheme that is delivered at the CSAD in the United Kingdom and at the SADI, Seoul, South Korea. Students study in Cardiff for the first semester from September until the end of January and then in Seoul for the remaining two semesters from February until August.

SADI is a private institution that is sponsored by the Samsung Corporation. This philanthropic activity aims to foster high-quality design education in South Korea. SADI is a highly respected provider of three-year design programmes. Competition for places is high and most applicants will also have a first degree in other subjects. SADI may be a relatively small institution by Korean standards with approximately 500 students but high-quality design education is comparable to the design philosophies at the CSAD at Cardiff Metropolitan University.

The CSAD is one of five schools at Cardiff Metropolitan University. It offers undergraduate, masters and research degrees in a wide variety of subjects including product design, graphic communication, illustration, textile design, ceramics, fine art and architecture.

Institutional Motivation

Collaboration between the two institutions developed amid a climate of financial austerity cuts introduced by the British government. These placed new financial pressures on universities. British 'home' students faced tuition fee increases of up to three times than previous levels (in some circumstances) and the government announced budget cuts for universities. These factors have already contributed towards universities placing greater emphasis on generating alternative sources of income and international students, whose importance to UK HEIs is now greater than ever, are often perceived as being well financed and used to paying higher tuition fees. Montgomery (2010) points to the tensions between the discourses of marketisation, the increasing commercialisation of higher education and the more altruistic motivations of internationalisation. In this economic climate the tensions between developing strategies that increase numbers of international students and approaches to internationalising the student experience to educate the global citizen may become even more acute.

These developments might be considered unfortunate. However, it does provide a significant opportunity for growth in international activity if universities embrace the benefits of internationalised education.

The temptation in the current economic climate, however, might be for university managers to develop international strategies that regard international students only as a source of additional (and lucrative) income. This strategy will undoubtedly encounter resistance from academic staff and students alike who might have reason to complain about the increasing commercialisation of education. It is often within this context that universities in the United Kingdom have been developing their internationalisation policies. Targets to increase the numbers of international students are sometimes perceived to have been set without consideration for the relevance of their learning experience or the impact of a larger international student cohort on 'home' students.

School Ambitions

As is the case for many UK universities, historically, the primary focus of the CSAD's international activities has been the recruitment of overseas students. More recently, however, the emphasis has begun to shift to recognise that the recruitment of good quality international students goes hand in hand with other elements of internationalisation such as the internationalisation of curricula. It is perceived that the need for internationalised curricula is particularly acute given that, on average, approximately 36 per cent of its students are from the immediate surrounding geographical area and some from socio-economic backgrounds where there have been relatively few opportunities for them to engage in cross-cultural activities and debate. The School has a complement of approximately 1200 students with five per cent of them being international students (from beyond the borders of the European Union) and only one per cent from the European Union. This is in contrast to the University as a whole where international students account for 10 per cent of the total student population. Of the remaining student population in the School, approximately 58 per cent are UK students from beyond the immediate surrounding geographical area. In line with the School's student demographics, it is perceived that a learning environment which recognises that students should appreciate the importance of learning within different cultural contexts that highlight alternative art and design influences, processes and strategies is highly beneficial.

Benefits and Requirements of Internationalisation

Despite the commitment of the School and the University to the potential that internationalisation has to develop responsible, capable, compassionate, self-aware and cosmopolitan citizens, better prepared to function effectively in a global society and global employment marketplace, the reality of the introduction of the concept can give rise to intense debate among staff. Fuel is added to the fire when central University agendas appear to emphasise the importance of internationalisation activities as income-generating activities and this central directive often eclipses the transformative benefits that internationalisation could bring.

A significant body of research exists putting forward a compelling series of arguments to reinforce the fact that organisations, at every level, should adopt the principles of internationalisation of curriculum. Schoorman emphasises, for example, 'the importance of internationalisation in institutional missions and in administrative efforts to engage in strategic planning for internationalisation' (2000, p. 5). Much of this research also underlines the fact that adopting these principles requires substantial change — or transformation — and seeing internationalisation as an 'add-on' is not an option. Morey, for example, explains that 'to bring about a truly transformed curriculum requires fundamental and systemic change in the organisation itself' and she goes on to argue that '[t]he framework entails the establishment of an enabling environment for change, including a shared vision of what is possible and a strategy for change' (Morey, 2000, p. 27).

Kitano (1997) identifies three specific levels of internationalised curricula and intercultural engagement. In the first of these, Kitano describes universities termed as 'exclusive', that is to say universities whose curricula embody traditional, mainstream experience and perspectives where academic staff act as the fountain of all knowledge with limited opportunities for alternative world views and perspectives and critical debate. The next level of engagement is described by Kitano as 'inclusive'. This level constitutes a radical departure from the first level in that internationalisation strategies are perceived as beneficial to all. The curricula in these sorts of contexts can be characterised by their drive towards cultural inclusivity as they strive to incorporate international perspectives and opportunities for cultural exchange. Within this model, alternative perspectives are put forward and a variety of teaching methods used to support active learning. The final level of participation described by Kitano is that of the 'transformed' university and this constitutes a dramatic paradigm shift. Whereas in the previous model of the 'inclusive' university, cultural interaction is based largely on observation, at the final level, academics and their perspectives are characterised by full engagement. In line with this, work is considered from the perspective of others and entirely new approaches are developed. Within this model, students and tutors are seen to learn from one another and new learning and assessment strategies are embraced, which include self-assessments, evaluation and reflection.

An environment of diverse perspectives and mutual respect prevails (Kitano, 1997).

As our own understanding of internationalisation developed within the School, we recognised that our pedagogic practices were ethnocentric in that the world was often viewed from a western perspective. This suggested that we were only achieving the second level of international engagement as described by Kitano — that of an 'inclusive' university. Our ambition was to achieve Kitano's third level of internationalisation, that of a 'transformed' university, if we were to reposition our School as a global institution and to enhance the student experience in the process.

The University's internationalisation strategy encourages the mobility of students but this activity is either as a part of, or in addition to, their studies. Our students were able to pick and choose modules or parts of courses from international partner institutions to enhance their studies. However, we recognised that these arrangements were somewhat ad hoc and a more developed and cohesive strategy was needed.

We recognised that to create a truly meaningful international experience for our students, we needed to change our learning and teaching strategies to embrace the unique skills and experiences that international students bring to the classroom. Academics can do this by including the perspectives of their international students in discussions and by creating a learning environment where no single cultural perspective has dominance. By creating a learning environment for international students, universities can also address the needs of local and home students who have relatively little experience of other cultures. Adapting curricula to provide international learning for all should ensure that all students are equipped with the skills needed to compete for work in a global marketplace.

Initiatives such as study placements overseas begin to give international perspectives to home students and the greater involvement of international students' ideas at the University also gives a wider perspective on cultural issues. An internationalised curriculum encourages home students to engage with other students without stereotyping or prejudice and this helps them to develop the perspective and confidence of a global citizen.

Challenges and Solutions

It is within this economic and changing educational context that co-operation developed between Cardiff Metropolitan University and the SADI. This collaboration had been under way since 2007 and began partly in an attempt to address some of the internationalisation issues discussed above. Academic staff had run various design workshops and provided guest lectures at SADI, and CSAD's design students visited SADI for week-long workshops where the students worked in mixed groups on various design creativity projects. What proved to be particularly successful about the workshops was not only the professional working compatibility of British and South Korean students, but that some understanding of cultural perspectives began to emerge through their academic work and social interaction. A close working relationship and mutual respect followed between the School and SADI and it was a logical 'next step' to develop a postgraduate degree together based on the success of the workshops.

International Learning Experience: Course Structure

The objective of the new Masters degree in Design was to prepare students to operate professionally and confidently in an international design arena by adopting the perspectives of a responsible global citizen. The international employment market for designers is highly competitive. Employers can afford to be selective by requiring applicants to have postgraduate qualifications and in specialised subjects that will directly contribute towards their business strategies. With emphasis on practice, the SADI MDes provides an opportunity for advanced design study in the context of a professional, international situation.

The structure of the SADI MDes recognises the specific expertise at each institution. CSAD has developed an excellent reputation for the world-leading international research that it conducts into design theory and practice. Students explore and develop design methodologies to create unique perspectives within their specialism. These perspectives emerge through academic and cultural investigation and interaction between 'home' and international students in a structured and measured way. This is achieved by addressing the learning outcomes of the module descriptors from a global context where design philosophies and practice are explored and discussed from the different cultural perspectives that exist in the lecture rooms and design studios. The students are required to develop their own critical creative position at CSAD which they later apply through design practice at SADI.

SADI is internationally recognised for the quality and professionalism of its students and their highly creative design capabilities. The emphasis at SADI is on design practice where students apply their newly formed design philosophies in the new environment of Seoul. This process encourages students and staff to evaluate cultural design perspectives through their work and prepares them for operating in a global professional context.

Challenges

The development of the SADI MDes was not straightforward. Questions were raised about the course's income-generating capacity as numbers of students were always going to be small compared with other trans-national educational programmes. However, support was gained thanks to cross-departmental recognition of the programme's unique embedded student mobility.

Another challenge has been how to ensure the quality of the student learning experience is maintained at both institutions. Measures such as both institutions using the same virtual learning environment have greatly helped and the involvement of the Internal Moderator who visits twice a year cannot be underestimated in ensuring parity of marking schemes and the quality and timing of assignment feedback for example. The different pedagogical approaches emphasising the different cultural approaches to learning and teaching have also presented challenges in terms of meeting the expectations of the partner institution. CSAD sometimes considers that SADI 'over-teaches' the students and, conversely, SADI might be of the opinion that we have too little contact time with them. I believe that the success of the programme is due in part to both partners' commitment to internationalisation at every level. This has been instrumental in fostering a working relationship of trust between the two institutions meaning that the different cultural approaches to learning and teaching are recognised and respected. Students are made aware of these cultural differences and are encouraged to exploit these in the development of their learning strategies.

The Impact of the Programmes

It is already clear that collaboration between SADI and CSAD has not only given students the confidence to work as designers at opposite sides of the world, but also given them the experience of another culture and the appetite to explore others. It has also allowed students to question some of their own cultural values and characteristics through their collaboration by understanding the perspectives others have on themselves and their professional design work. To some extent, this demonstrates that the programme is beginning to help us to reach our target of attaining the third level of internationalisation achievement as described by Kitano — that of a transformed university.

Other measures of the impact of the programme can be seen by analysing the destinations of its graduates. The SADI MDes is only in its second year of delivery but already graduates from South Korea are working for international organisations in Seoul, Europe and the United States.

The overall philosophy of the programme to 'internationalise' our 'home' students has also been a successes. Graduates of the CSAD MDes are employed in Seoul, Hong Kong and Beijing and another British graduate is now an associate tutor at Dong-A University in Busan, South Korea. A pleasing result has been that the students themselves have been active in driving the internationalisation agenda in the School by demonstrating a growing eagerness to engage internationally and there have been increased requests from 'home' students to conduct their major project at SADI during the third semester.

Concluding Thoughts

Although, on the one hand, the current financial climate has muddied the waters of the internationalisation of the curriculum debate, on the other it has inadvertently created significant opportunities for reflection and change. The theories and practices of internationalisation have the potential to play an important role in readdressing the balance between the commercial impetus to recruit international students and ensuring curriculum relevance for all students. However, a single strategy that unites the concepts of curriculum internationalisation and international development cannot be measured by a single programme alone. These strategies need to be adopted by a network of programmes across the University if internationalisation is to be at the heart of campus life. In light of this, the role that the University and School management need to play in this process should not be underestimated. In order to encourage adoption of internationalisation, it needs to be clear that the University at every level not only supports these important principles but also understands them.

References

Kitano, M. K. (1997). What a course will look like after multicultural change. In A. J. Morey & M. Kitano (Eds.), *Multicultural course transformation in higher education: A broader truth* (pp. 18–30). Boston, MA: Allyn and Bacon.
Montgomery, C. (2010). *Understanding the international student experience*. Basingstoke: Palgrave Macmillan.

Morey, A. I. (2000). Changing higher education curricula for a global and multicultural world. *Higher Education in Europe*, 25(1), 25–39.

Schoorman, D. (2000). What do we really mean by 'internationalisation?'. Retrieved from http://web.ebscohost.com/ehost/detail?vid+4&hid=3&sid=a5d015de. Accessed on April 3, 2008.

Chapter 2.3

Collaborative Reach: A Model for International Collaborations through Engaging Different Levels within Partner Institutions

Ian Willis

Internationalisation holds out the promise of a more connected world and is a response of many higher education institutions to increasing globalisation. There is increasing demand for high-quality higher education that impels higher education to build greater capacity globally. According to Bone (2008), a long-term collaborative view of internationalisation is required. International partnerships are one way forward.

The models of internationalisation collaboration that are outlined in this paper examine different elements of collaborations, including the social dimension. This was expressed by Homi Bhabha (2012), in the keynote address to the 2012 Going Global conference, as developing 'good neighbourliness' or the 'ability to live side by side'. He argued that we need to think beyond the nuts and bolts and self-interest of collaboration and to see it as 'immersing yourself in that which is not your own' in the 'continual labour of intercultural conversation' that seeks to negotiate convergence in international collaborations.

Taking these ideas as a starting point, this paper outlines out some of the meanings of collaboration. Collaboration is examined in more

Going Global: Identifying Trends and Drivers of International Education
Copyright © 2013 by Emerald Group Publishing Limited
All rights of reproduction in any form reserved
ISBN: 978-1-78190-575-3

detail by looking at different constituent layers or levels of interaction between partners. The international collaboration between the University of Liverpool (UoL), United Kingdom, and the University of Health Sciences (UHS) in the Punjab, Pakistan, is used as a case study in order to give practical examples of ideas and to build a model that may have useful applications in a range of settings. This model is extended to incorporate the concept of collaborative reach and to show some practical possibilities for developing the 'ability to live side by side'. It is argued that the model is applicable to a wider range of international collaborations. Finally, the achievements and impact of the UHS — UoL collaboration to date and the learning derived from the experience are summarised and related to the different levels of interaction.

The Nature of Collaboration

Collaboration has multiple meanings, centred on working together for mutual advantage. It includes the ability to achieve goals that could not have been gained by the organisations acting alone (Huxham, 2003). Inherent in international collaborations is the idea that as our world becomes more globalised and interconnected there is a corresponding increase in the possibilities for collaboration and the complexities of collaboration. However, simply deciding to collaborate is insufficient; there are numerous challenges to be addressed in order to create constructive possibilities (Walsh & Kahn, 2010).

This paper analyses these challenges by means of a model that specifically addresses the multi-levelled nature of successful international collaboration. The levels of interaction between partners are:

- the individuals involved, usually enthusiasts who build initial engagement
- the shared social space where these individuals, through professional dialogue, negotiate activities and understanding
- the institutional structures and agreements that are essential for sustainability.

Collaborative reach is introduced as a concept that enables partners to reach across divides such as geography, culture and organisational characteristics.

The Collaboration between UoL and UHS

UoL and UHS are partners in a British Council INSPIRE project (International Strategic Partnerships in Research and Education) that aims to enhance learning and teaching in medical education in the Punjab. UHS is a 'hub university' that controls the medical and dental examination system in most of the Punjab (population 80 million). This is achieved through its 30-plus affiliated colleges and universities that are dispersed though the province. It has been recognised as the top medical university in Pakistan by the Higher Education Commission of Pakistan. UoL is a research-led university with a strong medical faculty and a strategic aim to be globally recognised. Thus, there are some natural synergies in medical education and some differences in research focus and international recognition.

The case study is analysed through the lens of the levels of interaction between the partners:

- the individuals involved
- the shared social interactions
- the relevant institutional structures.

It is argued that attention must be paid to all of these levels in order to build a sustainable partnership that endures beyond the initial enthusiasms and funding. The early stages of a project usually require individual motivation and agency, progress is achieved through social or interpersonal interactions, and sustainability requires institutional commitment and benefit. Examining the different levels of interaction gives the partners in any collaboration a way of analysing progress, strengths and potential weaknesses.

The two universities had signed a Memorandum of Understanding (MoU) in 2009 in order to develop a mutually beneficial relationship in research and education, but tangible projects were required to give the MoU real meaning. The role of the British Council was crucial in providing initial seed funding to allow exchanges and discussions to start to shape concrete proposals. The project was founded on the notion of mutual benefit, 'aid not trade' (Bone, 2008). To achieve sustainability it was recognised that methods had to be found to ensure that both universities were able to benefit in ways that accorded with their strategic aims.

Levels of Interaction between Partners: Individual, 'Social' and Institutional

The Individuals Involved

Despite the existence of institutional MoUs it is often enthusiastic individuals who initiate collaborative activity through their personal connections. Bhabha (2012) argues that the passions of the mind are as important as the cognitive processes in collaborations. In a similar vein,

Gajda (2004) claims that the personal is as important as the procedural and that generally, in examining collaborations, attention is directed towards the institutional level. This tendency can downplay the importance of the motivations and actions of key individuals.

These motivations and actions can be expressed as agency, the ability to pursue personal projects. Supportive organisational structures, such as MoUs, can be seen as providing the opportunity for individuals to exercise their own agency and to advance projects that are important to them (Archer, 2003). These 'personal projects' are manifest as a personal and professional interest in international educational activity for one person and a desire to maintain and develop their career through personal and professional links in Pakistan and United Kingdom for another. For the four people most immediately involved there is the pleasure and the learning of the engagement. This affective dimension is not shown in any documentation but it is strongly argued that it is a key driver in the initial stages of the overall project and is under-represented in official reporting and researching. Indeed, Walsh and Kahn (2010) list the personal qualities required for effective collaboration including energy, commitment and determination but they pay little attention to the affective domain in terms of personal enjoyment and growth. This surely must contribute to personal choices about which projects to engage with and the depth of that engagement.

The Shared Social Interactions

This section discusses the interconnected elements that can be related to the social interactions. These are the professional dialogues, programme goals, emergent activities and reciprocity.

Collaboration is by nature social and it is suggested that there is a need to attend to the 'professional dialogues', where individuals come together to develop the activities and outcomes of the collaboration. Professional dialogues are characterised by criticality, professionalism and effective communication and the recognition that joint decision-making requires time, trust, negotiation and ongoing learning (Walsh & Kahn, 2010). Professional dialogues are the means whereby decisions are made and relationships are deepened. For successful international collaboration these relationships do matter and the resultant social networks are a valuable asset (Field, 2003). According to Putnam (2001) social capital refers to the value of our networks and their inherent reciprocity. This value can be both economic and personal/social (Woolcock, 2000). One function of the professional dialogues is the explicit building of networks within the overall collaboration as mandated in the British Council's INSPIRE funding bids and closely is aligned to Bhabha's (2012) 'continual labour of intercultural conversation'.

In international collaborations, building networks is one means towards the end purpose of meeting a project's aims. Projects are bounded by over-arching goals, but these are often deliberately framed to allow space for the development of specific outcomes that can be negotiated by the partners as their relationships deepen. Many important objectives cannot be pre-planned. They emerge from the professional dialogues and shared activities. Encouraging emergence creates opportunities for more creative endeavours that go beyond pre-planned objectives. In fact, planned goals are often written in order to be met and need to be inherently conservative in nature. However, it is not always possible to know in advance how enhancements may best be made. Opportunities arise from professional dialogue and shared activities that are based in reciprocity, trust and increasing understanding of each partner's needs and constraints.

In this case study, UHS's initial interests were well defined in developing learning and teaching in medical education, whereas UoL's goals were broader in developing capacity to operate internationally and in making a contribution. This is described as a responsibility of academics in privileged institutions to collaborate (Bretag, 2008) and that academics are motivated by a desire to 'contribute the greater good' (Willis, 2010). These motivations might be individual or institutional, but the process of finding ways to enact these motivations is worked out in the social interactions, the professional dialogues.

Professional dialogues have led to the joint development of an 'Introduction to Teaching in Medical Education' aimed at all new medical educators in UHS affiliated universities. This has clear benefits for UHS and hopefully for health outcomes in the Punjab. Also, a Post Graduate Certificate in Medical Education, based on UoL's experience but owned by UHS is being delivered. In isolation, the benefits were asymmetrical and had the potential risk of not securing UoL's long-term commitment. Ongoing dialogue and commitment to reciprocity, ensuring mutual benefit, has led to an agreement that UHS would direct a significant portion of its allocation of PhD funding to UoL. Immediately, this gave UoL a tangible benefit at an institutional level and cemented a longer-term research-based relationship that accords with all of UoL's strategic aims.

The Relevant Institutional Structures

For long-term success institutional support for the collaboration needs to become embedded. Critically, long-lasting collaboration requires mutual benefit, so that partners need to secure items that matter to the other partner as well as ensuring their own institutional benefit.

In this case, the beginning was an institutional-level MoU that provided the initial framework. Individual actions and specific projects were needed to take this further. The British Council funding specifically encouraged travel between institutions to facilitate relationship building at all levels. These visits created the space for discussions and have allowed a significant number of senior staff in both institutions to meet. As well as those shown above, outcomes that have derived directly from these meetings include a knowledge exchange project and the development of a virtual learning environment at UHS. The institutional agreement for the provision of PhD training for UHS staff commits the institutions to a long-term relationship that will endure beyond the initial enthusiasms. This aspect of the relationship has the potential to sustain ongoing research collaborations that meet UHS's commitment to improve health outcomes in the Punjab and UoL's strategy for international research and engagement.

These projects and agreements are manifestations of the relationship; they are founded on personal engagement and mutual benefit for the universities. The leaders of the project must be able to work within their institutions to build support and demonstrate benefit. While there is often a rhetorical desire for international collaboration and to 'contribute to the greater good', in order to be brought into reality these aspirations must be worth it in practical terms.

In summary, the model presents practical actions in order to build and sustain international collaborations, which are:

- to attend to the personal, social and structural layers of interaction
- to create multiple connections, individual and departmental, between the partners
- to build institutional agreements and support
- to identify and articulate mutual benefit.

There is an interesting aspect to the collaboration, as seen from UoL's perspective. The university is strongly research focused. There appear to be differences in the university's approach to teaching and research partnerships. Its primary teaching partnerships are driven from the top, as university-level relationships. However, many research collaborations are founded on individual academic or departmental relationships (Qualter & Willis, 2011). In this case, a small-scale teaching project has been able to lead to an institutional-level research partnership. This runs counter to the usual partnership configurations and yet offers an interesting possibility of using teaching-based projects to foster longer-term research-based activity.

Collaborative Reach

Collaborative reach is a term coined by Kahn, Petichakis and Walsh (2012) to draw attention to the divides or differences between partners in a collaboration that the collaboration must 'reach across'. Kahn et al. (2012) stress the importance of acknowledging 'the full range of ways in which partners must cross boundaries in working together' (p. 7). It means identifying areas where challenges and misunderstandings might occur. The intention is to identify in advance, and where possible to reach across, these divides. It can lead to a checklist of 'things I wish I had known in advance'; some of these are obvious, especially once really known, and some take time and dialogue to appreciate.

It is useful to pose the question: what impact might any of these elements have on any particular project? Or: how much is known about the partners with respect to these elements?

- Physical elements
  o geography, time zone, infrastructures
- Individual
  o aims, needs, positions, enthusiasms
- Social
  o culture, language, religion, identity, history, hierarchies
  o the social essentials, for example gift-giving, ceremony, food, family
- Institutional
  o priorities, decision-making processes, 'politics', drivers, resources

Practical examples for the UHS — UoL collaboration includes the different emphasis on gift-giving and hospitality. From a UK perspective, we were underprepared for the significance of gift-giving and it is challenging to use institutional funding in United Kingdom for gifts. Similarly, hospitality, food and family are central to Pakistani culture; that is easier to adjust to! However, there are implications when our Pakistani colleagues visit Liverpool. Interestingly, and in general, our Pakistani colleagues are far better attuned to UK culture than vice versa. Another example relates to the time taken in decision-making. As a devolved organisation UoL often takes considerable time in reaching decisions, whereas UHS can react quickly, if those in power choose to do so. At the very least each partner needs to understand the position of the other. Also, it is an ongoing learning process about the 'politics' of the Pakistani Higher Education system, the ramifications may be impenetrable to outsiders, but not to know anything in this area and not to be continuously learning is a grave oversight.

The notion of collaborative reach can be extended to other key constituencies in the collaboration. To build a sustainable institutional-level collaboration requires that we also 'reach within' our own institution. As part of collaboration building we are wise to pay attention to the 'politics' of our own institution; who needs to be informed, what media can be used for communication, whose support is needed, how does the project connect and contribute to institutional strategies and how do we demonstrate the contribution?

Similarly, 'reaching without' to external partners or interested parties. What plans do we have for current and future dissemination and how are we communicating with current and future funding agencies?

Impact

The collaborative partnership has had a number of important results. At UHS: the Introduction to Teaching in Medical Education programme, the Post Graduate Certificate in Medical Education and the development of a virtual learning environment. For UoL: agreement for funded PhDs and using the experience as a model for future partnerships. In addition, the Knowledge Exchange project has contributed, through the British Council, to national strategy in this area.

The main impact for the international education community is that the model focuses attention on the different intersecting levels of a collaboration and can be used to ensure that sufficient attention is paid to the key component levels. The notion of collaborative reach can be readily adapted to articulate and reach across the divides that might separate the collaborators and be applied to our own institutions and to external partners.

In Summary

The social nature of collaboration is shown to be a central element to successful international collaboration. This can be traced to theoretical concepts such as social capital and to the ideas around good neighbourliness and the intercultural conversations that underpin mutually beneficial collaborations.

The model incorporates a 'levels analysis' of collaboration and the notion of collaborative reach can be used to evaluate any partnership and to develop practical actions. The model is helping UHS and UoL to develop ideas and processes that can be replicated in Pakistan as a whole and as well as internationally. The work highlights the importance of explicitly intending to learn about the partner institution and country. It also shows that personal motivation and agency is an under-researched area that offers fruitful opportunities to contribute to knowledge of the key factors in international collaborations.

References

Archer, M. (2003). *Structure, agency and the internal conversation.* Cambridge: Cambridge University Press.

Bhabha, H. (2012). *Education: Connecting the future world.* Keynote address, British Council's Going Global conference: London. Retrieved from http://ihe.british council.org/going-global/sessions/education-connecting-future-world. Accessed on June 2012.

Bone, D. (2008). *Internationalisation of HE: A ten-year view.* London: Department for Innovation, Universities and Skills. Retrieved from http://www.british council.de/files/2012/11/Internationalisation_reprot_DBone_2009.pdf. Accessed on June 2012.

Bretag, T. (Ed.) (2008). Editorial. *International Journal for Educational Integrity,* *4*(1), 1–2.

Field, J. (2003). *Social capital.* London: Routledge.

Gajda, R. (2004). Utilizing collaboration theory to evaluate strategic alliances. *American Journal of Evaluation, 25*(1), 65–77.

Huxham, C. (2003). Theorizing collaboration practice. *Public Management Review,* *5*(3), 401–423.

Kahn, P., Petichakis, C., & Walsh, L. (2012). Developing the capacity of researchers for collaborative working. *International Journal of Researcher Development, 3*(1), 49–63.

Putnam, R. (2001). Social capital: Measurement and consequences. *Canadian Journal of Policy Research, 2*(1), 41–51.

Qualter, A., & Willis, I. (2011). Internationalisation policy and practice: The position of middle managers. *ISOTL/ISL 2010 Conference Proceedings,* Liverpool, UK.

Walsh, L., & Kahn, P. (2010). *Collaborative working in higher education: The social academy.* London: Routledge.

Willis, I. (2010). *How important is the local when thinking global? Internationalisation at a research led university.* Lancaster: University of Lancaster.

Woolcock, M. (2000). Social capital: The state of the notion. In J. Kajanoja & J. Simpura (Eds.), *Social capital: Global and local perspectives* (pp. 15–40). Helsinki: Government Institute for Economic Research.

Chapter 2.4

Malaysia's Twinning Programmes and the Challenge of Achieving (More) Reciprocal 'International Partnerships' in the Emerging Global Higher Education System

Cameron Richards and Mohd Ismail Abd Aziz

The Rhetoric vs. Reality of International Higher Education Collaboration

> One of the major peeves I have is when I see many private colleges advertising their twinning programmes as 'world-class' and are partnered with the 'top' universities in the various countries overseas ... These students who have paid so much more taking these twinning courses would have learnt more, and be better qualified for the job market if they had enrolled in some of the better local universities in Malaysia. (*Education in Malaysia Blogspot*)

It is perhaps a truism that emerging universities — and nations for that matter — generally prefer to 'partner' more established higher education (HE) centres, and also that perhaps none really prefers to partner 'beneath' unless there is at least commercial benefit. While various modes of transnational, cross-border and international higher education collaborative partnership are often rhetorically justified in rhetoric in the 'warm and

Going Global: Identifying Trends and Drivers of International Education
Copyright © 2013 by Emerald Group Publishing Limited
All rights of reproduction in any form reserved
ISBN: 978-1-78190-575-3

fuzzy' terms of 'cultural globalisation' (preparing students for a changing world, high-quality degrees, employability outcomes, fair exchange, integrating new ICTs, racial/cultural diversity, education as a noble ideal and public good, etc.), the reality of course is that as a matter of survival ultimately no university or country can ignore the often conflicting imperative of economic globalisation (national policy/economic imperatives; competitive markets, user-pays service models, the broker model of HE hubs or internationalisation; and imperatives for efficiency, standardisation and accreditation transfer which often encourage 'surface-level' rather than 'deep-level' education and research) (Nelson, 2008). This has especially been the case since the 1995 GATS provided definitive international recognition of education as a trade in services (e.g. Knight, 2006). In other words, global enthusiasm for the undeniable attractions and opportunities of the transnational HE model (Aihara, 2009; Altbach, Reisberg, & Rumbley, 2009) can also blind universities and related national policy imperatives to the challenges and dangers of not sufficiently reconciling cultural and economic globalisation and also the related distinction between the global commons and global marketplace for higher education (Mok, 2011; Newman & Jahdi, 2009; Stambach, 2012).

In this paper we explore how the development of and changes in the Malaysian twinning programmes over the last two decades epitomise global as well as local dilemmas for established and emerging partners in any international partnership collaboration. Such an asymmetrical or hierarchical relation is usually quite evident in various transnational education arrangements, but perhaps less so in relation to various models of student, staff and 'curriculum' exchange on one hand, and various forms of research collaboration or knowledge sharing on the other (Sidhu & Kaur, 2011; Ziguras & McBurnie, 2011). In contrast to the focus today on international students being attracted to study in Malaysia (i.e. a broker model), the initial justifications for the Malaysian twinning model tended to be generally framed (following the 1986 First Industrial Masterplan) in terms of national capacity-building, and focused on local students (Singh, Schapper, & Mayson, 2010). Before the expansion of the student mobility global market (and related economic opportunities to harness this) then, the initial model was thus generally understood as more a transitional rather than permanent (or possibly 'neo-colonial') arrangement. Yet in time the asymmetric typical model of Malaysian private colleges or university colleges linking to public universities overseas became more entrenched. This was as national policy began to be viewed through a new lens as more of a business partnership in which the Malaysian economy and society would ultimately benefit as well as international partners (Rahman, 2011; Wilkinson & Yussof, 2005). On such a basis, higher education in Malaysia became in 2010 a National Key Economic Area, linked to a related policy target of attracting 200,000 international fee-paying students by 2020 (Chi, 2011). In this way also the twinning model was supplemented by increasingly popular franchising arrangements of accreditation which extended to the embrace of off-shore and branch campus alternatives or options.

Malaysia's Twinning Programmes and Nationalist vs. Globalisation Dilemmas in International Higher Education

> With 2.5 million students, countless scholars, degrees and universities moving about the globe freely there is a pressing need for international cooperation and agreements. (Altbach et al., 2009, p. ii)

Western Michigan University (WMU) credits itself with launching the twinning programme in 1987 which 'helped Malaysia emerge as a Southeast Asian regional center for education' (Roland, 2012). However, in its formal guide to Malaysia's twinning degree programmes, the government agency Higher Education Malaysia (2009) points out how 'over the past 30 years' it has been the policy of the national higher education system to 'offer you an international qualification of your choice'. Both points are perhaps true. The initial WMU programme no doubt was a seminal influence on the Malaysian (and also arguably the global) transnational education model. However, the various changes in and framing of the twinning programme have not only reflected the national policy context, but also a diverse and changing context.

From the outset the emerging framework of Malaysia's twinning programmes have converged two distinct rationales which reflect a basic dilemma. The first rationale (to develop world-class higher education institutions) (Salmi, 2009) needs to be understood in terms of how in the 1980s there was a large and expensive exodus overseas of students who wanted to get an international 'world-class' degree rather than local degree accreditation. The 2010 national transformation strategy to make higher education a Key Economic Area for the future was centrally focused on private colleges and universities and, by extension, the twinning degree programme (Gooch, 2011). Such a development arguably represents the culmination of a series of emergent stages in the connection between the twinning degree programme and national HE policy. This includes the landmark Acts of 1996, which really gave impetus to the programme, and the 2007 National Higher Education Strategic Plan, which provided the focus of related developments such as the creation of the Malaysian Quality Assurance agency (Lee, 2007). In this way the strategy to attract international and not just local students to get world-class university accreditation elsewhere while also harnessing the cultural and economic benefits of studying in Malaysia has now become a major focus of not just higher education policy in Malaysia but the national Economic Transformation Program and related 'new economic model' as part of the Tenth Malaysia Plan, 2011–2015 (Rahman, 2011).

However, the twinning programme also needs to be appreciated as part of a second rationale (national economic investment), focused on the capacity-building of the Malaysian higher education system through international partnerships. As is evidenced in relevant policy documentation, much of which is still in place today, the perspective of this distinct framework was that international partnerships were generally to be regarded as a transitional stage as Malaysian higher education developed its capacity through a range of partnerships, which included but went beyond transnational degree programmes. This is typified, for instance, in how, in the upgrading quality assurance criteria for colleges, university colleges and universities in Malaysia, there have long been built-in requirements that institutions should get either direct or indirect assistance from international partners in improving existing curriculum, setting up new courses, and generally upgrading academic capacities such as teaching and administration. Such requirements are specified for instance in the MOHE (n.d.) guidebook *Criteria for upgrading IPTS from university college status to university* which was still operational in recent years (cf. also Richards, 2011a).

The tension between these two distinct rationales for international HE partnerships is further reflected in how changes in the twinning programmes over the years has been linked also to the growing popularity of new or additional modes of transnational education 'franchising'. The twinning model has also been extended in Malaysia in terms of 'branch campuses' established by Nottingham, Monash and other universities and the new 'education city' shared campuses in Iskandar (the Malaysian city near Singapore) and Kuala Lumpur (e.g. Whitehead, 2012). While various twinning degree study and accreditation arrangements are generally viewed as — and indeed function as — international collaborative partnerships, many such arrangements would be more accurately described as franchising. This change in practice has reflected how the concept of twinning has been increasingly influenced by a corresponding change in the reference for viewing higher education in Malaysia as a national investment — that is a transition from the critical reference point of outward local student mobility flows to inward international student mobility flows. On such a basis there has been a related change in typical patterns of international collaboration partnerships between institutions in Malaysia and elsewhere (Richards, 2011b; Richards & Ismail, 2012).

The History of the Malaysian Twinning Programmes as an Example of the Asymmetric Franchising vs. Reciprocal Partnerships Tension in the Emerging Global Higher Education System

> Unique degree programmes such as '2 + 1' twinning degrees (where students study two years in Malaysia and one year at the overseas host university) and '3 + 0' degrees (where the entire foreign university degree programme is taught in Malaysia) offer international students abundant overseas bachelor's degree options that meet their budget and academic needs (Higher Education Malaysia, 2009, p. 2).

As indicated above Higher Education Malaysia's (2009) twinning degree programme brochure indicates that there is a range of twinning options extending from 1+2 to 3+0 degrees of a typical three-year programme. In the early years as the programme attempted to assist and attract those who would have left to study a degree overseas there was a general focus on students doing an initial preparation at a local campus and then still doing a significant if not main part of their degree at the international partner institution. On closer inspection it is clear that over the years there was a gradual drift in many (although not all) programmes towards the 3+0 model, where students could get an international degree without leaving Malaysia. As Goh (2005) reports, 'By 2000 there were around 120 private colleges offering twinning programs and 30 with "3 + 0" programs in which all teaching was undertaken in Malaysia'. In this way as Knight and Morshidi (2011, p. 603) further point out, by 2008 there were 3218 programmes being offered in Malaysia by foreign HE institutions. In 2010 when off-shore students first outnumbered those international students studying at UK universities, a significant number of these were enrolled via the 3+0 option in the Malaysian twinning programmes. UK and Australian universities have been most active but there has also been significant involvement from the United States, New Zealand and others. For instance, as the Study Malaysia website (www.studymalaysia.com) records, over 50 UK universities have had a twinning relationship to Malaysian HEIs at one stage or another. More recently there has been an Asian turn with collaborative programmes being developed with Japan, Thailand, India and others.

In her detailed analysis of a twinning programme case study, Goh (2005) has usefully pointed out the underlying tendency of such programmes to encourage 'surface learning' as distinct from 'deep learning' and by extension notions of quality assurance which likewise tend to focus on issues of teaching and learning in terms of a content emphasis on curriculum provision and transfer (cf. also Woo, 2006). Critics do rightly point out how the increasing recent scrutiny of the MQA (Malaysian Qualifications Agency) in applying a national quality assurance framework has helped improved the overall quality of Malaysian twinning degree programmes. Yet their focus inevitably tends to be on curriculum rather than all the intrinsic, contextual and pedagogical aspects of educational quality. There is an additional contextual asymmetry recognised by Altbach (2011) related to how the 'quality of curriculum and education are very different issues especially when it comes to the often different needs and interests of emerging and developing countries in contrast to Western countries' (p. 3). In referring to the international tendency for HE franchising as the 'McDonaldisation of higher education', Altbach has cautioned that HE internationalisation 'short-cuts' cannot substitute for local cultural contexts of quality of education or actual experience.

The challenge of recognising and seeking to overcome either direct or indirect asymmetries in the international HE system is further emphasised when, instead of twinning programme partnerships, Malaysian HE institutions attempt other kinds of collaborative degree accreditation arrangements — including joint degrees and especially proper dual-degree arrangements. As indicated, while the abstract concept of dual degrees represents the 'reciprocal' ideal, which stands in contrast to how the twinning programmes slide between clearly asymmetrical franchising and some degree of reciprocation in collaborative degree programmes. The more successful international dual-degree programmes involving separate dual accreditation tend to be at the postgraduate rather than undergraduate level and also involve relatively 'equal' universities (i.e. usually not across the Western–non-Western and developed–emerging divides) (e.g. Obst & Kuder, 2011). As Obst and Kuder ultimately concede, even in the most successful models there are inevitably various asymmetrical tensions of interest, commitment, expertise, enrolment, and student support as well as teaching and curriculum development. These ultimately relate to which partner contributes most to the endeavour on one hand, and on the other who benefits (and where) from the collaboration.

There are a number of examples of dual-degree programmes offered by Malaysian HE institutions as a collaboration with a Western university. However, as typified by the example of UCTI's (Asia Pacific University of Technology & Innovation) arrangement with Staffordshire University, on closer inspection many of these are joint accreditation arrangements rather than the kind of dual-degree partnerships projected by Obst and Kuder. From our own experience we know — reinforcing Obst and Kuder's further concession that the current global enthusiasm for dual degrees is much more rhetoric than reality — that efforts by Malaysian universities to set up this more reciprocal model of dual-degree partnerships with Western universities is often a difficult and problematic process.

For all of the above historical and cross-cultural as well as organisational and academic reasons, the Malaysian twinning model provides a useful focus for attempting a more integrated HE internationalisation framework. As depicted in Figure 1, such a framework embraces but also attempts to 'go beyond' a tension between existing *asymmetric* relations and realities on one hand and *reciprocal* ideals on the other. Figure 1 further outlines an HE *institutional collaboration axis* which connects in time with what might be called the *student mobility flows axis*. The emergence of a '3+0' franchising tendency from the original '1=2' and '2+1' versions of the twinning programme model stands in contrast to the growing popularity of short study trips which are often for a week or short-term exchange study programmes typically for one term or semester. In this way undergraduate academic exchange often blurs into what might be called educational tourism for all students to get their 'taste' of HE internationalisation. In the horizontal axis we see the lateral tension between the *direct asymmetry* tendency for HE franchising in contrast to the rather *indirect asymmetry* of more collaborative versions of twinning programmes or joint degrees. This provides an additional basis for a fundamental distinction between *HE reciprocation* as a mere ideal and as a concrete possibility of exchange and dialogue where there is sufficient mutual good will and genuine collaborative intentions for knowledge sharing and student exchange as well as

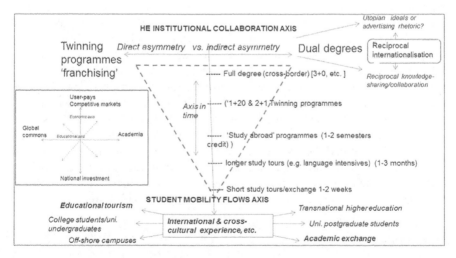

Figure 1: Towards a framework for recognising how Malaysia's twinning programmes also link to a basic asymmetric vs. reciprocal/dialogical tension in the emerging global higher education system.

academic staff exchange. The basis of this distinction really lies in taking a global rather than merely national or institutional view of higher education systems.

Conclusion

The twinning partnerships between local Malaysian colleges and typically Western universities represent a significant foundational as well as exemplary and interesting focus of the challenges and opportunities of transnational higher education over the last two decades. This paper has explored how the emerging Malaysian model usefully epitomises the nationalist vs. globalisation dilemmas of higher education expansion everywhere around the world as interdependent system. An associated rhetoric — reality gap was further identified in the associated 'surface' vs. 'deep-quality' education tensions between the competing rationales of degree franchising for profit on one hand, and human resource development for national industry capacity-building on the other. As discussed in relation to the challenges of 'going beyond' the Malaysian twinning model, the various challenges of a fast-changing, interdependent and indeed 'connected' world suggest that a more integrated paradigm based on strategic collaborative international partnerships is needed to reconcile associated challenges and harness new possibilities in higher education. This is order to transform into practice the rhetoric: (a) that formal education can complement growing imperatives of work-based education, lifelong learning and continuing professional development; (b) that such associated HE imperatives as marketisation, privatisation and the user-pays principle can be sufficiently reconciled with a residual and global affirmation of the principle that education might or should also be a 'public good'; (c) that HE internationalisation imperatives of global student mobility and academic networking can likewise be reconciled with policies which also view HE as a focus of national investment; and (d) that a 'reciprocal internationalisation' might be possible where academic staff and students from the West are also attracted to move to universities in non-Western including developing societies (and not just the reverse, as is often the case). In other words, aspects of change, diversity and innovation in education are not in themselves sufficient for achieving a 'world-class university' and a sustainable harnessing of the endless possibilities and potentials of the global HE system.

References

Aihara, A. (2009). Paradoxes of higher education reforms: Implications on the Malaysian middleclass. *IJAPS*, 5(1), 81–113.

Altbach, P. (2011). Franchising: The McDonaldization of higher education. *International Higher Education*, *66*, 7–8.

Altbach, P., Reisberg, L., & Rumbley, L. (2009). *Trends in global higher education*. UNESCO Report, Paris. Retrieved from http://unesdoc.unesco.org/images/0018/001832/183219e.pdf

Chi, M. (2011). Government aims to attract 200,000 international students by 2020. *Malaysia Insider*, *13*(September). Retrieved from http://www.malaysiainsider.com

Goh, P. (2005). *Perceptions of learning environments, learning approaches and learning outcomes: A study of private higher education students in Malaysia from twinning programmes*. Unpublished PhD, Adelaide University, Adelaide.

Gooch, L. (2011, October 2). Malaysia tries to rein in private education institutions. *New York Times*.

Higher Education Malaysia. (2009). *Twinning degree programmes: World class degrees, truly Asian values*. Kuala Lumpur: MOHE Publication.

Knight, J. (2006). *Higher education crossing borders: A guide to the implications of the general agreement on trade in services for cross-border education*. UNESCO Report. Retrieved from http://unesdoc.unesco.org/images/0014/001473/147363e.pdf

Knight, J., & Morshidi, S. (2011). The complexities and challenges of regional education hubs: Focus on Malaysia. *Higher Education*, *62*, 593–606.

Lee, M. (2007). Cross-border higher education and quality assurance in Asia-Pacific. *Accreditation for quality assurance: What is at stake*? (pp. 146–148). New York, NY: Palgrave Macmillan (Global University Network for Innovation).

MOHE. (n.d.). *Guidebook: Criteria for upgrading IPTS from university college status to university*. Kuala Lumpur: MOHE.

Mok, K. H. (2011). *Journal of Education Policy*, *26*(1), 61–81.

Nelson, J. (2008). Introduction. In J. Nelson, J. Meerman, & A. Rahman (Eds.), *Globalization and national autonomy: The experience of Malaysia*. ISEAS/IKMAS.

Newman, S., & Jahdi, K. (2009). Marketisation of education: Marketing, rhetoric and reality. *Journal of Further and Higher Education*, *33*(1), 1–11.

Obst, D., & Kuder, M. (2011). *Joint and double degree programs in the global context: Report on an international survey*. Institute of International Education.

Rahman, M. (2011). Malaysian institutional models in private higher education. *QS World Class Showcase*. Retrieved from http://www.qsworldclass.com/showcase/countryfeature10.php

Roland, C. (2012). President Dunn heads to Malaysia to celebrate 25 year partnership. *WMU News*. Retrieved from http://www.wmich.edu/news/2012/06/763

Richards, C. (2011a, February). Developing a 'win-win' quality assurance framework for the Malaysian private higher education sector in ever-changing times. *Refereed Proceedings of the 6th QS-APPLE*, pp. 53–89. Retrieved from http://www.qsapple.org/6thAPPLE2010Proceedings.pdf

Richards, C. (2011b). Higher education marketisation, privatisation, and internationalisation: Singaporean *vs.* Malaysian models of the Asian Education Hub policy, *Refereed proceedings of INCUE 2011*. Kuala Lumpur.

Richards, C., & Ismail, M. (2012). Sustaining the higher education hub model: The challenge of adequate academic and social support structures for international students. *Asian Journal of Higher Education*, *7*(2), 109–129.

Salmi, J. (2009). *The challenge of establishing world-class universities.* World Bank Report. Washington, DC.

Sidhu, G., & Kaur, S. (2011). Enhancing global competence in higher education: Malaysia's strategic initiatives. *Higher Education Dynamics, 36*(4), 219–236.

Singh, J., Schapper, J., & Mayson, S. (2010). The impact of economic policy on reshaping higher education in Malaysia. In M. Devlin, J. Nagy, & A. Lichtenberg (Eds.), *Research and development in higher education* (Vol. 33, pp. 585–595). Milperra: HERDSA.

Stambach, A. (2012). Two models of cross-border education. *International Higher Education, 66,* 8–10.

Whitehead, F. (2012, May 8). Inside Educity Iskandar: A university partnership in Malaysia. *The Guardian.*

Wilkinson, R., & Yussof, I. (2005). Public and private provision of higher education in Malaysia: A comparative analysis. *Higher Education, 50*(3), 361–386.

Woo, K. (2006) Malaysian private higher education: A need to study the different interpretations of quality. *IJASA: UCSI International Journal, 1,* 17–21. Retrieved from http://www.ucsi.edu.my/jasa/1/papers/10A-pg17.pdf

Ziguras, C., & McBurnie, G. (2011). International student mobility in the Asia-Pacific: From globalization to regional integration. *Higher Education in the Asia Pacific, 36*(2), 123–140.

Chapter 2.5

Going Agile — Agile Methodologies in the Education of Global Citizens

Jasmina Nikolic and Jelena Gledic

Challenges of the Higher Education System in the 21st Century

Higher education (HE) today is challenged to fulfil its purpose of developing a truly international social, cultural and economic future, given that it lacks the ethos and organisational strategies needed to efficiently and effectively respond to increasingly diverse societies in which the underlying constant is change. Responding to change becomes one of the main responsibilities of HE, as stated in the UNESCO's World Conference on Higher Education: 'Faced with the complexity of current and future global challenges, higher education has the social responsibility to advance our understanding of multifaceted issues, which involve social, economic, scientific and cultural dimensions and our ability to respond to them. It should lead society in generating global knowledge to address global challenges...' (UNESCO, 2009). HE institutions (HEIs) have to endure in the global nature of the competitive environment and the rise of global universities, as well as to respond to the growing call for both internationalisation, in terms of student body, staff and curriculum, and personalisation of individual educational goals and settings. 'The most successful institutions will be those that can respond quickest and offer a high-quality education to an international student body' (Levine, 2000). To that end, HEIs must develop their capacity for change and transform their strategies, from constructed-beforehand to permanently-in-construction.

Going Global: Identifying Trends and Drivers of International Education
Copyright © 2013 by Emerald Group Publishing Limited
All rights of reproduction in any form reserved
ISBN: 978-1-78190-575-3

Bridging the Gap — Going Agile

If academia is expected to deliver a highly skilled, creative, adaptable workforce, that is personally motivated, globally oriented, ethical world citizens, ready to successfully move around fast-paced, changing job markets with vague distinctions between jobs, then it cannot do so through an institutionalised system with limited diversity, flexibility and national constraints, which in no way resembles the truly international real-life work experience most students have, or are required to have, after graduating. HEIs need to assess their paradigms and structures against client-driven values, to step out of isolation, and to become more responsive to changes in society in motion but also in their competitive environment.

Responding to change and development are two main drivers of an agile business approach to maintaining a presence in competitive environments, and at the same time are the main purposes of HE. The concept of 'agility' as an attribute of work organisation arose in response to the requirements of modern business to operate in predictable ways, even in the face of extreme system or technological complexity. By embracing change, it radically departed from the mass production-based model that extracted profit from stability, standardisation and economies of scale (Charnitski, 2002).

The adoption of characteristics that reflect society's prevailing economic model is not unusual for education and HEIs should introduce Agile methods to truly implement institutional responsiveness to change brought by increasingly international and diverse environments, and especially to facilitate the process of thorough renegotiation of the established work practice with new stakeholders.

Basic Principles of the Agile Approach

The concept of Agile emerged with the shift from mass production to economy based on constantly evolving technology, knowledge and market. Technology has rendered customisation of products and services an affordable reality. International competitive environments required a change in management, that is doing more with less. Focusing the work on delighting the client led to working in self-organised teams (most likely to generate continuous innovation) and client-driven iterations, since positive outcomes are best achieved by the successive approximations of perceived client needs. The fundamental concept of product has changed — it has become negotiable, that is iteratively fulfilling changing requirements. Client-driven iterations focus on delivering value (through constant prioritisation) by the end of each iteration. They enable frequent client feedback. Self-organising teams that work iteratively both enable and require radical transparency, which also assists them in improving their performance. An underlying prerequisite of all of these principles is interactive communication (Denning, 2010). Agile methodologies enable high-performance, geographically distributed, international teams and structured networking and co-operation.

Agile principles as exposed above are summarised in the seminal declaration, the Manifesto for Agile Software Development (Agile Alliance, 2001). One of the most prominent characteristics of the Agile Manifesto is that it is worded as a comparative value statement, not as a list of principles: 'We value: individuals and interactions over processes and tools, working software over comprehensive documentation, customer collaboration over contract negotiation, responding to change over following a plan. That is, while there is value in the items on the right, we value the items on the left more'.

There are various methods that are collectively known as Agile, as they promote the values of the Agile Manifesto and are consistent with the stated principles. The most popular ones are: Dynamic Systems Development Method (DSDM), probably the original method; Scrum, the most popular and widely adopted, relatively simple to implement; and Extreme Programming (XP). These and other methods have caused Agile to be widely adopted across a variety of industries. All Agile methods allow project teams to adapt working practices according to the needs of individual projects/tasks (Highsmith, 2002; Larman, 2004; Martin, 2003), and provide a shared set of values that allow even the most diverse teams to thrive in working towards a common goal.

Scrum is an iterative and incremental Agile development method conceived for managing software projects and product development, first described and implemented in the early 1990s.

Work organisation is split into small, cross-functional, heterogeneous, often geographically distributed, self-organising teams that spend defined periods of time (time-boxed iterations called Sprints), working on different settings (both virtual and physical space) and time zones. They work on specific tasks (small, concrete deliverables, sorted by priority in the visible backlog) that support the building of a product increment (relevant to the customer), that is then presented to the customer and stakeholders to elicit feedback (and influence further development).

The method includes pre-defined core and auxiliary roles that enable smooth workflow. Meetings are strictly pragmatic and have set guidelines (time-boxed daily project status meetings to check what is done, the impediments and what will be done; Sprint review meeting to review completed work and present it to the stakeholders; Sprint retrospective, where all team members reflect on the past Sprint). As many other Agile methodologies, Scrum visualises the workflow (Adkins, 2010; Kniberg, 2009).

Kanban is a concept related to lean and just-in-time production. It is a scheduling system devised by Toyota in the 1950s that helps determine the production process. Kanban uses cards to visualise the workflow (the work is split into pieces, each item is written on a card and put on the wall — today in the online software). The main characteristic and most powerful asset of Kanban is that it limits work in progress. Its efficiency is based on frequent delivery (from 'to do', through 'doing', to 'done') and prioritisation (critical, high, normal, low), which helps understand the team's real capacity. It provides transparency in communication, workflow, and effects of (in)actions. Such visualisation has proved to be very psychologically rewarding and motivating (Anderson & Reinertsen, 2010).

Scrum is more prescriptive than Kanban. In Scrum, work is divided into Sprints that last a certain amount of time, whereas in Kanban the workflow is continuous. Scrum and Kanban often combine in a new development model called Scrumban.

These Agile methods can be supported by innovative open communication techniques based on a core assumption that knowledge, wisdom and responsibility of the group are greater in non-hierarchical but structured settings. The most efficient one is Open Space Technology (OS), an approach for hosting any sort of gathering focused on a specific and important purpose or task, but beginning without any formal agenda. Participants create and manage their own agenda of parallel working sessions around a central theme of strategic importance. It is highly scalable and adaptable, it can last from two hours to several days, it can host from dozen to thousands participants, and it can be equally used in physical and virtual space, which allows for massive international, global conversations. OS works particularly well in moving from planning to action. OS has five guiding principles and one law (the law of two feet): 'if [...] you find yourself in any situation where you are neither learning nor contributing, use your two feet, go someplace else' (Owen, 2008).

Going Agile throughout the System

All principles underlying agility as a paradigm can be applied to HE in all essential phases of the education/learning process: organisational and communication management, learning management and curriculum design. Highly adaptive, extremely international and massive open online courses are already a reality, as well as new brands of high-quality certified education providers (e.g. Udacity) that work in the best agile, growth-oriented manner: iteratively and incrementally through constant real-time cycles of inspection and adaptation. Agility fosters creating a truly global and international HE model with the most appropriate common values and work ethics.

Agile can be a platform for strategic planning. It allows easy monitoring, self-assessment and improvement. More prescriptive Agile methodologies such as Scrum could be implemented at the managerial level, allowing a smooth transition from the existing strict, closed hierarchies through team roles, while Kanban could be introduced at the level of communication and organisational management and used for curriculum design. Curricula can be designed so that they can be customised, and regularly inspected and adapted, with adaptation mechanisms built in (not waiting for long-span accreditation processes or broad labour market surveys). Tasks and iterations are not much different from knowledge objects, an increasingly recognised modular unit of HE. A lifelong learning concept needs agility.

Through Agile, HE can transform in many ways:

- from high assurance and strict standards culture set to reduce the unknown to rapid and iterative production of small chunks of value that will inform, and thus control the unknown future, and embrace the diverse present (by tailoring the Scrum method)
- from uncommunicated and prescribed processes to using values to empower individuals to work in, putting trust in them (by applying Agile ethos)
- from reductionist, predefined structures of independent and inflexible units and curricula to holistic cross-functional self-responsible teams and modular, customised curricula (by using Kanban and Scrum)
- from representational to inclusive participation and communication (by using Open Space)
- from standardised, long-lived outcomes to individualised, transitory and adaptable outcomes (by using Scrum artefacts such as User stories)
- from hierarchical relations, based on control and tradition, to heterarchical relations, based on competence and assessment (by introducing Scrum roles)
- from a criticising culture to a self-improving culture (by self and peer-assessment and real-world feedback)
- from teaching/learning to problem solving (by introducing Scrum roles and practices such as value negotiation)

Case Study 1: Agile Reform in HE — Reforming Foreign Language Studies in Serbia (REFLESS)

The REFLESS project is part of the TEMPUS IV family of EU projects in Serbia (2010–2013). The main goal of this high-priority national project is to harmonise the existing university language degree programmes and to develop new Masters degrees at a national level in order to facilitate the process of EU integration. More than 150 professionals from 18 public, private and governmental institutions (including 10 HEIs) from six countries work in distributed international Scrum teams. The co-operation is based on the REFLESS Agile Manifesto (refless.rs), and no contracts are signed between the partner institutions. The project is managed using a tailor-made combination of Scrum and Kanban, and efficient meeting styles, such as OS and World Café. OS was used several times to discuss the issues concerning the project goals and to make an action plan (Sprint and project backlogs). The elements of Scrum are used for Sprint planning, and solving the issues. Scrum artefacts, such as User stories, are used for writing learning outcomes. The REFLESS teams use online Kanban software daily to schedule and prioritise the work and to communicate in real time and transparently (emails and telephone calls are discouraged). The use of Kanban is rewarding since it builds the trust and negotiation capabilities of team members. Although most team members were used to traditional HE settings, they quickly and easily accepted the proposed work methods and stated they were more efficient working in an open setting, in the creation of which they actively participated. The project is successful, especially in building up the community that owns what it produces and feels responsible for it.

Case Study 2: Agile Student Representation

The two-day OS was first successfully used in HE in Serbia in April 2011 for working with student parliaments from Serbia to encourage them to solve their political conflicts and create a backlog of priority tasks necessary for the improvement of the educational situation. It was organised and facilitated by the Serbian Higher Education Reform Experts team. The students discussed 18 topics proposed by themselves and produced a backlog of 34 tasks to be done. Through Scrum negotiation methods they came up with three urgent or priority tasks and pulled them onto the wall Kanban board into the 'doing' lane. All three tasks were moved to 'done' and the process is ongoing. Several students said the OS changed some of their beliefs.

The second OS was used at an EU students' representatives gathering in Serbia in November 2011. Through discussion in open space circles and negotiation the students fulfilled their mission, which was to produce a joint declaration on future challenges and perspective of the Bologna Process. The declaration was then adopted by the Serbian Parliament.

At the start of each process, different representative bodies and stakeholders were believed to have irreconcilable interests and values, but through Agile negotiations and communication they managed to reach common goals.

Case Study 3: Agile High School Science Seminar

At a science centre for extracurricular high-school education, Petnica Science Centre (PSC), the Agile approach was used to implement a Social Sciences Seminar. From 29 March to 4 April 2011, 27 students from significantly different backgrounds were asked to define their interests, and then blend them into the lecture programme. Although PSC has a tradition of learning innovation and disruptive educational models, the added value of the Agile approach was noteworthy.

Scrum roles provided an excellent replacement for traditional teacher–student roles. Students embraced viewing education as a product that they are responsible for and that has personal value. They noticed that they are more creative and efficient when given a specific goal rather than a sequence of steps to follow, and that it is more interesting to do something when you know why you are doing it. The daily meetings proved excellent for dealing with procrastination.

In an OS organised to teach the benefits and pitfalls of self-organisation, students were asked to define topics related to social science, which allowed them to blend out-of-school interests with traditional education. They applied the basic principles throughout the seminar — especially the importance of viewing things as they are, not what they could have been.

Although PSC programme participants usually form close bonds, students showed a new level of closeness. They kept changing their seating order and there were no smaller common-interest groups. When asked, they responded that the OS taught them the creative potential of mobility.

Conclusion

Agile philosophy could impact the international education community by enabling it to envision a new, truly international system of education through our outline of an Agile model of education policies, instructional design, curriculum development and institutional management. By providing the framework for dignifying harmonisation of backgrounds, world-views, needs and ideas of local and international students, staff and other stakeholders, it leads to relevant and truly international HE, as well as the advancement of knowledge essential to engendering progress and true democratic participation.

The presented framework and case studies show that Agile methodologies could bring both short-term and mid-term advantages for the HE community, by allowing for:

- global (virtual or physical), inclusive and transparent communication and collaboration of HEIs through direct involvement of all stakeholders and their partnership in distributed teams
- building or reforming education systems by utilising value detection, prioritisation, change and test-driven development (empirical approach)
- continuous processes quality control (small pieces of effort, applied frequently) replacing the traditional practice of quality control after completion
- efficient conflict and seemingly irreconcilable difference solving through transparent decision making and efficient value negotiation
- visualised, transparent and limited work in progress/workload (ECTS)
- reduction of waste creating processes
- space for artefacts for planning, monitoring, assessing, and estimating
- modular and fractal curriculum and organisational structures
- good quality-control mechanisms, suitable for an international environment.

Although the agile era is at an early stage, the very nature of an approach based on continual reprioritisation of requirements ensures success of the long-term life cycle, even in unpredictable and turbulent environments.

References

Adkins, L. (2010). *Coaching Agile teams: A companion for ScrumMasters, Agile coaches, and project managers in transition*. Boston, MA: Addison-Wesley.

Agile Alliance. (2001). *Manifesto for Agile Software Development*. Retrieved from http://agilemanifesto.org/

Anderson, D. J., & Reinertsen, D. G. (2010). *Kanban: Successful evolutionary change for your technology business*. Sequim, WA: Blue Hole Press.

Charnitski, C. W. (2002). *Gauging the readiness of an institution of higher education to implement change in its distance education program in ways that are consistent with the paradigm of organizational agility*. Retrieved from http://dspace.library.drexel.edu/handle/1860/25

Denning, S. (2010). *The leader's guide to radical management, reinventing the workplace for the 21st century*. San Francisco, NY: Wiley.

Highsmith, J. A. (2002). *Agile software development ecosystems*. London: Addison Wesley.

Kniberg, H. (2009). *Scrum vs. Kanban, how to make the most of both*. Retrieved from http://www.infoq.com/minibooks/kanban-scrum-minibook

Larman, C. (2004). *Agile and iterative development: A manager's guide*. London: Addison-Wesley.

Levine, A. E. (2000). The future of colleges: 9 inevitable changes. *The Chronicle of Higher Education, 27*(October), 10–11.

Martin, R. C. (2003). *Agile software development, principles, patterns, and practices*. Upper Saddle River, NJ: Prentice Hall.

Owen, H. (2008). *Open space technology: A user's guide*. San Francisco, CA: Berret-Koehler Publishers.

UNESCO. (2009). *Communique UNESCO world conference on higher education*. Retrieved from http://www.unesco.org/fileadmin/MULTIMEDIA/HQ/ED/ED/pdf/WCHE_2009/FINAL%20COMMUNIQUE%20WCHE%202009.pdf

Chapter 2.6

Setting up an Entrepreneurial University — Lessons from Sri Lanka

Chandra J. Embuldeniya

Origins

In 2004 the Sri Lankan government invited a businessman to set up a university that would cater to the market needs particularly for global economic opportunities, avoiding the prevailing drawbacks of the system. The university was named after the remote underdeveloped province where it is located.[1] Having accepted the invitation, a location was found within the province, the concept was developed, the university built, and staff members recruited and trained. They recruited six batches of students and conducted the first convocation for the students to graduate. The University has drawn attention from several international universities for its unique model. This experience is unique in the history of establishing a new academic culture in Sri Lanka, and is symbolic of Sri Lanka's growing internationalisation.

Challenges

In setting up the University there were several major challenges to overcome. The foremost was to develop the new vision and strategy to pave the way for global market access. The Government wanted to reduce the unemployment of graduates, to quell sporadic unrest in the university

1. Uva Province is the second least populated and the last but one poorest province in Sri Lanka.

Going Global: Identifying Trends and Drivers of International Education
Copyright © 2013 by Emerald Group Publishing Limited
All rights of reproduction in any form reserved
ISBN: 978-1-78190-575-3

system, to bring harmony, cater to economic and inclusive development through the academic programmes, identify and serve the needs of a global market for higher education (HE) and industry needs, conduct research and innovate, commercialising research innovations, reducing dependence on state funds, improving access to a greater population in Sri Lanka and improving on the productivity of resource use. Therefore, the challenge was to break away from the traditional system of a silo-based education system built on the Oxbridge model.

Strategy

Starting in October 2004 the founding vice-chancellor developed a strategy with the vision for the University to 'become the renowned centre of knowledge and expertise for value addition to the national resources base', subsequently revised to 'be the centre of excellence for value addition to the national resource base'. This theme had a magnetic effect on the country proud of national growth while catering to global markets. National policies resonated with this theme, effectively neutralising only destabilising strategies and providing the space required for developing a desirable culture. The mission was to produce well-rounded leaders in economic activity capable of using scientific and technological approaches to value addition that would invariably pave the way to global markets, and enable Sri Lankan graduates to be part of the international scene, and compete for jobs internationally. The University collectively set up the major goals: to effectively deliver new broad-based programmes with unique combinations of subjects relevant to economic development; to use innovative mechanisms to deliver programmes; to develop an environment conducive for the pursuit of academic excellence; to produce well-rounded students matching the demands of society; to become a model employer; and to fulfil fiduciary responsibility as a higher education centre to the government.

Value Proposition

The stakeholder[2] value proposition[3] consisted of three key aspects. Knowledge and skills development on adding value to the national resources

---

2. Stakeholders are students, employers, parents, government, society and employees.
3. Value proposition defines the stakeholder value delivered through the internal processes using learning and growth elements.

base took the key position, along with mentoring students to solve their academic, personal, financial and career problems. Market-relevant entrepreneurial knowledge supported by scientific and technology knowledge delivered with practical experience was a hallmark of the value proposition. Essential skills development and broad general education were part of the core curriculum. Relationship development with the external and internal environments was the second key element of the value proposition. The third element of the value proposition was to develop the image of the University as a responsibility shared among everyone. The results were seen with the many innovations produced by students and when graduates found lucrative jobs as they graduated (Jayathilake et al., 2011). This enabled the graduates to compete internationally with graduates from universities around the world for research and employment.

Internal Processes

Three new processes for academic, administration and research activities deliver the value proposition. The academic process was developed to deliver the academic outcomes of the university by breaking away from the silo-based system of traditional Sri Lankan universities with a powerful interdisciplinary system. This was achieved through including a combination of disciplines within each academic programme. They combined this with the compulsory essential skills development programme and the broad general education programme as part of the core curriculum. Faculty-based department structures were a hindrance but some elements were retained only in order to fulfil statutory requirements under the Universities Act (Universities Act, No. 16, 1978). The academic processes were driven by Course Committees headed by Course Directors of the various academic programmes. Course Committees were made up of Subject Co-ordinators from numerous disciplines combined into the curriculum. The system enabled breaking through the once impregnable department and faculty silos prevalent in the university system. The Course Directors ensured the market orientation of the programmes and the employability of graduates while each Subject Co-ordinator ensured the value inputs of the discipline. This process has drawn attention from UK universities, and grew out of the experiences of the University Senior Management at the Entrepreneurial University Leadership Programme held at the Saïd Business School, University of Oxford for university leadership training. The vice-chancellor was invited by the International

Education Exchange Council[4] in Edinburgh in 2009 to deliver a keynote speech on his experience in setting up a truly entrepreneurial university. These international experiences have been of considerable benefit to the Sri Lankan University. The University's vice-chancellor is also currently retained by the University of Central Lancashire as the Consultant for their internationalising efforts in setting up a campus for 10,000 students on a 130-acre plot in Sri Lanka. This experience of transnational education has opened up the Sri Lankan HE landscape considerably.

This academic process delivers skills and entrepreneurial content. Special emphasis is laid on providing the opportunity to students to learn entrepreneurial skills and acquire knowledge through research, training and observations. The essential skills in the curriculum are communications, quantitative reasoning, information technology, English and language skills. The essential skills programme is compulsory for all students. Sinhala-speaking students must learn Tamil and vice versa. While all programmes are conducted in English, the ethnic language skills promoted social harmony.

The academic process makes continuous assessments of students and stringently enforces above 80 per cent attendance at all academic programmes. Continuous assessment was allocated 60 per cent; the rest 40 per cent weight in the grade point average (GPA). The internationalisation of qualifications through universal GPAs has had a major impact on student motivation. The impact on students was outstanding. Also this assessment had a powerful countervailing effect on student radicalism.

In order to give students universally recognised and applicable skills, the students were trained in private sector companies for a period of up to about five months. During this industrial training period their performances were evaluated by an academic supervisor and a company supervisor. The students had to conduct research projects on value addition, focusing on national resources, and produce research papers published at the annual research symposium. Students were encouraged to develop lab-scale prototypes of innovative research outcomes and engage with the private sector through exhibitions and competitive events.

Academic Programmes for Value Addition

A significant differentiating factor at the University is the 'interdisciplinary' nature of the academic programmes. The interdisciplinary programmes

---

4. For further information see: www.ieec.co.uk/previous-conferences/2009-edinburgh/parallel-sessions.

break through the silo-based focus within departments and faculties and pave the way for internationalisation of knowledge.

The University developed 11 degree programmes, based on value addition to the national resources base theme, within the first six years of operation. The resource base included agricultural, mineral, aquatic, tourism, ICT and management resources. Of course, at the centre there is a focus on human resources and value addition is to human capital. The programmes are unique to this University. This is a step in the technology ladder to grow the national economy by entering global markets with value-added resources.

Leadership

The key to success in managing change is astute leadership. The University has emphasised its vision and strategy at training sessions for students, academia and administrators. The University, through strong training, has managed to develop future leaders aligned with the vision and strategy. Strong leadership and good management have led to this University being the only government organisation in Sri Lanka without any unions, unrest or payment claims for overtime.

Three Pillars of Service

The University itself has also taken seriously the importance of its environment, underlying the fact that the University is the centre of excellence for value addition. The 'Three Pillars of Service' are celebrated here as Teaching and Mentoring, Research, and Social Responsibility. The first pillar clearly provides for student education and mentoring. The Mentoring process assigns seven to ten students to each lecturer. The second pillar requires every lecturer to conduct at least one research project for value addition at all times. With the third pillar, Social Responsibility, lecturers contribute to the inclusive development of the province. Every lecturer has to support at least one project at all times aiming to develop the region. The lecturers produce a self-evaluation based on the three pillars during the year for performance evaluation.

Spirit of Innovation and Entrepreneurship

A significant phenomenon at the University is the remarkable number of innovation prototypes produced by students demonstrating their strength in 'value addition to the national resources base'. This is an outcome of the entrepreneurial culture combined with scientific and technological skills and the commitment to value addition. A collection of students' research work is published and a research symposium and prototype exhibition is held annually by the University. A leading newspaper, *Ceylon Daily News,* carried a series of articles focusing on student innovations in the year 2010.

The students have demonstrated their outstanding skills in winning competitive events such as the HSBC Youth Enterprise Awards (see *Daily Financial Times*, 26 April 2012) and *Ideators* (see *Ceylon Daily News*, 1 May 2012) conducted by the British Council.[5] They have also won at a competitive robotics event conducted by the Sri Lanka Institute of Information Technology.[6]

Administration Process

The administration process is driven by multifunctional staff for operational success. All administrative jobs are labelled to emphasise the operations driven for outcomes. The administration process is run by the Registrar, entitled as Chief Operating Officer and others are entitled Manager Operations. All administrative staff members are trained on multifunctional duties to deliver results aiming the stakeholders.

The non-core services are outsourced through a statutory procurement process. The operations staff officers are trained on procurement of non-core services and hiring people for core activities. They excel in managing outsourced services such as transport, security, caretaking, cleaning, ICT, catering and lodging. It is the responsibility of officers to manage essential services as a 24/7 operation without interruption.

Learning and Growth (L&G)

Most L&G is made up of intangible assets, which depend on skills, technology and culture. The L&G raises three key elements — human capital, information capital and organisation capital.

---

5. For further information see: www.britishcouncil.org/srilanka-projects-ideators-2011.htm
6. For further information see: www.youtube.com/watch?v=jVk5b9XsrrY and www.sliit.lk/index.php/content-joomla-default/101-front-page-news/1358-sliit-robofest-2011.html

Human Capital

Staff members are selected through a structured process and trained to perform the functions of the entire value chain in delivering the value proposition. Thus it is important to recognise competence in addition to qualifications at the HR selections. The three pillars of service are the basis of evaluating performance of academic staff members.

Astute leadership plays an important role in motivating and driving the teams of academics and students on track delivering the value proposition. The first vice-chancellor of a university is appointed by the President of Sri Lanka on the recommendation of the University Grants Commission and the Ministry of Higher Education. The founding vice-chancellor was appointed after a head hunt by the Grants Commission, and is also the first private sector executive to be appointed as a vice-chancellor in Sri Lanka.

Information Capital

The second L&G asset information capital comprised the IT system that integrated the organisation strategy. The IT system plays several roles, particularly as a knowledge base, a management information system and a university resource planning instrument. The knowledge base is fundamental to the role of the University since the organisation grows by retaining past experiences and the knowledge so developed.

Organisation Capital

The third and the most intangible asset in the L&G perspective is the organisation capital where organisation culture, leadership and team play become crucial. Organisation culture is the social fabric that keeps developing incessantly, driven by the leadership. The vice-chancellor introduced a unique innovation here by appointing a young senior academic as a 'Culture Thermometer' to pick up problem signals and take prompt remedial measures. This device served as a useful performance driver.

The University Family

The concept now familiar to all as the University Family is another asset in the social fabric that binds the university community. The family label naturally has its implicit value and galvanises the community, seeking to strengthen 'togetherness'. The family develops a powerful feeling to motivate students to uphold the University values without being influenced by external radical elements.

Student Integration

Students' integration into the University begins with the articulation of the vision and the overarching theme of the university from day one with the welcoming Integration Programme. Parents and guardians come on board to share responsibility for the student conduct. The vice-chancellor and a few senior academics conduct an interactive session with parents on the first day. Thereafter, for about nine days, the sessions are divided into giving students the value of the University's heritage, programmes, discipline, 'dos and don'ts', talent shows, team building, law enforcement, governance, etc. This is managed and conducted by the University with the help of some senior students, local administrators, police and the judiciary.

Final Assessment

Academic pursuit for global needs at the University required a modern mechanism for delivery and an environment conducive without distraction. This necessitated a strategy with innovative processes and developing a culture enhancing learning and growth. It was driven strategically through deliberate activity until it became a self-driven process entrenched into the social fabric. Within a short period of seven years, this strategy has captured international attention. Several innovative outcomes are identified as lessons for global higher education system from this Sri Lankan experience:

- producing entrepreneurial leaders for the 21st century
- building strong relationships with industry
- being socially and economy relevant in academic programmes
- being a driver for inclusive development
- developing innovative processes for stakeholder value
- breaking through silos of knowledge for an inter-disciplinary (etc.) set of programmes.

There is more credence given to this fact by the external quality assessment of the University, carried out by an independent team of six senior professors. In their final conclusions they wrote: 'The unanimous view of the review team is that during the past five years, the rate of development of the University is nothing short of a miracle, mainly due to efficient management and administration'.

References

David, M. (2012, April 26). HSBC British Council launch 'Youth Enterprise Awards 2012'. *Daily Financial Times*. Retrieved from http://www.ft.lk/2012/04/26/hsbc-british-council-launch-youth-enterprise-awards-2012/. Accessed on October 11, 2012.

Jayathilake, L., Lakshman, W. D., Gunasena, H. P. M., Wijeyaratne, M. J. S., Karunaratne, V., & Dahanayake, K. (Eds.). (2011, 10–14 January). Overall judgment of the level of confidence in the university quality assurance arrangements (p. 21, Section 5). *Institutional Review Report of Uva Wellassa University*. Retrieved from http://www.qaacouncil.lk/qaa_doc/IR/IR%20-%20UWU.pdf

Jayawardana, R. (1 May 2012). Udana, the last one standing, behind the scenes of 'Ideators', Episode 14, *Ceylon Daily News*. Retrieved from http://www.dailynews.lk/2012/05/01/fea20.asp. Accessed on October 11, 2012.

Universities Act No. 16 and amendments to date. (1978). Retrieved from http://www.ugc.ac.lk/en/policy/universities-act.html. Accessed on October 11, 2012.

Chapter 2.7

Do Networks Work?

Tim Gore, Dinos Arcoumanis, Colin B. Grant, Julia Haes, John Hearn, Alex Hughes and Maurits van Rooijen

Universities are unusual institutions that are born and nurtured in close connection with their local communities but are also expected to be global in nature and aspiration. Globalisation has seemed an unquestioned part of our lives over the last few decades but there are many who see the financial and social events of the past few years starting to reign in the advance of globalisation and some who see its retreat in the face of growing national protectionism; shrinking international budgets and the retreat of globalised business models as localism and 'glocality' (Meyrowitz) take hold. Against this backdrop, higher education continues to expand globally, and global mobility as well as international co-operation in research continue to grow. Yet although the opportunity is there to see, few universities have the budgets and appetite for risk to be able to engage as aggressively as they would like in this agenda.

The sort of comprehensive internationalisation advocated by John Hudzik (2011) in his NAFSA report is perhaps unreachable for many. We do see examples such as New York University establishing its 'portals' in Abu Dhabi, Shanghai and elsewhere to establish their own 'circulatory system'. Similarly international co-operative arrangements have long been an established feature at Freie Universität Berlin[1] as an 'International Network University'. The university is supported by its seven international

---

1. Berlin Free University — http://www.fu-berlin.de/en/kooperationen/hochschulen/index.html

Going Global: Identifying Trends and Drivers of International Education
Copyright © 2013 by Emerald Group Publishing Limited
All rights of reproduction in any form reserved
ISBN: 978-1-78190-575-3

liaison offices, located in Brussels, Cairo, Moscow, New York, New Delhi, Beijing and São Paulo. These offices provide support to scholars, scientists and researchers affiliated with Freie Universität who wish to explore co-operative opportunities in these regions. They also serve as a point of contact for researchers, instructors and students. But universities such as these are the exception rather than the rule.

Strategic partnership networks could be a logical alternative to help universities secure a global presence more economically and with more acceptable levels of risk. There are a large number of university networks. Some are regional groupings such as the ASEAN University Network; others are based around a concept such as the Joiman network for joint, dual and collaborative projects and some are based around a commonality of purpose such as the World University Network, which tackles large global research projects.

There is a bewildering range of networks and it may help to introduce the nature and rationale of a few of these and then discuss how they function.

Global Initiatives Partnership

The Global Initiatives Partnership includes the University of Kent, Virginia Tech, Universiti Teknologi Malaysia, Ghent University, Tongji University and the University of Technology Sydney. It was formed after discussions between Professor Alex Hughes, Pro-Vice-Chancellor External at the University of Kent (UK) and Professor John Dooley, Vice President for Outreach and International Affairs at Virginia Tech, suggested that bringing together a small, engaged group of partner institutions bore the potential to render more powerful previously bilateral partnership projects. The group first met in Canterbury in 2010 and met again in Blacksburg, Virginia in 2011. The next meeting is in Johor Bahru, Malaysia, in 2012. Current group initiatives are focused on student mobility, short and longer term, and on the sharing of good practice in internationalisation.

The Worldwide Universities Network

The Worldwide Universities Network[2] (WUN) comprises 18 research-intensive institutions spanning five continents. Its mission is to be one of the leading international higher education networks, collaborating to accelerate the creation of knowledge and to develop leaders who will be prepared to

---

2. Worldwide Universities Network — http://www.wun.ac.uk/

address the significant challenges, and opportunities, of our rapidly changing world. The WUN creates new, multilateral opportunities for international collaboration in research and graduate education. It is a flexible, dynamic organisation that uses the combined resources and intellectual power of its membership to achieve collective international objectives and to stretch international ambitions. Dr Indira Samarasekera, President of the University of Alberta and Chair of the WUN says: 'The WUN network is dedicated to making significant advances in knowledge and understanding in areas of global concern, bringing together the experience, equipment and expertise necessary to tackle the big issues facing societies, governments, corporations and education'.

The University Global Partnership Network

The University Global Partnership Network[3] (UGPN) sets out to create a foundation for international collaboration enabling academics and students from some of the world's top universities to work together on issues of global importance. UGPN priorities embrace a holistic understanding of internationalisation across all academic disciplines. The UGPN is a multilateral network of 'preferred partners', that is global in reach but local in scale. Its core founding partners are the University of Surrey, the University of São Paulo and North Carolina State University. There are additional partnership relationships with Seoul National University (College of Engineering initially); Banco Santander, through the Santander Universities Network; and Fapesp (the São Paulo State Research Funding Council). The main aims of the network are: promoting global graduates; student experience and employability; student mobility and placement opportunities across the network; curriculum innovation; dual and multilateral awards; promoting research with global impact; networked research in key themes; pump-priming of research; and innovation partnerships with industry.

The World Cities World Class University Network

The World Cities World Class University Network[4] (The WC2 University Network) was established in 2010 by City University London with the goal of

---

3. University Global Partnership Network — http://www.ugpn.org/
4. WC2 University Network — http://www.city.ac.uk/international/international-partnerships/wc2-university-network

bringing together top universities located in the heart of major world cities in order to address cultural, environmental and political issues of common interest to world cities and their universities. By promoting closer interaction between universities, local government and business communities, WC2 helps to create a forum where universities can be more responsive to the needs of their stakeholders in the context of world cities.

Founding WC2 members confirmed to date, in addition to City University London are: City University of New York (CUNY); Hong Kong Polytechnic University (HKPolyU); Northeastern University (NU); Politecnico di Milano; St Petersburg State Polytechnic University (SPSPU); Technische Universität Berlin (TUB); Tongji University; Universidad Autonoma Metropolitana (UAM); University of Delhi; University of São Paulo (USPi). Meetings have already taken place in London, Hong Kong, Berlin and São Paulo.

Each of the founding members brings together local expertise in issues of common interest to world cities such as: transport; global health; cultural/ creative industries (global culture); and business. The aim is to advance understanding and recognition of the role of universities in world cities and the matters that are of common interest to them, not only locally, but internationally through collaboration. The flow of staff, students and information across borders and through levels of local government results in a more comprehensive understanding of world cities, their universities and how they may impact and aid each other.

WC2 member universities are at the heart of a world city and recognised locally as a major university; committed to international activities; cosmopolitan in perspective and strategic direction; committed to close and intense two-way interaction with their local society and economy; strong academically, and in research, in areas particularly relevant to world cities; driven to meet the development of new areas of knowledge and technology; civically engaged with the broader community in the public and private sectors; committed to act as a local hub for the WC2 network; open to involving others in their city (business, community organisations, city hall, etc.) in WC2; endorsed projects including relevant collaboration with other experts.

Creating Successful Networks

Despite an increasing number of such global partnerships, there seems to be a lack of consensus on what these networks are seeking to achieve and how they do it. Some would argue that these networks offer crucial engagement with peers across a wide spectrum of activity, while others would condemn them as either exclusive membership clubs or, at the extreme, irrelevant.

This can be confusing for institutions that wish to join or start a network themselves. It seems that a number of factors dictate the relevance and success of a network.

Firstly, there needs to be a clearly stated and understood purpose for the network that permeates all its member institutions. Merely to share a geographic proximity or region is probably not enough to knit an association together; indeed, many successful networks report that the more distant collaborations work best. Equally, too diverse a set of objectives is likely to lead to dispersal of effort. Having a clear focus on tackling certain types of research problems; or removing barriers to student mobility; or arranging dual and joint degree collaborations are the areas likely to work best. The Worldwide Universities Network and the University Global Partnerships Network both concentrate on tackling global issues through networked research, building on the range of research strengths around each network, while the Global Initiatives Partnership focuses on student mobility and other internationalisation issues.

Secondly, the governance and management of networks is crucial. Very often in the early stages of a network it is one or two committed and enthusiastic individuals who make the running; in other cases it's the university presidents who meet and decide on a 'good idea'. In all cases, the network will only succeed if this early enthusiasm is spread throughout all parts of the participating universities. A 'top-down' network may allow presidents to discuss their big issues but is unlikely to lead to real co-operation, whereas a group of enthusiastic academics can run the risk of becoming a victim of funding restrictions or other constraints to building real partnerships.

Successful networks involve members from all parts of the participating institutions and their events are firmly established far in advance in the institutional calendar. For a truly participative network, network governance needs to be taken seriously by each member institution. Ownership of the relationship with the network needs to be at the president level, but engagement needs to be at all levels.

Needless to say, a sense of reciprocity and mutuality of input and outcomes is essential to achieve. Communication and trust are crucial parts of network development. The events and activities of the network need to foster this sense of connectedness. Most networks have a regular annual meeting in the diary that rotates around various locations. For example, WC2 holds two meetings a year. In addition, efforts are made to involve a broad range of staff from each institution in project-oriented work throughout the year. This is perhaps easier where there is a clear and focused aim for the network. As an example, the Worldwide Universities Network bids for research projects in globally challenging areas where a single institution would not be able to cover the scope needed. The activity of preparing bids necessarily involves a range of members across the network. In addition, the funders require evidence of solid governance and leadership which provides another stimulus for cohesion of the network.

Size also seems to be important. The importance of the network to a university's strategic interests would seem to be higher in those networks with small numbers of members. Most of the examples considered here have between eight and 18 members — WC2, as an example, has 11 members. This size range is probably the limit for a network run by and for its members in a democratic and participative fashion. The University Global Network Partnership has a very small group of three founding members and half a dozen other members. The Worldwide Universities Network has 18 members. Any larger and it's likely that a secretariat will be necessary to serve the membership, and the nature of members' involvement would be different.

Specialist types of networks do operate with larger numbers of members. For example, the University of London International Programmes, which is an access-driven programme of degrees available through distance and flexible learning, has a network of over 70 recognised centres (and 50 more in the process) for the purpose of supporting the learning of their students around the world. The network also offers prospects for student and staff mobility as well as knowledge sharing. Larger networks like this can work if they have clear and focused aims and standardised approaches to agreements.

One of the key factors in creating sustainable partnerships is getting the dynamic tension between similarity and difference right. Similarity of culture and aims makes communication and setting of goals easier. However, complementarity of strengths is also important. Good partnerships have a good spread of expertise between the member organisations that is clearly recognised so that each member plays to their strengths but gains from the strengths in complementary areas in their partner institutions.

One of the areas of diversity that is crucial for a network to have truly global relevance is getting the cultural or geographical representation right. A network like WC2 has members from a very wide range of developed and developing economies, including the United States, Russia and India. Cultural diversity brings challenges to the organisation and running of a network as different calendars, contractual forms, approaches to budgeting, working styles and languages all need to be accommodated. But without a good geographical spread a network cannot claim to be globally relevant.

Taking part in a partnership network brings its own costs. Apart from the administrative load, there is also a commitment to travel involved which can add to an already costly travel budget for institutions, and this has been a reason for institutions leaving networks. However, this investment should bring other returns. Members of networks like WUN report that they get research funding opportunities through the network connections and for networks with good student mobility opportunities this can help with student recruitment. More importantly, through networks, institutions can claim the type of global reach that only a few larger and well-funded institutions can claim on their own.

To give an example of a project undertaken by a network, the WUN Spintronics Consortium consists of more than 30 partners, including 10 WUN universities. The consortium brings together the expertise of the partners and carries out collaborative research with the aim of having a significant impact on science and society by achieving major breakthroughs in the exciting but challenging area of spintronics, which is playing an increasingly significant role in high-density data storage, microelectronics, sensors, quantum computing and bio-medical applications, among others. It is expected that the impact of spintronics on the microelectronics industry could eventually be comparable to the development of the transistor more than 50 years ago. The multi-disciplinary nature of spintronics requires expertise in electronics, material science, physics and computer science. The UGPN ran its own Research Collaboration Fund for 2012. With more than US$180,000 contributed from the UGPN partners, eight proposals were selected after an evaluation process across the three universities. The UGPN Fund is designed to support high-quality research collaboration across the partner universities — North Carolina State University, University of São Paulo, and the University of Surrey. Successful proposals include a tri-lateral research project between the three partners, which examines the integration of smart materials with pattern recognition and nanofabrication techniques for the development of novel electrochemical disease diagnostics.

In summary, the successful network seems to be one that is of small to moderate size; that has agreed clear aims for its work; that has the commitment and involvement of all its members; and that has a good balance of complementarity and similarity. This approach offers cost-effective global reach to universities that would be hard to achieve otherwise.

References

Hudzik, J. (2011). *Comprehensive internationalisation, from concept to action.* Retrieved from http://www.nafsa.org/resourcelibrary/default.aspx?id=24045. Accessed on September 17, 2012.

Meyrowitz, J. (2008). *The rise of glocality.* Retrieved from http://21st.century.phil-inst.hu/Passagen_engl4_Meyrowitz.pdf. Accessed on September 10, 2012.

SECTION 3
STUDENTS AND
INTERNATIONALISATION

Chapter 3.1

Editors' Introduction to Section 3

Going Global 6 introduced international students as a key theme in the discussions and subsequent Going Global Conferences looked at various aspects of the student experience and mobility. This section combines a number of articles that argue that students should be seen to be at the centre of discussions about the internationalisation of higher education.

Joan K. Stringer opens this section with an argument that transnational education is in many ways coming of age after a false start in the 1990s, when its reputation was somewhat tarnished and it was seen as a transient means to an end in most countries. Stringer argues that this is no longer the case and TNE is establishing a sustainable role that is not necessarily in contradiction with the local development of capacity. She makes the point that TNE providers need to carefully consider the nature of the experience they are offering their students and the extent that prepares students to be the global citizens of the future.

Christine Humfrey takes this theme further by arguing that the quality of the student experience is solidly rooted in the strategies and policies of the providing institution. While the experience is necessarily different from an experience on the home campus of the institution, it is not necessarily a poorer experience. However, universities need to take responsibility for thinking through the various aspects of that experience and for using the resources they can deploy to ensure it is a positive one.

Alejandra Ma. Vilalta y Perdomo looks at the way the Tecnológico de Monterrey endeavours to instil global citizenship value sets and thinking into its students through a series of active study abroad and joint international programmes, partly through the Universitas 21 network and also through a network of 400 partner institutions across 40 countries. This commitment to internationalisation goes as far as setting up a series of alumni liaison offices in a range of countries where Monterrey alumni have taken root.

Going Global: Identifying Trends and Drivers of International Education
Copyright © 2013 by Emerald Group Publishing Limited
All rights of reproduction in any form reserved
ISBN: 978-1-78190-575-3

Mohd Ismail Abd Aziz and Doria Abdullah use the context of internationalisation in Malaysia to discuss how countries like Malaysia could derive greater and deeper benefits from the presence of international students. David X. Cheng argues that study abroad programmes are crucially important for the internationalisation of Hong Kong universities. Most universities in Hong Kong are relatively young and have difficulty attracting full international students, so the combination of sending some students abroad and receiving foreign students in exchanges is a vital part of the internationalisation mix. This paper reports the findings of a survey of both inbound and outbound students with largely positive results — with nuances in the areas of quality of facilities and gains in certain soft skills.

Graeme Atherton discusses the efforts of some universities to address under-represented and disadvantaged students in their internationalisation strategy. Then Jayasree Anitha Menon looks at student-led internationalisation initiatives at the University of Zambia. She argues that internationalisation in developing contexts such as this should be primarily about preparing home students to function in an increasingly globalised professional environment. The paper describes how students have engaged in the process of analysing and re-aggregating internationally focused curriculums to allow more relevance to the local context, while preserving the international nature of the experience — a delicate balancing act.

It seems appropriate to end this section with student-centred projects and for us all to ask whether we have truly developed our institutions and policies with the student at the centre of this thinking.

Chapter 3.2

Growing Global Citizens: A Personal Perspective on the Future of Transnational Higher Education

Joan K. Stringer

Transnational Higher Education Today

The history of transnational higher education (TNE) over the last 30 years has been a story of assumptions challenged and expectations surpassed. The view of the market today from the perspective of traditional provider institutions in the West is arguably quite different from that which prevailed in the early days of growth in TNE and different even from the view in the mid-2000s.

TNE has developed through an initial phase of growth from a historically low base in the 1980s; diversification into mature and emerging markets in the 1990s; and a period of some instability through the 2000s tainted by concerns about quality, cost and return on investment. A new phase of development has begun and it looks set to be bigger, and potentially transformational compared with what has gone before.

Some of the new TNE activity is supply-driven. Institutions in some established Western provider countries in particular are planning to grow TNE as an income stream to diversify their business and reduce their reliance on diminishing state funding. In some cases, notably in the United Kingdom, renewed interest in TNE has been a response to concerns about tighter controls on student immigration and the risk to overseas student

Going Global: Identifying Trends and Drivers of International Education
Copyright © 2013 by Emerald Group Publishing Limited
All rights of reproduction in any form reserved
ISBN: 978-1-78190-575-3

recruitment arising directly and through changes in the perception of the United Kingdom as a destination which may result.

These supply-side incentives to grow TNE may carry risks similar to those which attended the more opportunistic approaches to expansion of TNE in the 1990s when several poorly researched and poorly executed initiatives tarnished the image of TNE and led some providers to withdraw from the market. However, the big picture today looks rather different compared to ten, or even five years ago.

Until quite recently there has been a quite widespread assumption that TNE enrolments would decline in the mature markets as a result of dramatic improvements in the scale and quality of local provision (e.g. McBurnie & Ziguras, 2007). Therefore, future growth in TNE would be limited and largely in the emerging TNE consumer countries. However, it appears that demand for TNE is growing strongly across all markets. TNE enrolments at UK institutions in 2010/2011 were up 23 per cent compared with 2010/2011, having grown by over 5 per cent between 2008/2009 and 2009/2010 (HESA, 2012). The entry into the market of new private providers attests to their confidence in the future growth potential of TNE.

While consumer countries are ambitious to achieve dramatic improvements in the scale and quality of local provision, domestic education systems in those countries struggle to deliver. India plans to triple enrolments in tertiary education as part of her 2020 vision but only 12 per cent of high school students go on to college and the qualifications awarded by universities do not in many cases meet industry needs (India Education Review, 2011). Similarly in Hong Kong employers complain that their needs and expectations are not being met. It has therefore become apparent that TNE has an enduring role to play working with and in partnership with the domestic system in consumer countries. That now seems to be a realistic assumption. The pedagogical innovation which has led to the high-quality, student-centred offering from Western institutions today, with its emphasis on graduate attributes and employability, has been built over decades and will continue to develop. Those institutions can therefore play a role in the development of education systems overseas and not ultimately or inevitably in competition with those systems.

Globally, TNE is recognised as an agent of international and inter-cultural relationship building and influence. It is also increasingly recognised as a source of prestige and a valuable export in its own right. Consequently more countries are seeking to become TNE providers, including some which are already consumers. The Hong Kong government has stated its intention of developing the territory into a regional education hub, both recruiting international students and providing international higher education. This is a development TNE providers in Hong Kong can play a part in and which will extend the matrix of relationships between providers and consumers across the East Asia region.

Developments in technology which facilitate new modes of delivery, particularly in distance learning, have intermeshed with developments in TNE. Hitherto assumptions (or expectations) about the potential future growth in distance learning and the application of technology to replace more traditional modes of delivery have not been matched by the extent of real change. Human capacity and cost have been important inhibiting factors. However, there are reasons to believe that we might be approaching a turning point. The collaboration between Harvard University and MIT to deliver edX — a non-profit joint venture to offer online, interactive courses which can be studied by anyone anywhere — has the potential to be transformational in delivering low-cost, mass-market higher education. In the coming decade or two the innovators in educaional delivery will be from a generation who grew up with social media and a technology-rich environment. We might reasonably expect that they will approach the needs of learners with fresh paradigms and hitherto unimagined solutions.

The Purpose of TNE

While some aspects of current developments in TNE seem familiar and thus point to learning lessons from the past, much of the landscape is fresh and offers considerable new opportunity. When considering the future of TNE, the starting point must be our understanding of the purpose of TNE. If it is not a transient support or substitute for still developing education systems, what is its enduring value?

The key to a positive future for TNE is the understanding that it exists for the shared and enduring benefit of all parties, that is governments, societies, institutions, employers and learners.

Second is the understanding of the importance of fair trade in TNE. Western institutions providing in-country TNE for the benefit of locally based overseas students is only one part of the perfect picture. There is a pressing need to address the balance of trade in higher education exemplified by the recently estimated 33,000 UK students who study at overseas institutions compared with the 370,000 overseas students studying with UK institutions (*International Focus*, 2010). The development of TNE and the delivery of international higher education more widely, by more providers and through new modes of delivery, offer a framework within which greater student mobility in all directions could be achieved.

The Future of TNE

With that understanding the distinction between providers and consumers and the perceived risk of exploitation which comes with it become blurred. TNE becomes more clearly about building alliances and long-term collaboration which enables more people in more places to acquire the kind of high-quality international higher education which will make them successful global citizens.

That is the basis of a positive future for TNE, but what does that imply for institutions seeking to deliver TNE and for the range of models of delivery?

There is much concern, and much academic discourse, about the proliferation of providers and types of TNE. There is concern that effective student choice is undermined by the absence of a universal quality framework or standardised information about course content and qualifications. There is a concern that an increasingly complex and confusing market will obscure low-quality, exploitative provision.

We may be some way from a universal quality framework. However, a lesson from the past is that exploitative, low-quality or poorly planned provision doesn't survive for long, whether at the hands of home or host country regulators or students voting with their feet. If the future of TNE is as a much more integrated part of home and host country systems, as it must be, opportunistic, poor-quality offerings will find it even harder to take root.

Institutions seeking to provide TNE will need to carefully assess and be clear about the markets they are seeking to provide for, the nature of their role and they must place TNE at the heart of their institutional strategy.

Providers will increasingly have an obligation to see themselves as part of the education systems in the countries in which they operate and not simply as service providers to them. Equally they will increasingly see TNE as an integrated part of their business as relevant to home students as to international students. They will need to be adaptable and avoid making assumptions about which models will work for particular markets.

The established models doubtless all have an enduring role to play but equally have limitations.

Overseas delivery through partner institutions including the use of 'flying faculty' is a well-established and successful model which promotes quality and a shared understanding of pedagogical approaches. However, for any one institution there is ultimately a human resource constraint on growth. Branch campuses have been successful for some institutions and a number of new branch campuses are being planned by UK universities, but the risks associated with capital development can be high for a single institution to manage and there have been some notable failures. Online and distance learning have a growing place in the market but barriers to start-up and scale-up can be high.

Regardless of concerns about immigration controls, exchange rate fluctuations and other factors which can affect student mobility, the logic of a greater physical in-country presence by provider institutions seems irresistible, but not of course limited to Western providers in non-Western countries. If TNE is truly to become an integrated part of the world's education systems then TNE providers will become not only international but in a sense multi-national organisations. A branch campus will reflect the ethos of its parent, be responsive to the aspirations of the local government and may recruit students from the originating country, the host country and the surrounding region.

A more dynamic market and a growing market raise issues of scale and risk and capacity for providers. There is therefore an opening for a paradigm shift from competition to collaboration. Historically Western provider institutions have been uniquely competitive in their approach to international and transnational education. Collaboration in research, in pedagogy, comes naturally but in the scramble for vital income the potential for collaboration in internationalisation has largely gone unrecognised.

The scale of the opportunity which is now available through TNE will change that. Through collaboration, institutions will be able to pool their resources and share risk. Learners will benefit from a richer offering drawing on a wider pool of intellectual and other resources. The collaboration between the University of Warwick and Monash University — committed to provide a richer offering to all of their students across all of their campuses and facilities — captures the motivation which will be at the heart of the future of TNE.

Such collaborations will take different forms to meet the needs of different markets and to be sustainable and responsive in different contexts. They may develop into more extensive federations with offerings from multiple institutions being available through multiple campuses. Technology will play a role, and having overestimated its potential for the last 20 years or so now seems precisely not the time to underestimate it.

These are postulations, but they are far from incredible. They are a logical inference from what is already happening. If this vision for TNE comes to pass the result will be greater integration and interdependence between higher education systems, long-term partnerships which will deliver more, which will be clear about their motivation and responsive to the needs of diverse markets and countries. A global approach to growing global citizens.

References

Higher Education Statistics Agency. (2012). *HESA SFR 169: Higher education student enrolments and qualifications obtained at higher education institutions in the*

United Kingdom for the academic year 2010/11. Retrieved from http://www. hesa.ac.uk/content/view/2355/161/. Accessed on June 28, 2012.

India Education Review. (2011, January 3). Sibal targets 30 per cent GER in higher education by 2020. Retrieved from http://www.indiaeducationreview.com/news/ sibal-targets-30-ger-higher-education-2020. Accessed on June 28, 2012.

McBurnie, G., & Ziguras, C. (2007). *Transnational education: Issues and trends in offshore higher education*. Abingdon: Routledge.

Motivating outward mobility. (2010, January 20) *International Focus*, (50), p. 1.

Chapter 3.3

Transnational Education: Examining and Improving the Student Experience

Christine Humfrey

Transnational Education (TNE) in Context

The UK university sector is now responsible for the academic achievement and overall learning and living environment of nearly one million international students. The gradual but steady increase in 'traditional' international students on UK-based programmes over the last 40 years has not been managed without considerable debate on principles, strategy and operation. This debate continues. Several points are, however, clear. The United Kingdom has achieved a great deal in its international recruitment aspirations and has refined its approach from the 'recruitment to survive' stage, to the desire to internationalise its institutions in the most sophisticated and sensitive manner.

Figure 1 indicates the steady growth in international student numbers in UK institutions and the additional spurt in growth of TNE in 2010/2011. Over the last 10 years, however, the concept of TNE (before then recognised by the General Agreement on Trade in Services or GATS), and visible through e-learning, validation, franchise, partnerships, joint and dual degrees and limited overseas campus development) has become a reality, and a fast-growing and immediate challenge. In *Vision 2020*, the British Council's report from 2004 which forecasted international student mobility to 2020, the expansion of TNE was addressed, but it still came as a considerable surprise to most higher education institutions (HEIs) (but perhaps

Going Global: Identifying Trends and Drivers of International Education
Copyright © 2013 by Emerald Group Publishing Limited
All rights of reproduction in any form reserved
ISBN: 978-1-78190-575-3

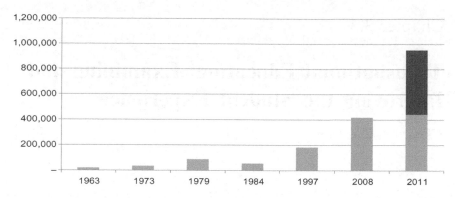

Figure 1: Numbers of international students pre-1981 and post-1981 and full-cost fees.

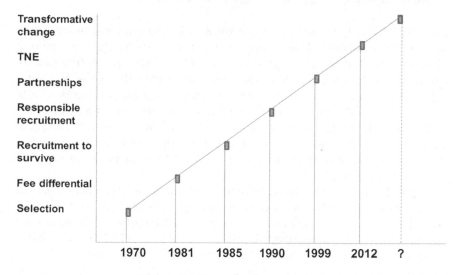

Figure 2: Growth of sensitivity.

not the British Council), when the figure exploded to over half a million TNE students in 2010, a significant increase on the previous year.[1]

That progress continues. Figure 2 indicates the growth in sophistication in the UK institutional response to internationalisation, its concept of partnership leading to TNE and beyond.

---

1. The British Council's *The shape of things to come* is a 2012 report which forecasts international mobility and TNE trends from 2010 to 2020.

TNE statistics were first collected formally in the United Kingdom by the Higher Education Statistics Agency (HESA) in 2007/2008 and the acknowledged size of the activity helped to increase interest in, and concern for, its development. The international student experience, particularly as it related to these students at institutions in the United Kingdom, had been accepted as critical to student satisfaction, institutional ranking and branding, commitment to quality, and an indicator of internationalisation in its response to student need.

The major problem is now to explore what the student experience could or should be for those TNE students who may never visit the United Kingdom to be immersed in English language, never mix with UK students, rarely will leave or will have left the dominant culture of their own country.

TNE Activity and Institutional Motivation

TNE, like other aspects of internationalisation, is not the sole domain of the United Kingdom, and the increase in TNE activity experienced by the United Kingdom is reflected across many of our 'usual' competitor and collaborator countries, including Australia and the United States.

In the United Kingdom, TNE is high on the risk register in any of a university's international activities for well-understood reasons. In a time of turbulence in tertiary education for domestic students, increased competence in traditional international education, and demanding debate on the function and future of universities, why are UK institutions across the mission groups so interested in TNE in all its forms? The answers cover both the pragmatic and the altruistic, and most institutions understand the need for the two. A quick rehearsal of the former includes government policy on net migration to include international students, the experience of UK Border Agency requirements, limited capacity of plant in the United Kingdom to meet all possible demand, a desire to raise profile in a selected region and, sometimes, a misguided expectation of potential income generation, and the resource and effort required to obtain it (Cavanagh & Glennie, 2012). The more laudable rationale is based on the emerging ideas of international partnership which is the real basis of TNE, the belief in widening participation for students outside as well as within the United Kingdom, and the desire to engage in internationalisation in as complete a manner as possible. This latter aspiration would include an opportunity for enrichment of domestic students and staff. Neither group of drivers stands completely separate from the other.

Successful TNE does assist with networking and, therefore, reputation; it can increase registered student numbers and diversity from a greater variety of national and socio-economic groups; it should enhance the potential for research collaboration and outward mobility of staff and students. It might protect the institution from some of the strictures of immigration compliance. It is the natural progression for the internationally facing institution, but that does not mean that overseas campuses should be the natural choice, from the wide TNE portfolio, for all of them.

The fundamental point of all of the above is the understanding of 'successful' in the context of TNE, and particularly with regard to the student experience.

TNE Activity and Student Motivation

While the challenges to and potential advantages for the institutions that offer successful TNE are clear, the benefits for sponsors, students and indeed the partnering nations are also considerable. The United Kingdom has recruited intellectually able international students to its universities and, through scholarship provision, has been able to accommodate some international students of equal ability from lower income groups. Students with a more liberal background, or those with more international experience, have been able to flourish in a different culture, while some of those with less international expertise or maturity have needed considerably more support, or stayed at home, or in like-minded countries in their region. That group, too, may have wanted or needed an international experience leading to a highly regarded qualification, but circumstances have not allowed it through traditional recruitment. TNE in all its forms offers a route to the desired qualification for the academically qualified who perhaps:

- cannot afford the full international fee and cost of living overseas
- want part-time attendance
- are unable to leave the family
- are discouraged by religious, gender or political reasons from staying in the United Kingdom
- have a disability and feel they need special support
- have extensive domestic and/or professional responsibilities.

TNE, through its gradation of the requirement for physical presence in the providing institution, is a way of offering this quality of education. For these groups, the student experience could well be an even more important yet difficult to define aspect of their higher education.

TNE and the Student Experience

The student experience is evaluated in the *Times Higher Education* (*THE*, April 2012), for English undergraduate students by scoring for:

- quality, helpfulness and interest of staff, small group tuition, workload
- well-structured courses and personal relationships with teaching staff
- social life, community atmosphere, extracurricular societies/activities
- environment on campus and around the university, security
- facilities, catering for personal requirements, student union
- support and welfare facilities, accommodation, library quality and opening hours
- convenient/centralised facilities, cheap shop and bar facilities, sports facilities
- industry contact.

This heterogeneous list, which seems to include fundamental Quality Assurance Agency (QAA) and professional accreditation requirements with package holiday attributes, is depicted by the Survey Supplement as the result of higher fees, so 'student expectations are rising and young people are increasingly looking for ways to get the most from their investment ... Although universities must never put the student experience before their mission for academic excellence, its value to young people — the ability to take stock, make friends and connections, learn and have fun — cannot be underestimated'. It goes on to stress that with increasing levels of competition between universities 'the experiences of the student "consumer" demand more attention than ever before'.

The international student experience has been a concern of the UK Council for International Student Affairs (UKCISA), among other organisations, for many years, and has concentrated on preliminary information to students, assistance with application, pre-arrival preparation, orientation, accommodation, study and language support, financial, welfare and career advice, pedagogy, curriculum, and reorientation. It has also, importantly, developed continuing professional development (CPD) for all categories of staff in order to deliver this desired experience. Satisfaction rates in the benchmarking studies have been high yet with acknowledgement that improvement is always possible. The Minister of State for HE and Intellectual Property said in 2008 in UKCISA's *Mobility Matters*, 'The international student experience which we offer, is, I believe, one of the United Kingdom's great success stories and it is because of the investment which we make in this area that our reputation and satisfaction ratings are as high as they are today' (UKCISA, 2008, 2011).

Surveys and insights from i-graduate have also alerted universities across the world to international student views and levels of satisfaction and areas of dissatisfaction, and the need for improvement. The Student Barometer allows institutions to compare their provision in this area with that of others in similar institutions in the United Kingdom or across the world. The efficacy and benefit of all of this to institution, sponsor and traditional international students is not difficult to recognise and sits well with other quality measures, but cannot be so easily identified and secured for TNE students.

The fundamental question here relates to the product that UK universities are offering in their name to students who may never come to the United Kingdom or at best spend only a part of their degree programme at the awarding university. In successful TNE activity the quality of the award is the same as that offered in the United Kingdom, and in many instances the curriculum will be exactly the same as that in the United Kingdom, with the same assessment at the same time and the same external examiner. The academics are unlikely to be the same people unless the course is delivered by the 'parachute' pattern or through a virtual learning environment. All of these are academic quality issues and, while vital to the student, are the concerns of validating, accrediting and quality assurance agencies with disastrous and highly publicised outcomes when they fail to safeguard quality.

It is that part of the product that falls outside the main academic offering that now needs to be considered. What differentiates the student experience in a Heriot Watt Approved Learning Partner Institution in the Caribbean from the experience offered on a similar course by the University of the West Indies, or other international providers with the same course offering available as TNE? How does the experience of a UCLan University of Central Lancashire 2+1 franchise student in China differ from that offered to a compatriot travelling to Preston from Beijing, or studying at a university in Hong Kong? How does Lancaster manage its students on the 3+0 programme with Sunway University College, or Reading its 1+2 programme with Taylor's University College? What does Nottingham expect to impart on its degree under 2+2 arrangements with Thammasat University in Thailand. Some of these institutions in the United Kingdom have now launched overseas campuses, the existence of which makes the student experience question all the more complicated and demanding (Humfrey, 2009).

Why should the student select a UK TNE programme? If we leave aside the academic quality which is vital in the conferment of a UK degree, what else is implied by that award, and how is it evidenced in the student experience which supports it? This is where it can be argued that the strategy which underpins all the internationalisation activity of the awarding institution can help to provide this experience. The experience is based on the quality of relationships between partner and partner and student and partner, the consistency of delivery offered between the home campus and all TNE outlets, the transparency of the arrangement that supports the TNE and the respect and integrity with which it is delivered, together with the imagination and sensitivity with which the programmes are managed and the relationships enhanced.

Support for this belief in the strength of strategy in internationalisation is evidenced in Elkins, Farnsworth, and Templer (2008) in his case studies with university business schools in which it was shown that a complete strategic focus leads to success in internationalisation, and a consequent desire to achieve even greater levels of internationalisation in the future. To achieve this, the university must be robust in its belief that internationalisation should be integral to the university mission and identity, and the international strategy should complement, and not compete with, those other key strategies for teaching and learning, research, community engagement, and the student experience. Without this holistic approach it is more difficult for the university to deliver in the complex area of the TNE student experience. TNE activity should be a natural development in the internationalisation strategy, and has been classified as the third wave of internationalisation; the first being traditional international student movement form home to the awarding institution and the second some adaptation of the 'flying faculty' model.

If the student experience is secured by a robust internationalisation strategy, then that strategy, particularly in the case of TNE, is built on an awareness of and commitment to four key concepts debated by educational commentators — control, cost, return and risk.

Control indicates a willingness to manage and to accept accountability for the students, any partnership and outcomes. It signifies an understanding of the constraints and the importance of quality assurance and the implications of failure.

Cost is a commitment to make the product work, and a clear recognition that expenditure at the appropriate level will be for the long term. Expenditure under this heading is agreed for the benefit of all parties, and not simply for the awarding institution. Cost is planned and a part of the institutional budget but calculated with the flexibility to survive change in short-term circumstances. Cost includes both significant management stretch and the calculation of opportunity cost.

Return is based on a vision of internationalisation of which TNE is one part. The activity will not be undertaken solely or even primarily to secure a large return on financial expenditure, but a real return in academic advancement, collaborations, networks, the diversity of the student community, international research opportunities and possible outward mobility.

Risk is an understanding of the institution's strengths and aspirations and a belief that the infrastructure, management, resource and spirit of the institution can accept the challenge of this internationalisation activity. The ability to manage risk is an indication of leadership strength, based on solid forecasting and ability to acquire and handle data, and inspire the university community. In a *THE* article on the recent decision by the University of Central Lancashire (UCLan) to extend its TNE portfolio the vice-chancellor stressed these points: 'We are not simply franchising out our name for short-term gain, which is where ventures like this can easily go wrong: we are making a long-term commitment by establishing campuses that we control and maintain [...] The new campuses will help us to expand our international links [...] and bring UCLan's superlative student experience to students in these regions [...] At the centre of our university's strategy is a commitment to internationalisation' (*THE*, 1 March 2012).

The idea that the quality of the student experience is borne of and secured by the quality of the strategy upon which it is founded, is emphasised in the recent OBHE report by Gore (2012), 'Higher education across borders'. Here the syntax of the successful private corporation and the successful internationalised university are brought together in 'sense of community, brand and protection of reputation, aims and transparent values, sensitivity to cultural differences, analysis and acquisition of knowledge [...] and core competencies'. The author goes on to regret that 'few universities have well-articulated global strategies' and yet fewer 'a compelling vision'. Yet it is this vision of its essential nature, and whether this nature can be a part of overseas activity, that dictates the success of the TNE endeavour, and in that success lies the quality of the student experience.

Conclusion

Undoubtedly all our students need access to the kinds of support structure, the quality of teaching and learning, the calibre of physical infrastructure that can be assessed and measured and ranked, and indeed, should be the best it is appropriate to provide. In the end, however, that is not sufficient to ensure the quality of the student experience. That experience, especially for our international TNE students, whose perception of the country and university conferring their award may be partial or needs to be sustained and assured by a strategy for internationalisation. That strategy needs to reflect and implement that comprehensive internationalisation first arti-culated by Jane Knight and most recently by Hudzig, quoted by Gore, as 'a commitment, confirmed through action, to infuse international and comparative perspectives throughout the teaching, research and service mission of higher education. It shapes institutional ethos and values and touches the entire higher education enterprise [...] It not only impacts all of campus life but the institution's external frames of reference, partnerships and relations'.

With adherence to such a vision, we stand more chance of succeeding in the complicated and sensitive matter of the TNE student experience.

References

British Council. (2004). *Vision 2020*. Retrieved from www.britishcouncil.org/eumd_-_vision_2020.pdf

Cavanagh, M., & Glennie, A. (2012). *International students and net migration in the UK*. Institute for Public Policy.

Elkins, G., Farnsworth, J., & Templer, A. (2008). Strategy and the internationalisation of universities. *International Journal of Educational Management, 22*(3) (Emerald Group Publishing).

Gore, T. (2012). *Higher education across borders: Models of engagement*. OBHE.

Humfrey, C. (2009). *Transnational education and the student experience*. London, UK: UKCISA.

THE. (2012, March 1). Taking the plunge.

THE. (2012, April 26). Student experience survey supplement.

UKCISA. (2011). *International student services 2010–11: A benchmarking survey*. ISBN 1 870679 58X

UKCISA. (2008). *Mobility matters: Forty years of international students. Forty years of UKCISA*. Retrieved from http://www.ukcisa.org.uk/files/pdf/about/mobility_matters.pdf

Chapter 3.4

The Education of Global Citizens in Mexico through International Programmes: The Tecnológico De Monterrey Case

Alejandra Ma. Vilalta y Perdomo

For many years now there has been discussion about the importance of internationalisation and education for citizenship. Simultaneously, in some countries nationalist sentiments are increasing and some regions are polarised on religious or economic variables. Questions are asked about globalisation from both economic and social standpoints. Now, more than ever, the preparation of the next generations must be aimed at enabling young people to feel comfortable working as a team with people in and from different cultures and nations, while encouraging them to reconcile their interests so as to improve their respective societies in a harmonious way.

The internationalisation programmes developed by many educational institutions aim to facilitate greater student mobility, as well as generating possibilities for joint projects such as those on research that have emerged in the last two decades. However, more work on genuine and real internationalisation of globalisation concepts is needed. There is a discernable difference between a group of people who just work together on a project and a real integrated teamwork. Developing a productive team from people with different backgrounds, focused on a common interest, is one of the great challenges of internationalisation. It is all part of producing citizens with both a national perspective and an international perspective, with

Going Global: Identifying Trends and Drivers of International Education
Copyright © 2013 by Emerald Group Publishing Limited
All rights of reproduction in any form reserved
ISBN: 978-1-78190-575-3

a global understanding that promotes greater tolerance and openness for future international strategies.

Definitions of citizenship, whether academic and non-academic, are hugely varied — it is described as a quality, a condition, a status, a value, a mission, a profession, an activity, a commitment or an inspiration. Words like co-existence, participation, equity, democracy, freedom, equality, solidarity, integration or collaboration are mentioned in the same breath. Whatever the approach, producing good citizens is about developing co-operation so that people assume their life values as part of responsible citizenship. In society we need to design programmes to help individuals learn, appreciate and put into practice rights and social obligations from their own community and to be able to understand others that could be foreign to them. Although different countries have different legal frame-works, there are some common elements in societies that contribute to social co-existence and human well-being in respect of the individual and the institutions. Young people should know and understand these common elements.

As in any educational process, preparing a responsible citizen implies developing not only knowledge but also attitudes and values that allow young people to participate actively in the development of the communities in which they live. In this regard, academic institutions have a great responsibility to train citizens, in the same way that families and other institutions and organisations are responsible.

There are a great number of initiatives in Mexico to build citizenship among young people: the programme CONSTRUYE-T ('Build yourself') has an enrolment close to million and a half students aged between 15 and 18, from more than 1600 schools in all states of the Mexican Republic; IMAGINA-T ('Imagine yourself') and CONSTRUYE TU MUNDO ('Build your world'), enjoy the participation of hundreds of adolescents in Mexico City.

Mexico is by no means alone in working to this end. The United Nations declared 2010 the international year of youth, with the slogan: 'Dialogue and mutual understanding', encouraging young people to devote their potential economic, social and cultural development to the promotion of a shared consensus. It was also intended to promote dialogue and under-standing between the generations and to promote the ideals of peace, respect for human rights, freedom and solidarity. These are some of the examples of the many initiatives carried out with teenagers to draw attention to the immense potential of this population group, who are both important actors and recipients of the major social change going on in Mexico. The empowerment of young people allows them to recognise the contribution they make to their community and their country. Teenagers must be the basis for the construction of a culture of peace, inclusion and equality they must grow and be prepared to develop to their maximum potential and creativity — especially in a country like Mexico with a population of 112 million people and an average age of 26. We are facing the future with a very young community, so we must be engaged to prepare them to be the best citizens this society needs. To this end the Tecnológico de Monterrey educational model pursues the development of social commitment and community responsibility.

Developing Global Citizenship

Mexico offers great opportunities to young people. With its geographical position, a regulatory and legal framework friendly to foreign investment and competitive production costs, Mexico needs global understanding for business. Mexico has 12 free-trade agreements, providing an opportunity to reach 44 countries, an equivalent to 1200 million people (PROMEXICO Report). Mexico manufactures and exports a large number of sophisticated products, which will increase in the near future, helped by the 115,000 engineers graduating every year from careers in science and technology, so enterprises and industry need people who will embrace globalisation.

Exposure to multiple cultural identities makes students appreciate the elements of global citizenship and gives them the opportunity to take advantage of global opportunities for their future. New generations are comfortable using all those new technologies which decrease or eliminate physical and geographical boundaries, so they see themselves more and more as a part of a new world construction. Travel, knowledge of languages, international mobility and the membership and activity in social networks can be also important ways to explore the individual as a citizen of a global world.

In terms of international mobility, the Tecnológico de Monterrey accounts for about two per cent of the population of higher education in Mexico and its students represent 20 per cent of Mexican students abroad. Yearly data for 2011 shows that 7528 students spent one semester or summer term studying in a university abroad; 603 faculty members participated in projects, summer courses, seminars or congresses abroad. Up to January 2011, 28 per cent of alumni 5 years after graduation have had at least one international professional experience and 25 years after graduation this percentage was close to 25 per cent. This is a key point to prepare students as global citizens in order to satisfy the future needs of global societies.[1]

---

1. For more information about the Tecnológico de Monterrey see: http://www.itesm.edu/wps/wcm/connect/ITESM/Tecnologico + de + Monterrey/English

Since international collaboration is needed to develop global pro-grammes it is important to develop an international network with prestigious universities and consortiums. This has been a crucial engine to ignite internationalisation at the Tecnológico de Monterrey. From this international collaboration several highly compelling and successful programmes have resulted, such as the certificate of globalisation, the Global Issues Programme (GIP)[2] offered by the Consortium Universitas 21, in which students from the Tecnológico de Monterrey and other participating universities may take courses online through the Tecnológico de Monterrey Virtual University (one of the compulsory subjects of the certificate). They may also take other courses on their own campus as well as abroad in the partner universities from the GIP group (Melbourne and Queensland Universities in Australia, Lund University in Sweden, Notting-ham University in the UK, and the University of British Columbia in Canada). This is an international honours programme of excellence designed to give students a global context through the study of several issues critical to this interrelated world. Top academic students from all undergraduate programmes in business, social sciences and humanities at the Tecnológico de Monterrey can apply and 20 of them are chosen. On completion of this programme the students should have a global and intercultural vision, both from the content of the materials and from the interaction with other students from partner universities. They should develop a better understanding and tolerance of different cultures and international working environments, and should also have learnt to apply knowledge in global affairs to their professional activities. Students are awarded an official certificate by the Consortium Universitas 21 after taking classes with specialist teachers on a high-level curriculum from the participating institutions, using the most advanced technologies for education through the Internet, and having the opportunity to interact with peers from different universities. To be eligible for this GIP students should have completed the third semester of their undergraduate programme and/or have accredited 18 courses from their own academic programme.

These programmes strengthen others offered on campus to all students to prepare them for global knowledge and a global social accountability so they may focus on improving their quality of life for their communities, develop their human potential and respect human culture in its diverse manifestations.

---

2. Global Issues Programme (GIP) offered by the Consortium Universitas 21 http://www.universitas21.com/article/students/details/62/global-issues-programme

Personal Skills Training

The Tecnológico de Monterrey educational model seeks to prepare students for life. Marketable skills increase chances to find better jobs. Educational institutions must give an extra importance to this challenge especially in these days of economic crisis in a wide range of countries. The World Commission on the Social Dimension of Globalization pointed out that: 'All countries which have benefited from globalisation have invested significantly in their education and training systems' (2004).

The Tecnológico de Monterrey, the educational model, offers students multiple opportunities to actively participate in professional environments, both national and international. This also requires special national and international training programmes for faculty members who are engaged with the continuous improvement processes performed by the institution.

Promoting entrepreneurship, innovation, creativity, new management practices and technologies, sustainable development, practical education and labour market training programmes and focusing on productivity all increase competitiveness in the global economy. But this is not enough as a part of an academic programme. Other important issues must be considered: those related to human and social aspects, because globalisation provides not only benefits to some countries but also inequality to others.

Double degrees, among other international programmes, offer students a comprehensive developmental experience in an international environment. This in turn gives them an opportunity to develop their capacity to adapt in diverse contexts in social, economic, cultural and professional areas. Students in an international academic programme may have the opportunity to graduate with both a degree from Tecnológico de Monterrey and a degree from the foreign university where their academic exchange took place. To qualify, students must comply with a 1–2-year stay in this foreign institution, successfully undertaking between 12 and 16 courses. To be admitted and to graduate from those programmes, students must fulfil different requirements from both institutions. At this moment, there are 49 international agreements for double degrees in different academic areas with universities from 12 countries and more are in the pipeline.

International on-the-job training or internships and business projects also give students the opportunity to be trained to global labour standards. These eligible programmes run during regular semesters or during the summer. They allow students to get credits on their undergraduate programme by working, or combining this work experience with attending courses at the partner universities abroad.

Professors have a key role in developing multicultural skills, so the Tecnológico de Monterrey also encourages international mobility among them. In 2011 there were 603 faculty members who participated in projects, summer courses, seminars or congresses abroad and 544 visiting international professors were received to teach on different campuses.

Creating an International Culture for Students and Alumni

The Tecnológico de Monterrey offers students the prospect of a comprehensive developmental experience in an international environment through attractive programmes at different levels in more than 30 countries. This in turn gives them the opportunity to develop their capacity to adapt to diverse contexts within social, economic, cultural and professional areas and thus have a better future for themselves and their families — this also helps to build a better society. Every year Tecnológico de Monterrey alumni gain more international experience. In 2011, 40 per cent of graduating students had studied abroad at some point during their academic programme.

The 2011 *Student Mobility Report* shows a 12.3 per cent increase in the number of students from the Tecnológico de Monterrey who studied abroad — in total 7528 (25.12 per cent from high school, 72.97 per cent from undergraduate programmes and 1.91 per cent from graduate programmes). The student destinations ranged from 55.14 per cent to Europe, 29.29 per cent to North America, 7.43 per cent to Asia, 4.72 per cent to Central and South America, 3.40 per cent to Oceania and 0.03 per cent to Africa. Though English as a second language has great importance in the curriculum so that students have more options to study abroad, they still want to improve their knowledge of French, German or Chinese, allowing the possibility of international academic experience in these countries.

Innovation and collaboration on international programmes are necessary to develop new academic possibilities to students and professors. Programmes offered by the Tecnológico de Monterrey rely on academic co-operation agreements with some of the best universities in the world. Successful international mobility is possible due to the international agreements with 450 universities in more than 40 countries. In the last 11 years the Tecnológico de Monterrey has sent more than 70,000 students abroad and received more than 45,000 students from universities all over the world. This mobility creates an international culture for students and alumni. At least 25 per cent of high school students should have an international experience, 50 per cent of undergraduates and 100 per cent in some high school and undergraduate programmes where international experience is mandatory. Each campus of the Tecnológico de Monterrey aims at five per cent of students from foreign universities, which is a challenge for an institution with 31 campuses and a student population close to 90,000.

Impact of Alumni Liaison Offices Abroad

Because of the large number of alumni living and working in other countries having an international experience during their studies at the Tecnológico de Monterrey, there are 29 liaison offices in 15 countries. They are all very active, organising meetings and giving support to alumni in different professional services. The EXATEC community is promoted by the office of alumni relations through events at liaison offices and through print and electronic media. This concept of global citizenship being developed by the Tecnológico de Monterrey enhances campus and institution diversity through the internationally networking alumni provided to the liaison offices. There are regular meetings and also big annual conventions, such as those celebrated yearly in autumn in Europe, generating an attractive space to exchange for those alumni living and working in European countries. Many of those alumni offer opportunities to new generations in their own companies abroad in that they recruit younger alumni or receive current students for internships or business projects. This is a win-win situation.

Institutions like the Tecnológico de Monterrey can prepare students as global citizens in order to satisfy the future needs of global societies in a different connected world. Transnational education will have a significant impact on institutions and host countries and their collaboration and partnerships will shape and create global networks and global opportunities.

References

Promexico Report. (September 2012). 'México es oportunidad. Retrieved from http://www.promexico.gob.mx/work/models/promexico/Resource/1000/1/images/Presentacion_Mexico_es_Oportunidad.pdf

Student Mobility Report. (2011). Tecnológico de Monterrey. Retrieved from http://viewer.zmags.com/publication/04ef4be3#/04ef4be3/1

World Commission on the Social Dimension of Globalization Report. (2004). A Fair globalization: Creating opportunities for all. Brief review of policy issues, Geneva, p. 275. Retrieved from http://www.ilo.org/wcmsp5/groups/public/—dgreports/—integration/documents/publication/wcms_079151.pdf

Chapter 3.5

Shaping the Internationalisation of Higher Education through Student Mobility: Focus on Malaysia

Mohd Ismail Abd Aziz and Doria Abdullah

There was an interesting question posed by a delegate in one of the plenary sessions of Going Global 2012: 'Can we summarise "internationalisation of higher education" in one page?' Internationalisation is a buzzword these days, and it is difficult to separate the 'international, global and inter-cultural' (Knight, 2007) elements from all the core businesses of the system. Moreover, the 'flat' world and the rapid cross-border flow of talents, programmes and providers have made definitions of the concept disputable. Should we even attempt to summarise the phenomenon if it is synonymous with higher education systems these days?

Higher education institutions have begun to structure their operations around internationalisation, and are mindful of the complexities, consider-able risks and the impact of the phenomenon on higher education. One of the visible activities symbolic to internationalisation is the flow of students across borders, reflecting the major implications of student mobility in stimulating the growth of international higher education globally.

This paper explores student mobility as a means in shaping internatio-nalisation of higher education, with a focus on Malaysia and its efforts in intensifying student mobility in the country.

Going Global: Identifying Trends and Drivers of International Education
Copyright © 2013 by Emerald Group Publishing Limited
All rights of reproduction in any form reserved
ISBN: 978-1-78190-575-3

Winners and Losers in Student Mobility?

Altbach, Reisberg, and Rumbley (2009) observation on the increase in international student mobility is echoed by major international organisations. Asia is a major importer of higher education, with over 52 per cent of students from the region enrolled worldwide. Student mobility is also reflective of the 'global workforce development' phenomenon in the job market, as the workforce is now drawn from a global community instead of a single nation. Both students and employers are optimising opportunities in international higher education in developing the right skills set and competencies to work and solve global issues in a complex and intercultural environment.

Regions with great resources and expertise in higher education will attract students in significant amounts, thus becoming central nodes in higher education exports. In 2011, the Institute of International Education (IIE) reported that there is a critical outflow of students in the South, West and Central Asia, while the Western Europe and North America regions recorded a greater inflow of students. Walker (2010) also highlighted the increasing poverty and wealth gaps between richer and poorer countries, as the former tend to attract talents from the latter, and have greater advantage when forming knowledge partnerships with the latter.

The emergence of global ranking leagues has also highlighted the race for higher education institutions to move ' ... into the higher reaches of the academic hierarchy' (Bok, 2003) by leveraging on a critical mass of top foreign talents in building 'world class universities' (Salmi, 2009). The outcome-based measurements of success in higher education often disregard the actual process of students' learning and the students' contribution towards productive learning in higher education institutions. Student development is also more defined along the lines of human capital development instead of the actual and imperative process of 'humanising' higher education (Dzulkifli, 2011).

Student Mobility: the Malaysian Context

The Malaysian Government views higher education as a means of achieving both income generation and global competitiveness in transforming Malaysia to a high-income developed nation by 2020 (NEAC, 2010). Malaysia aims to be an international education hub, generating an estimated RM 4.5 billion from the 150,000 international student enrolment in 2015 and RM 6 billion (200,000 international students) in 2020, building the country's capacity in knowledge-led activities through increased mobility of students and faculty members and international collaborations in the areas of research and development.

Underlying the growth of the Malaysian higher education is the National Higher Education Strategic Plan 2020 (NHESP, 2020), embodying the essence of Malaysian higher education transformation in a four-phase implementation from 2007 to 2020 (MoHE, 2007). Internationalisation of higher education is highlighted as one of the strategic thrusts under this plan; initiatives in place will focus on building a strong global network and international academic collaboration, increasing the attractiveness of Malaysia as a choice destination for higher education and positioning Malaysian higher education as a relevant, competitive and sustainable system contributing to the development of communities locally and abroad.

Knight and Morshidi (2011) have classified Malaysia as a 'student hub' with its growing international student volume, international collaboration and initiatives in development of strategic regions in the country such as the Educity at Iskandar Malaysia. The affordable cost of living, competitive fee structure and international recognition of qualifications are some of the reported pull factors in attracting students to Malaysia for higher education (Jani, Zubairi, Tat, & Ngah, 2010). There is an increase of 65 per cent international student enrolment in the country in an eight-year period, from 30,397 international students in 2003 to 86,919 in 2010, with private higher education institutions enrolling more than 70 per cent of the students. Malaysia is a destination of choice for students from Asian, Middle East and African regions with approximately 65 per cent of the total enrolment from 2008 to 2010. Morshidi (2008) noted an increased enrolment of students from the Middle East countries post-9/11. The political instability and the difficulties for the students in applying for post-secondary education in the United States have, to an extent, directed these students to Malaysia for their education.

Of emerging interest is Malaysia's transnational education profile as host of international branch campuses (IBCs). Malaysia played host to seven IBCs by 2011 and has captured 25 per cent of the global market share of students in IBCs. The average number of students enrolled per IBC is 2189; 75 per cent of students are Malaysians and the rest come from other countries (24 per cent) and the IBC home country (1 per cent). While there is no substantial data supporting this argument, it can be inferred that IBCs in Malaysia have immense potential in retaining domestic students seeking affordable options for international degrees and stimulating greater inflow of students to the country.

The Ministry of Higher Education (MoHE) has also emphasised the implementation of short-term mobility programmes in public higher education institutions to democratise mobility for students, through development of short programmes, generally completed within one to two weeks. Such programmes offer more flexibility and provide greater equity by eliminating or reducing barriers, particularly those related to financial and time constraints, which are commonly cited as key inhibitors for participation. A total of 9107 students from public higher education institutions participated in short-term mobility programmes in 2010 and the current figure stands at 7382 students (May 2012). It is becoming a priority for public higher education institutions to provide international experience to their students through short-term mobility programmes, as their experience abroad, regardless of duration, will have an impact on the students' personal and professional development.

Reflection: Putting Student Mobility in Perspective

Kell and Vogl (2012) described Asia Pacific as one of the active regions in student mobility, stating ' … they are very often the basis for making the shift from higher education system in nation building … '. In their study of student mobility trends and issues across Singapore, Hong Kong and Malaysia, they highlighted the need to value the presence of international students as agents promoting 'greater mutual interest from participating institutions'. Malaysia is a popular host for students from Islamic and developing countries in the Asian region. The incoming students have helped the country establish itself as a higher education exporter — in 2010 it played host to students from more than 167 countries. However, Malaysia has yet to fully explore its impact on the development of the students' home countries and communities, particularly countries in the ASEAN region, following the region's development blueprint towards a united and harmonised ASEAN community by 2015. Malaysia should capitalise on its current standing and see beyond surface-level economic, human capital and scholarly benefits to be more relevant regionally, building a 'higher education diplomacy' by expanding its outreach and influence in the region.

The student 'voice' appears to be lacking in the decision-making process concerning institutional internationalisation. Both local and international students are critical actors in providing context to the international character of an institution. The policy dissonance became apparent between the students' perceived value of an 'international' higher education and the processes implemented by institutional management in creating an 'international' higher education. Policy analysis and evaluation which take into consideration the students' perspective would provide insights into underlying issues affecting participation and successful implementation of internationalisation efforts of an institution.

The presence of international students should stimulate improved services and infrastructures in higher education institutions as the value of a service may be perceived through the experience students have had in obtaining the service, and the cumulative effort expended in getting it (Brenders, Hope, & Ninnan, 1999). Following Malaysia's aspiration to become an education hub, there should be a comprehensive review into the country's capacity and capability to manage the growing international student population in building its higher education profile internationally. A commitment to recruiting international students should also come with a commitment to ensuring a conducive environment for the students at the institutional level.

There is also a need to establish proper engagement opportunities between internationals and locals in stimulating 'internationalisation at home', particularly to a larger proportion of students who are not mobile internationally. Are institutions making use of the presence of international students to the benefit of local students and the local community? Jani's (2010) research on international students in Malaysia has indicated the lack of interaction between international students and the locals. Her findings echo similar researches on international student interaction in different settings globally for the past decade, such as the UK (Montgomery, 2010), Australia (Briguglio, 2000), and the United States (McLachlan & Justice, 2009). International students look for both academic opportunities that would enhance their employability and career advancement and educational and social experiences that would enrich their personal growth. Institutions should stimulate greater social interaction between international students and the local population as this would enhance local students' intercultural abilities, a much sought-after skill in the global market today. The international students' interaction with the local population would also contribute to greater social and academic well-being and their overall experience as sojourners.

The international student population should be considered as a 'talent capital', with the potential of driving Malaysia towards its high-income, innovation-driven aspirations. A good case study is Singapore: the country is able to capitalise on the available international population in their higher education system as a feeder for the nation's high-skilled talent needs (Sidhu, Chong, & Yeoh, 2011). As such, each institution is responsible for creating the right ecosystem to enable and support student mobility, as academic performance has been singled out as the indicator for student success (Australian Vice Chancellor's Committee, 2005). The students' feedback on student mobility in a plenary session of Going Global 2011[1] illustrated some of the avenues in which higher education institutions can work on to enhance students' experiences. For example there should be proper organisation in facilitating student mobility at every stage of implementation and recognition on students' academic learning and effort in undertaking mobility opportunities. Recognition for enabling mobility should also be given where it's due, especially to enablers of mobility programmes; incentives should be made available to students, faculty members and administrators who have gone the extra mile in making mobility happen in respective faculties.

Summary

This paper has attempted to highlight the place of student mobility in internationalisation of higher education, focusing on Malaysia as a case study. Malaysia is in the position to capitalise on student mobility because of its efforts in the internationalisation of higher education, particularly with regard to enabling student mobility in its higher education institutions. Internationalisation of higher education can, and should, be looked at from a practical, student-centric standpoint by focusing on effective management and the implementation of student mobility. Having said that, there is still room for improvement for the country in ensuring more effective student mobility, whose success is dependent on collective and systematic efforts by relevant stakeholders involved at all levels in higher education institutions.

It is appropriate to end this paper by reminding fellow practitioners of the principles of high-quality higher education from Sharing Quality Higher Education across Borders: A Statement on Behalf of Higher Education Institutions Worldwide released by the International Association of Universities (IAU) in 2004. There are eight core principles put forward in the document; however, of interest in the context of this discussion are four principles: (1) contributing to broader economic, social and cultural well-being of communities; (2) strengthening developing countries' higher education capacity to promote global equity; (3) providing access of higher education to all; and (4) expanding mobility opportunities for students, faculty and researchers. These principles should always be embodied by higher education institutions in welcoming, and accommodating to,

---

1. See http://ihe.britishcouncil.org/going-global/sessions/turning-tables-international-student-mobility

the increasing volume of students going across borders not just for higher education, but also for personal, professional and home country development.

References

Altbach, P. G., Reisberg, L., & Rumbley, L. E. (2009). *Trends in global higher education: Tracking an academic revolution.* Report prepared for the UNESCO 2009 World Conference on Higher Education. Retrieved from http://unesdoc. unesco.org/images/0018/001831/183168e.pdf. Accessed on 6 July 2011.

Australian Vice Chancellor's Committee (AVCC). (2005). *Provision of education to international students: Code of practice and guidelines for Australian universities.* Canberra, Australian Vice-Chancellors' Committee (AVCC).

Bok, D. (2003). *Universities in the market place: The commercialization of higher education.* Princeton, NJ: Princeton University Press.

Brenders, D. A., Hope, P., & Ninnan, A. (1999). A systemic, student-centered study of university service. *Research in Higher Education, 40*(6), 665–685.

Briguglio, C. (2000). Language and cultural issues for English-as-a-second/foreign language students in transnational educational settings. *Higher Education in Europe, 25*(3), 425–434.

Dzulkifli, A. R. (2011). Re-envisioning future roles of universities. Paper presented at Global Higher Education Forum (GHEF), Penang, 14 December.

International Association of Universities (IAU). (2004). *Sharing quality higher education across borders: A statement on behalf of higher education institutions worldwide.* Retrieved from http://portal.unesco.org/education/fr/ev.php-URL_ID = 31950&URL_DO = DO_TOPIC&URL_SECTION = 201.html. Accessed on 24 May 2012.

Jani, R. (2010). International students' view of Malaysian higher education. Paper presented at Internationalisation and Marketing of Higher Education Malaysia Seminar, Ministry of Higher Education, Putrajaya,17 June.

Jani, R., Zubairi, Y. Z., Tat, H. H., & Ngah, A. H. (2010). International students' views of Malaysian higher education. Paper presented at Internationalisation and Marketing of Higher Education Malaysia Seminar, Ministry of Higher Education, Putrajaya, 17 June. Retrieved from http://jpt.mohe.gov.my/PENGUMUMAN/ mohe%20seminar%202010/SPEAKER%206%20-International%20Students% 20Views%20of%20Malaysian%20Higher%20Education.pdf Accessed on 19 September 2012.

Kell, P. M., & Vogl, G. (2012). *International students in the Asia Pacific: Mobility, risks and global optimism.* Netherlands, Dordrecht: Springer.

Knight, J. (2007). Internationalisation: Concepts, complexities and challenges. In J. J. F. Forest & P. G. Altbach (Eds.), *International handbook of higher education* (Vol. 18, pp. 207–227). Dordrecht: Springer.

McLachlan, D. A., & Justice, J. (2009). A grounded theory of international student well-being. *Journal of Theory Construction & Testing, 13*(1), 27–32.

Ministry of Higher Education Malaysia (MoHE). (2007). *Pelan Strategik Pengajian Tinggi Negara Fasa 1 2007–2010*. Putrajaya: MoHE.

Montgomery, C. (2010). *Understanding the international student experience*. Hampshire: Palgrave Macmillan.

Morshidi, S. (2008). The impact of September 11 on international student flow into Malaysia: Lessons learnt. *International Journal of Asia-Pacific Studies, 4*(1), 79–95.

National Economic Advisory Council (NEAC). (2010). *New economic model for Malaysia: Part 1*. NEAC: Putrajaya.

Salmi, J. (2009). *The challenge of establishing world-class universities*. Washington, DC: The World Bank.

Sidhu, R., Chong, H. K., & Yeoh, B. (2011). The global schoolhouse: Governing Singapore's knowledge economy aspirations. In S. Marginson, S. Kaur & E. Sawir (Eds.), *Higher education in the Asia-Pacific: Strategic responses to globalization* (pp. 255–271). Dordrecht: Springer.

Walker, M. (2010). A human development and capabilities 'prospective analysis' of global higher education policy. *Journal of Education Policy, 25*(4), 485–501.

Chapter 3.6

Assessing Student Exchange Programmes: Putting Students at the Centre of Internationalisation Efforts

David X. Cheng

Our students on campus today will live and work in a global economy and multicultural society after they graduate. Many of them will have to interact and work with colleagues and organisations abroad on a regular basis. However, when universities around the world are driving towards internationalisation, programmes under such an umbrella are not always designed with students' interests in mind. On the contrary, many institutions find that the temptations to pursue the glamour of staying on top of various league tables or profit through international student tuition are simply too strong to resist.

Altbach and Knight (2007) examined institutional initiatives in the name of internationalisation, such as branch campuses, cross-border collaborative arrangements, programmes for international students, English-medium programmes and degrees, etc., and found motivations for such activities ranging from commercial advantage, knowledge and language acquisition to curriculum enhancement with international content, plus many others. Focusing on internationalisation as related to student learning, Cheng (2011, p. 161) maintains that, 'although political, economic, and institutional considerations of internationalisation are well justified, these rationales can only be meaningful when students become the primary beneficiaries'.

Going Global: Identifying Trends and Drivers of International Education
Copyright © 2013 by Emerald Group Publishing Limited
All rights of reproduction in any form reserved
ISBN: 978-1-78190-575-3

It is worth noting that colleges and universities are no strangers to the idea of putting students at the centre of educational activities. In the United States, institutions have long embraced the idea of multiculturalism, believing that higher education institutions ought to prepare students for active participation in future society, which is becoming increasingly diverse. When discussing the concept of justice, Sandel (2009, p. 171) makes the argument for diversity in the name of the common good: 'a racially mixed student body is desirable because it enables students to learn more from one another than they would if all of them came from similar backgrounds'. Defending the affirmative action case for the University of Michigan, Gurin (1999, p. 36) maintains that 'diversity is a critically important factor in creating the richly varied educational experience that helps students learn and prepares them for participation in a democracy that is characterized by diversity'. Cheng (2011) believes that the same diversity argument also offers justification for adding an international dimension to the multicultural education agenda, where students should be at the centre of the institutional attention.

However, increasing international diversity on campus is a task easier said than done, especially for the countries and regions that are not traditionally viewed as study-abroad destinations. Altbach and Knight (2007, p. 291) rightfully point out that '[i]nternational academic mobility similarly favors well-developed education systems and institutions, thereby compounding existing inequalities'. In recent years, although Asian countries have experienced a significant increase in international student enrolment, the direction of student flow is still mainly from Asia and the developing world towards North America, Western Europe and Australia. 'But there is growing recognition that, to take their place in a global economy, countries must increase their engagement with the peoples and economies of other parts of the world' (Doyle et al., 2010).

It is in this context that the Hong Kong government began to actively promote internationalisation in higher education less than a decade ago. For historical reasons most universities in Hong Kong are relatively young, so it will take time before they can attract highly talented degree-seeking students from overseas. As a result, building student exchange programmes has become the only viable option, at least for now, for Hong Kong universities to diversify their student body in order to enhance students' international exposure. Through the exchange programme, not only can a student travel to and study in an institution outside their own region, but the university can also receive the equivalent number of international students to their campus. For those who are not able to study abroad for various reasons, this means internationalisation without crossing borders. Such a win-win situation is created without serious financial implications, because exchange partners, through their arrangements of tuition fees, reduce study-abroad costs for each other's students.

Literature Review

There exists a broad literature on college students' study-abroad experience (e.g. Brustein, 2007; Rotter, 1982), and researchers have compiled convincing evidence to demonstrate the benefits of international exposure (e.g. Maiworm, Steube & Teichler, 1991; NAFSA, 2003).

Researchers have used the social learning theory as a tool to evaluate both individuals studying abroad and study-abroad programmes (McLeod & Wainwright, 2009). Specifically, they seek to match what students expect with what they actually experience from their study-abroad programmes, with the hope that matching expectations with reality would lead to a more positive experience. Nahal's (2012) list of student expectations includes travel, interacting with international students, taking courses on different countries and cultures and participating in co-curricular programmes focusing on unique cultures and countries. Others found that students are quite conscious of exchange programmes being 'an effective way to develop international competences' (Nelson, 2003, p. 25). For instance, exchange programmes offer opportunities to learn critical academic and professional skills, including self-awareness, self-knowledge, more patience, greater openness, interpersonal skills and communication skills (Clyne & Rizvi, 1998; Doyle et al., 2010).

Studies on students' overseas experience report issues and obstacles related to exchange programmes (e.g. Messer & Wolter, 2007). While financial problems often top the list, researchers also found that language barriers, feelings of personal or cultural isolation and worries about academic performance had a negative impact on their overseas experience (Doyle et al., 2010). At the programme level, some complained about lack of 'strategic planning or process development at an institutional level that would facilitate or motivate [student] participation' (Doyle et al., 2010, p. 484), and others found that, sometimes, universities focus so much on sending students abroad that they overlook tapping into the international students on their campus who, in turn, can provide a different kind of global experience to domestic students (Nahal, 2012).

Survey Design and Research Method

The institution studied is a public, highly selective research university in Hong Kong. Committed to putting students at the centre of internationalisation efforts, the university's exchange programme is designed to prepare graduates who will have the knowledge, skills and cultural awareness to succeed in the global workplace. However, despite the popularity of the programme, there is so far little evidence that the exchange programme is achieving its desired outcomes. Therefore, this study was designed to gather empirical evidence on the effectiveness of and issues related to its student exchange programme. A parallel design of both inbound and outbound exchange student surveys was implemented, aimed at comparing inbound students' academic and social experiences in Hong Kong and that of outbound Hong Kong students in their host universities overseas and in mainland China.

The data was collected through two web-based surveys of inbound and outbound exchange students enrolled in spring 2012. Among the inbound population of 309 students, 147 of them responded to the survey, and of the 414 outbound students, 199 responded, yielding a response rate of 48 per cent for both surveys.

The major items in the two surveys are identical so that comparisons can be made regarding student experience in the host institutions and the home institution. Specifically, the author of the study sought to answer the following questions:

1. What did students expect from their exchange experience? To what extent did the exchange programme meet their expectations?
2. What capacities have students developed as a result of their exchange experience?
3. What are students' academic and social experiences at the host institutions?
4. What are the obstacles faced by exchange students?

A 10-point scale was applied to the items in the surveys, making it easier to conduct analysis based on means and standard deviations. *T*-tests were performed on each item to compare the experience of inbound and outbound students. Tests of significance were used only to help us better understand the difference between the two groups, not for the sake of statistical inference, since the populations, not the samples, were used in the surveys.

Results

Five items top both inbound and outbound students' list of expectations: becoming independent; travelling and seeing the world; having a better understanding of different cultures; making friends from different back-grounds; and understanding more about the host countries. Looking back, both inbound and outbound students seem to have gained what they set out to achieve. For Hong Kong students, being independent is a much stronger reason for exchange, while inbound students give a higher priority to gaining better understanding of different cultures (see Table 1).

Table 1: Student expectations and reported gains from exchange experience.

	Expectations[a]			Gains[b]		
	Inbound mean(SD)	outbound mean(SD)	Sig.	Inbound mean(SD)	outbound mean(SD)	Sig.
Have a better understanding of different cultures	8.86(1.34)	8.53(1.25)	*	8.73(1.30)	8.74(1.22)	
Become more independent	8.19(2.14)	8.76(1.41)	**	8.58(1.66)	8.95(1.36)	*
Sharpen my foreign language skills	7.62(2.27)	8.31(1.40)	**	7.36(2.28)	8.16(1.55)	**
Look for intellectual stimulation	7.57(2.14)	7.90(1.44)		7.41(2.07)	7.97(1.57)	**
Make friends from different cultural backgrounds	8.71(1.63)	8.47(1.47)		8.76(1.34)	8.35(1.77)	*
Attend a prestigious university	6.85(2.51)	7.54(1.90)	**	6.26(2.63)	7.62(1.94)	**
Enhance career competitiveness	7.69(2.17)	7.57(1.71)		7.61(2.01)	7.60(1.83)	
Travel and explore the world	8.73(1.52)	8.75(1.39)		8.89(1.25)	8.91(1.38)	
Plan for further studying abroad	7.04(2.85)	6.96(2.19)		8.14(2.03)	7.55(2.07)	**
Prepare for overseas job opportunities	7.06(2.59)	6.63(2.22)		7.72(2.10)	7.70(2.02)	
Understand more about the host country	8.05(2.06)	8.43(1.61)		8.43(1.79)	8.81(1.29)	*

* $p<.05$; ** $p<.01$.
[a] Scale: 1 = strongly disagree and 10 = strongly agree.
[b] Scale: 1 = not at all; 10 = to a great extent.

In terms of student development, both inbound and outbound students experienced improvement in the areas of cultural awareness, interpersonal skills and communication skills. Compared with the inbound, Hong Kong students were more positive about their experience in developing skills in problem-solving and critical thinking, and being proactive and innovative, and they reported gains in knowledge in their fields of study and in motivation to learn (see Table 2).

Inbound students reported a higher level of satisfaction with university academic resources than those outbound. While both groups reported a positive experience in communicating with instructors and participating in academic activities in host institutions, Hong Kong students found the learning environment in host institutions more stressful (see Table 3).

Regarding social experience, Hong Kong students reported a higher level of integration into the local community. Both groups felt that they had adapted to host institution well and had a sense of community with others around them, and they also perceived being stereotyped by others because of their cultural backgrounds (see Table 4).

Asked to identify issues related to exchange programmes, Hong Kong students reported significantly higher levels of academic and financial problems (see Table 5).

Table 2: Extent to which exchange helped develop capacities.

	Inbound		Outbound		
	Mean	SD	Mean	SD	Sig.
Intellectual curiosity	7.73	1.99	8.09	1.49	
Critical thinking	7.22	2.38	8.03	1.50	**
Logical reasoning	7.12	2.15	7.83	1.48	**
Knowledge in field of study	6.83	2.49	7.65	1.73	**
Learning motivation	6.60	2.53	7.84	1.71	**
Capacity to innovate	6.87	2.38	7.80	1.64	**
Self-confidence	8.02	1.90	8.44	1.34	*
Communication skills	8.20	1.66	8.51	1.34	
Ethical awareness	7.80	2.19	8.22	1.54	
Cultural awareness	8.62	1.41	8.78	1.31	
Interpersonal skills	8.13	1.75	8.57	1.33	*
Being proactive	7.59	2.13	8.28	1.29	**
Problem-solving skills	7.46	2.23	8.64	1.25	**

Scale: 1 = not helpful; 10 = very helpful. $*p < .05$; $**p < .01$.

Table 3: Students' academic experience.

	Inbound		Outbound		
	Mean	SD	Mean	SD	Sig.
Host institution offered a wide range of courses for exchange students	7.53	2.19	7.39	2.18	
I was able to take the courses as planned	7.46	2.51	7.35	2.21	
I was satisfied with host institution's academic resources	8.43	1.67	7.81	1.82	**
I was satisfied with host institution's academic support services (e.g. tutoring)	7.53	2.33	7.58	1.87	
My fellow students were helpful to me in academic work	7.20	2.45	7.63	1.96	
I felt comfortable participating in class activities	8.05	2.11	7.87	1.75	
I felt comfortable communicating with my instructors	8.19	1.87	8.25	1.47	
The teaching was stimulating	6.91	2.61	7.77	1.81	**
I found learning environment at host institution stressful	4.76	2.94	5.63	2.69	**

Scale: 1 = strongly disagree; and 10 = strongly agree. $*p < .05$; $**p < .01$.

Table 4: Students' social experience.

	Inbound		Outbound		
	Mean	SD	Mean	SD	Sig.
I could use English to communicate freely with local students	6.95	2.41	7.53	2.11	*
Most of my friends were students from my own culture	6.19	2.87	5.56	2.59	*
I felt uncomfortable about people stereotyping me or my culture	5.06	3.06	5.10	2.42	
I felt integrated into local culture	5.86	2.51	7.06	1.77	**
I had a sense of community with others around me	7.18	2.23	7.44	1.63	
I made good friends with local students	6.65	2.60	7.47	1.99	**
I felt lonely	3.83	2.83	3.94	2.33	
I was able to adapt myself well to the host institution	8.02	1.91	7.86	1.63	

Scale: 1 = strongly disagree; and 10 = strongly agree. $*p < .05$; $**p < .01$.

Table 5: Issues encountered during the exchange period.

	Inbound		Outbound		
	Mean	SD	Mean	SD	Sig.
Academic issues	5.06	3.08	6.04	2.67	**
Financial issues	3.97	2.80	5.89	2.63	**
Culture shock	4.52	2.66	5.05	2.57	
Communication problems	5.42	2.65	5.08	2.61	
Accommodation problems	3.52	2.69	4.84	2.86	**
Homesickness	3.46	2.73	4.16	2.65	*
Diet problems	4.66	3.26	4.31	2.68	
Health issues	3.65	2.76	3.83	2.58	
Safety issues	2.30	2.26	4.21	2.73	**

Scale: 1 = not an issue; 10 = major issue. $*p<.05$; $**p<.01$.

Conclusions and Implications

Acknowledging the substantial benefits of internationalisation of higher education, colleges and universities in different parts of the world are nonetheless faced with very different challenges when it comes to internationalisation. What is unique about Hong Kong is that, though it is a well-recognised international finance and business centre and its university faculties are mostly recruited internationally, the college student population is anything but international. Therefore, building exchange programmes and making them work are not only desirable but also necessary.

Institutions running exchange programmes have strived to enhance their students' experience overseas. But for the institution studied here, improving inbound students' experience is as important, since the majority of its local students' continued international exposure depends on the steady incoming stream of exchange students. Therefore, the parallel design of inbound and outbound surveys offered insights into the exchange programme from both sides, leading to possible improvements not only in outgoing students' experience but also of campus environment at home institutions.

This study provided empirical evidence to support the argument for putting students at the centre of internationalisation efforts. Both inbound and outbound students consider learning about other cultures and making friends from different backgrounds the most important reasons for participating in the exchange programme. Their satisfactory rating of gains in these areas demonstrates the value and success of exchange programmes designed with students' interest in mind.

While confirming most of claimed benefits of studying abroad, this study also shows Hong Kong students' unique needs for, and perspectives on, exchange programmes. Compared with their inbound counterparts, they attach more importance to sharpening language skills, learning to be independent and even preparing to attend graduate schools overseas after graduation. In terms of competence building, Hong Kong students also reported a higher level of gains in problem-solving, critical thinking, as well as learning to be proactive and innovative. The latter may reflect a weakness in Hong Kong's college education, since similar anecdotal criticism has been heard in the past, but it has been dismissed for lack of evidence.

It is worth noting that inbound students reported significantly higher levels of satisfaction with university academic resources than Hong Kong students attending overseas institutions. Though still not considered a prime destination for studying abroad, Hong Kong is obviously ready to offer first-class college education to the international community, at least in terms of academic resources available to students.

In summary, it is our firm belief that students' college experience should top the priority list of any institution's internationalisation agenda. After all, students should be the major reason why an institution wants to embrace internationalisation. Meanwhile, any institutional initiatives to build international presence and reach out to overseas students should serve to support student learning and development.

Acknowledgement

The author wishes to acknowledge the invaluable contribution to this paper by Simon Lim, who helped to prepare the survey data for analysis.

References

Altbach, P. G., & Knight, J. (2007). The internationalization of higher education: Motivations and realities. *Journal of Studies in International Education, 11*(3/4), 290–305.

Brustein, W. K. (2007). The global campus: Challenges and opportunities for higher education in North America. *Journal of Studies in International Education, 11,* 382–391.

Cheng, D. X. (2011). International education in the context of multiculturalism. In S. Chen (Ed.), *Diversity management: Theoretical perspectives and practical approaches.* New York, NY: Nova Science Publishers.

Clyne, F., & Rizvi, F. (1998). Outcomes of student exchange. In D. Davis & A. Olsen (Eds.), *Outcomes of international education: Research finding* (pp. 35–49). Canberra: IDP Education Australia.

Doyle, S., et al. (2010). An investigation of factors associated with student participation in study abroad. *Journal of Studies in International Education, 14*(5), 471–490.

Gurin, P. (1999). Selections from the compelling need for diversity in higher education, expert reports in defense of the University of Michigan. *Equity and Excellence in Education, 32*(2), 36–62.

Maiworm, F., Steube, W., & Teichler, I. (1991). *Learning in Europe.* The ERASMUS experience, a survey of the 1988–1989 ERASMUS students, Higher Education Policy Series 14. London: Jessica Kingsley Publishers.

McLeod, M., & Wainwright, P. (2009). Researching the study abroad experience. *Journal of Studies in International Education, 13*, 66–71.

Messer, D., & Wolter, S. C. (2007). Are student exchange programs worth it? *High Education, 54*, 647–663.

NAFSA. (2003). *Securing America's future: Global education for a global age: Report on the strategic task force on education abroad.* Washington, DC: Author.

Nahal, A. (2012, May 10). Study abroad trends in the U.S. and at HBCUs. *Diverse* p. 43.

Nelson, B. (2003). *Engaging the world through education: Ministerial statement on the internationalisation of Australian education and training.* Canberra: Commonwealth of Australia.

Rotter, J. B. (1982). *The development and applications of social learning theory.* New York, NY: Praeger.

Sandel, M. J. (2009). *Justice: What's the right thing to do?* London: Penguin.

Chapter 3.7

Breaking Down the Borders? Widening Access to Higher Education and International Student Mobility

Graeme Atherton

Inequality in access to higher education is a global issue. It unites countries across all continents. There is considerable research that shows how, while definitions of who constitutes the most important under-represented groups in higher education may differ across nations, inequalities of access by socio-economic group appear a common phenomenon (even in countries which are otherwise seen to be more equal) (OECD, 2010). However, for policy makers and higher education institutions (HEIs) especially, these inequalities are perceived primarily as a domestic issue. There is an increasing wealth of evidence, however, that shows how such inequality applies to international activities as well (Brooks & Waters, 2011; HEFCE, 2009). Those who benefit from being able to study at tertiary level either for part of or for the whole of their studies appear to be far more likely to come from the more advantaged strata of societies.

This paper will explore the implications of internationalisation of HE for social inequalities globally both within and outside HE. The ability of some to participate in a 'global student experience' positions them increasingly favourably where accessing high-value employment is concerned. Internationalisation of HE is not merely reinforcing existing social inequality but contributing to its reconstruction by enabling existing elite groups to retain their dominant positions. Work to promote access to and the internationalisation of HE needs to be brought together to enable all groups of

Going Global: Identifying Trends and Drivers of International Education
Copyright © 2013 by Emerald Group Publishing Limited
All rights of reproduction in any form reserved
ISBN: 978-1-78190-575-3

students to experience HE in an international way. There are good examples of how this is happening and several are described in this paper. To integrate 'internationalisation' into the experience of all students will require more creative and radical work from those in HE, though in terms of both practice and advocacy.

Added Value for the Affluent

'To sum up, those who apply for university abroad [from England] are: academic high-performers, from the higher social-class backgrounds, disproportionately concentrated in private schools and have "mobility network" connections abroad' (King, Findlay, & Ahrens, 2010, p. 31).

The dominance of those from higher socio-economic groups in those who study abroad at tertiary level is by no means confined to England. Desoff (2006), looking at the United States, finds strong evidence of similar inequalities combined with huge differences by ethnic group. Research by Woodfield (2009) examining the situation in Germany, Waters (2008) in China and Puwar (2004) in India all point to studying abroad as being an experience almost solely available to students from higher socio-economic groups. Brooks and Waters (2011) in particular have drawn upon empirical work with students in both Europe and Asia to highlight how international study is dominated by students from more advantaged groups, and also serves as a means by which these groups seek to position themselves favourably in what are perceived as increasingly competitive global labour markets. There are other distinguishing features of the international student body that stem from their socio-economic position. These are, in particular, relatively high levels of prior qualification and especially for those from western countries studying abroad, attendance at more research-intensive universities with relatively high positions in global university ranking tables (King et al., 2010).

Brooks and Waters (2010) argue that the relationship students from higher socio-economic groups have with the international experience can be explained by drawing on the work of French sociologist Pierre Bourdieu on social and cultural capital. They argue that the decision to study abroad reflects the 'habitus' of those from higher social-class groups. 'Habitus' is a concept developed by Bourdieu and described by Archer, Hollingworth, and Halsall (2007) as:

an amalgamation of the past and the present that mediates current and future engagement with the world, shaping what is perceived as ab/normal, un/desirable and im/possible.

Hence the decision to study abroad draws upon the specific set of norms and values held by those from higher-class groups regarding the economic and social importance of learning about other cultures and in other countries. Study abroad allows them to enhance both their social and cultural capital in terms of improving their ability to relate to different cultures and the extent of their networks which can then be translated into financial capital in the labour market. The global student experience is more than just a matter of obtaining a qualification from another country or being able to add 'study abroad' to one's résumé. It is a combination of both academic and non-academic experience with both having key roles to play.

Globally Mobile Students: 'Riding the Second Wave'

The value of this global student experience is likely to increase as the nature of the world economy changes. Brown, Lauder, and Ashton (2008) argue that the early 21st century is seeing the beginning of 'second wave' globalisation. First wave globalisation was marked by transnational companies (TNCs) separating low-skilled and high-skilled work with the latter increasingly outsourced to developing nations. Second wave globalisation will see not only a broader spread internationally of high-skilled work but also increasing differentiation among the higher skilled. Brown et al. found a common perception among the TNCs they spoke to in their research: that they were involved in a 'war for talent', that is a fight for a global elite of skilled workers, who would increasingly both work in more than one country in their careers and on an almost daily basis with an international set of colleagues. The preparation for being part of this elite is a tertiary student experience with an international element.

It is also likely that even in the levels below this mobile global elite, high-skilled work will require a kind of social and cultural capital which has an international element built into it. Predictions of economic trends in the 21st century echo Brown and Lauder, pointing to greater global interconnectivity and increasing numbers of students completing tertiary education in forth-coming years (Oxford Economics, 2011). The picture is one of a more and more competitive labour market for those graduating from higher education, where the possession of international experience is increasingly important.

Widening Access and Student Mobility: What Governments and Universities Are Doing (or Not Doing)

The international knowledge base regarding how different countries across the world tackle access to higher education in national policy terms and institutionally is patchy. There have been some good attempts to map the extent to which specific policies and practices exist across nations, but they do not provide great detail as to exactly what priorities are and how they are addressed. The UK, the United States, Australia, until recently Canada and several African nations, for instance, have all made concerted attempts at a state level to reduce inequality in access to HE in the last decade (Lihamba, Mwaipopo, & Shule, 2006; National Audit Office, 2008; Hare, 2012). However, the focus has been heavily on entry to HE and less on what happens when students are actually in HE. The main exception is the United States and more recently England. The United States has the most explicit linkage between the access and internationalisation agendas at the national programme level. The TRIO programme began in the United States in 1964. It is a federally funded initiative that aims to support those from disadvantaged backgrounds to both enter HE and succeed while they are there. It serves over 800,000 students per year with an annual budget of just over US$900 million. TRIO focuses on providing additional activities and programmes to help learners improve their attainment, understand better the financial aid available to them and to cope with the challenges they face while actually studying at HE level. TRIO has its own study abroad programme that aims explicitly to give disadvantaged learners an international student experience. As it is available only for TRIO students, this ensures that the beneficiaries of the programme are from less advantaged backgrounds.

Individual universities offering scholarships for their students to study abroad are relatively common across countries. Moreover, there are good examples of universities constructing such scholarships with a view to embedding a widening access element into their international student experience work. The University of East London (UEL) in England has recently instigated its Going Global Bursary scheme. The university is providing approximately 200 bursaries to enable students to go abroad for a short period of time (usually less than one semester for a field-trip or work placement, for example). The bursaries are not targeted specifically at students from disadvantaged backgrounds, and provide only part funding. UEL is, however, one of the most socially diverse universities in England with over 40 per cent of its learners coming from lower socio-economic groups. The university is using the funds it does have to support study abroad opportunities, spreading the benefits to as many students as possible. There are also examples of universities aiming to be one of the global elite, who also display significant commitment to enabling their students to study abroad. The University of Melbourne is very research intensive, and has one of the smallest percentages of students from lower socio-economic backgrounds in Australia (James, 2007). Melbourne does offer though over

10 different forms of scholarship and support, including over 1,000 Melbourne Global Grants and a Melbourne Global Financial Assistance Scheme. While only a small number of students from lower socio-economic groups enter Melbourne, for those who do there are opportunities to study abroad.

There are efforts being made by individual universities to allow as many of their students as possible, from a wide range of backgrounds, to have an international higher education experience. However, they are still touching only a minority of learners. To really address the new inequalities that increasing internationalisation is bringing requires a strategic and innovative approach.

Access Beyond Borders and the 'Global Classroom'

The starting point is greater integration at a policy level. National policies to address widening access should as a matter of course include objectives related to extending opportunities for international mobility for under-represented groups and vice versa; policies to extend international mobility in particular should have explicit targets within them regarding participation by those from under-represented groups. Many countries have adopted high-profile attempts to enable more of their students to study abroad in recent years. The US$2 billion Science without Borders programme in Brazil is an excellent example (Gardner, 2011). It aims to give 75,000 Brazilian students studying science, technology, engineering or mathematics (STEM) the opportunity to study in different countries. It should aim for a set percentage of these to come from disadvantaged backgrounds. Brazil is not alone here: the United States and the European Union have also initiated new approaches in recent years to increasing mobility without setting such targets explicitly. The priority in virtually all cases appears to be to increase the level of student mobility per se, with references to the social background of the students as a second-order consideration to be tackled when overall numbers are increased. This is the wrong approach. Unless diversity is built in at the outset it is far harder to include it later down the line.

Technological innovation could provide some answers. The increasing prevalence of online learning means the 'global classroom' at tertiary level could be the reality for more and more learners into the 21st century (Gourley, 2012). Recent years have seen some high-profile attempts at global higher education level courses, most notably from Harvard University and the Massachusetts Institute of Technology with their US$60 million edX platform (Coughlan, 2012). An internationalisation of the student experience may become much more prevalent if online learning becomes the solution to increasingly expensive HE provision. It is not, however, likely to confer on students the same broader benefits enabling entry to the highest skilled occupations. The risk is that universities and governments are able to point to a democratisation internationalisation by showing how their students are engaging in cross-country dialogue in increasing numbers, but in reality inequalities in the nature of international education experience are becoming entrenched.

The global classroom could be more effective at reducing inequalities in access to international education; however, if it can be introduced at the pre-HE stage as a part of the activities that universities, schools, colleges and community organisations deliver to support more learners from more disadvantaged backgrounds to apply to HE. It is not just economic constraints, but differentials in cultural and social capital that make those from disadvantaged backgrounds less likely to seek and demand international study opportunities (Findlay & King, 2010; HEFCE, 2009). It is this differential that needs to be addressed. The opportunities presented by online communication tools and learning materials may be a means of doing this. If learners have contact with learners from outside their own country then this may embed in their understanding of what HE is the international dimension that many of their peers already hold.

For internationalisation to be integrated into access work however, the development of much stronger relationships and partnerships between access practitioners in different countries will be essential. However, linkages between those involved in access in different countries are much weaker than between those working in international education. Access practitioners in individual universities need international education colleagues to use their networks to link them with their access counterparts in other countries. But even this will not be sufficient. Access practitioners need to develop a global community of their own if they are to build internationalisation into their pre-HE work. Better university-to-university connections between access practitioners across countries constitute the threads, but they will need to be woven together in a more coherent pattern to achieve the kind of shift in thinking and action described here.

Finally, changing what potential students demand from HE as a strategy to change what universities do is likely to have increased impact as students bear increasing amounts of the cost of their studies into the 21st century. As research from Marcucci and Usher (2012) shows, greater dependence on investment from students is a global trend. Access practitioners should look in the light of this not just to build better alliances between international colleagues and in their own community but with organised student movements nationally and internationally.

Conclusions

This paper has argued that international education is the new frontier for access to HE work. The growth in international mobility as a key part of the 'student experience' for some of those in HE threatens to echo a familiar trend in how relationships of inequality between social groups renew themselves. As more students from a greater range of backgrounds enter tertiary education across the world, those from existing powerful groups find ways of differentiating themselves from these new entrants via international HE experiences. The equality those working on access to higher education strive for therefore proves elusive as the rules of the game continually change. This challenge can only be addressed by HE international education and widening access becoming integrated both strategically and operationally. If borderless higher education for all is to become a reality in the 21st century, then the boundaries within HE itself have to come down.

References

Archer, L., Hollingworth, S., & Halsall, A. (2007). 'University's not for me — I'm a Nike person': Urban, working-class young people's negotiations of 'Style', identity and educational engagement. *Sociology, 4,* 219–237.

Brooks, R., & Waters, J. (2010). Social networks and educational mobility: The experiences of UK students. *Globalisation, Societies and Education, 8,* 143–157.

Brooks, R., & Waters, J. (2011). *Student mobilities, migration and the internationalization of higher education.* London: Palgrave Macmillan.

Brown, P., Lauder, H., & Ashton, D. (2008). *Education, globalization and the knowledge economy: A commentary by the Teaching and Learning Research Programme.* Retrieved from http://www.tlrp.org/pub/documents/globalisation comm.pdf. Accessed on 28 June 2012.

Coughlan, S. (2012). Top US universities put their reputations online. *BBC News,* 20 June. Retrieved from http://www.bbc.co.uk/news/business-18191589. Accessed on 6 July 2012.

Desoff, A. (2006). Who's not going abroad? *International Educator, 15,* 20–27.

Findlay, A. & King, R. (2010). *Motivations and experiences of UK students studying abroad.* BIS Research Paper No. 8. Book Department for Business, Innovation and Skills, London.

Gardner, E. (2011). Brazil promises 75,000 scholarships in science and technology. *Nature,* 4 August. Retrieved from http://www.nature.com/news/2011/110804/full/news.2011.458.html. Accessed on 5 July 2012.

Gourley, B. (2012). No room for complacency in emerging market HE. *University World News,* February. Retrieved from http://www.universityworldnews.com/article.php?story=20120210094821617. Accessed on 5 July 2012.

Hare, J. (2012). Flagship education partnership schemes take $18m knock. *The Australian*, 9 May. Retrieved from http://www.theaustralian.com.au/higher-education/flagship-education-partnership-schemes-take-18m-knock/story-e6frgcjx-1226350387328. Accessed on 5 July 2012.

HEFCE. (2009) *Attainment in higher education: Erasmus and placement students.* Bristol: HEFCE.

James, R. (2007). *Social equity in a mass, globalised higher education environment: The unresolved issue of widening access to university.* Faculty of Education Dean's Lecture Series 2007. Melbourne: Centre for the Study of Higher Education.

King, R., Findlay, A., & Ahrens, J. (2010). *International student mobility literature review: Report to HEFCE, and co-funded by the British council, UK national agency for Erasmus.* Bristol: HEFCE.

Lihamba, A., Mwaipopo, R., & Shule, L. (2006). The challenges of affirmative action in Tanzanian higher education institutions: A case study of the University of Dar es Salaam, Tanzania. *Women's Studies International Forum, 29*, 581–591.

Marcucci, P., & Usher, A. (2012). *2011 Year in review: Global changes in tuition fee policies and student financial assistance.* Toronto: Higher Education Strategy Associates.

National Audit Office. (2008). *Widening participation in higher education.* London: National Audit Office.

OECD. (2010). *Economic policy reforms: Going for growth 2010.* Paris: OECD.

Oxford Economics. (2011). *The Hays: Oxford economics global report: Creating jobs in global economy 2011–2030.* Oxford: Oxford Economics.

Puwar, N. (2004). *Space invaders: Race, gender and bodies out of place.* Oxford: Berg.

Waters, J. (2008). *Education, migration and cultural capital in the Chinese Diaspora: Transnational students between Hong Kong and Canada.* New York, NY: Cambria Press.

Woodfield, S. (2009). *Trends in international student mobility: A comparison of national and institutional policy responses in Denmark, Germany, Sweden and the Netherlands.* Retrieved from http://www.iu.dk/filer/markedsfoering/Trend%20rapport.pdf. Accessed on 5 July 2012.

Chapter 3.8

Internationalisation of African Higher Education: Case Studies of Student-Led Initiatives from the University of Zambia

Jayasree Anitha Menon

Internationalisation at universities refers to awareness and interactions within and between cultures across the globe, through teaching, research and service functions (Yang, 2002). The ultimate aim of internationalisation would be to achieve mutual understanding across cultural borders and to provide an educational experience that truly integrates a global perspective. While internationalisation is being recommended and practised at many universities globally, there is a need for empirical knowledge on the issue of internationalisation, so as to explore its possible impact on higher education.

When we consider the present — and future — universities in Africa, they should be able to afford opportunities for students to prepare for the challenges that they will face as graduates in the working force in a global environment. Universities, therefore, need to be innovative in their strategies and learning styles to prepare the new generation to be successful in the competitive world. This paper examines internationalisation occurring from international partnerships at the University of Zambia in which students played a lead role. This type of internationalisation has the potential to improve curriculum and learning experience, to enhance the learning environment and facilitate career development. The challenges and successes of two case studies from the Department of Psychology at the University of Zambia are presented here. Both the case studies are based on international

Going Global: Identifying Trends and Drivers of International Education
Copyright © 2013 by Emerald Group Publishing Limited
All rights of reproduction in any form reserved
ISBN: 978-1-78190-575-3

partnerships of a multi-disciplinary nature in which the students played a leading role in implementing the partnerships. The case studies will introduce the project, discuss the process highlighting students as change agents and then bring out the benefits, challenges and sustainability of the initiative. The paper will conclude by discussing the national and international impacts of such initiatives and their value in contributing to internationalisation of universities.

Case Study 1: Student-Led Curriculum Change[1]

A challenge that many universities face is resolving the contradictory image of internationalisation of higher education: is it to prepare graduates to participate effectively in a global society (Leask, 2001) or to recruit more international students into the university (Yang, 2002)? This paper argues that, in developing countries, the internationalisation of higher education is more to do with preparing graduates to function and contribute effectively in a globalised society. This, therefore, entails the need for the university to provide them with the experience and skills to become international citizens.

The University of Zambia, through a collaborative venture between the Schools of Humanities and Social Sciences, Medicine and Education, partnering with NORAD Masters Programme (NOMA) introduced a Master of Science degree in clinical neuropsychology. The programme commenced in October 2008 and the first cohort of graduates completed in 2010. Clinical neuropsychology is a new field in Zambia that bridges the knowledge between physical and psychological parameters.

The curriculum was developed with the input of national and international experts and had the objective of enhancing the scientific skills of clinicians and to provide non-clinical graduates with insight into clinical problems by working alongside clinicians. At the end of offering the newly developed curriculum to the first cohort of students, an evaluation exercise was carried out. The curriculum in its initial format was designed for an international community; the experiences of the first cohort of students expressed some concern with items in the curriculum that were not applicable to the current local scenario. A number of issues were raised to make the learning process more useful through the direction of the students on the programme.

---

1. Lisa Kalungwana contributed to this section. She was a student in the first cohort of the programme being presented here and is now a faculty member in the Psychology Department, University of Zambia.

In order to counter these problems and still be able to operate in the global community, students initiated and engaged in focus group discussion to identify how the curriculum could be overhauled to be more relevant to the local scenario, as well as maintain its international perspective. For example a need to have local norms for international test battery used in the programme was identified and the students, through collaborative effort of the Masters theses, collected data that was used to develop local norms. Students were also involved in revising some of the contents of the course work. The students also identified books that were useful to them; and from this discussion the required readings were changed and new ones that would be more useful on the programme were incorporated.

The above exercise initiated by the students also had input from national and international experts. The students, therefore, interacted with the experts in the field and thereby built on their skills, not only in their subject area, but also for personal development. Through the student-led curriculum review, a learning framework was established that has yielded a more diverse learning programme. It also increases ownership of the programme by the nation, with an understanding that the programme has a local element and, while it does not ignore issues that are happening in the country of implementation, it still maintains an international element. Being involved in such extracurricular activities to bring about some change leads students to be change agents and effect changes to their learning experience (Dunne, 2012).

One of the major advantages resulting from this is the creation of a benchmark which other African or non-Western countries may use in making a fast-growing field like clinical neuropsychology useful to the local community. It also makes the field of neuropsychology less country or culturally centred, but instead helps integrate cross-cultural issues in the field of clinical neuropsychology. It also opens up more areas of research and increases the diversity of the field by giving an international theme to the programme of study.

Another notable advantage of this process has been the identification of research and areas of clinical placements. Because the students actively participated in the review process, they were able to explore more research areas and produce information that was useful locally, regionally and internationally. The integration of the information in the international curriculum fused with local ideas from the students produced a document that can not only be used locally but also prepare students well to explore their careers internationally as early scholars, researchers and clinicians. This is also likely to improve the employability of students, in fact eight out of the nine graduates from the first cohort are working in the field of neuropsychology in Zambia and many of them have continued to be involved in research in collaboration with national and international researchers.

One of the major challenges of such initiatives is the sustainability of the programme. The field of clinical neuropsychology is constantly growing and changes emerge each year. Incorporating new ideas each year may be a challenge and a costly method. The idea of using a student-led curriculum review is said to increase student ownership of the project, but it is important to be aware that students are not the experts and the method may dilute the content of the curriculum in order to suit their views and opinions. Implementers of the curriculum must, therefore, be fully aware of new trends in the field in order to maintain the strength of the course both locally and internationally.

Another challenge in this process is maintaining a local and international element in the curriculum. According to Serpell (2007), African universities have inherited from the West a number of institutionalised arrangements for learning that are imperfectly designed for students in Africa so as to empower them to transform the world and pioneer social progress. In certain instances international methods are given priority because they have been used over a period of time, while the local integration takes on more of an experimental direction. The failure of some local integration may lead to a lack of trust in the sustainability of the local ideas. However, the opposite is also true. In some instances the internationally validated methods may not be useful for the local community and this creates a challenge of coming up with local ideas, which may take years to be validated, creating a research and practice gap in the programme of study.

Case Study 2: Service-Learning Project[2]

Service learning is an approach to teaching and learning that combines community service with formal classroom teaching. An important focus of this approach is on critical, reflective thinking as well as personal and social responsibility.

The National Youth Leadership Council (2008) released the K-12 Service-Learning Standards for Quality Practice that used research in the field to determine eight standards of quality service-learning practice: meaningful service, link to curriculum, reflection, diversity, investigation,

---

2. Owen Kabanda contributed to this section. He is a founding member of UNZA service learning club and now a registered PhD student of the Psychology Department, University of Zambia.

partnerships, progress monitoring, project design, action, demonstration and recognition. These are skills which are equally essential to success in any organisation but they cannot be learnt in a classroom. Therefore, being a part of service learning gives students the opportunity to learn, reflect and practise these skills; and being on a programme initiated by them, it can be presumed that they would be motivated to make maximum use of the situation. This paper argues that being involved in a student-led service-learning programme would contribute to internationalisation of higher education through providing relevant learning experience and personal development.

The service-learning programme began at the University of Zambia (UNZA) in 2005, and was co-ordinated by the Psychology Department. This project involved 30 UNZA undergraduate students of psychology and 15 San Jose State University (SJSU) graduate students of counsellor education. It was aimed at building a partnership between the two universities and enhancing cross-cultural awareness between the Zambian and American students (UNZASLC, 2006).

At the end of the first service-learning project, UNZA students expressed the need for such a learning experience to continue, and established the University of Zambia Service Learning Club (UNZASLC). This is a club registered with the University of Zambia Dean of Students and it spearheads the implementation of the community service learning projects that are carried out in the communities under the University of Zambia Community Service Learning Programme. The club has a membership of registered UNZA students from various Schools at the UNZA and it is committed to helping students apply their university-acquired knowledge in mitigating community problems. Since then, UNZASLC, in partnership with the Psychology Department, has taken a lead role in initiating and implementing service learning at UNZA.

In 2006, 22 UNZA students and 11 SJSU students undertook the second community service-learning project in community schools in the Kalinga-linga, Chainda and Ng'ombe compounds that have care and support programmes for orphans and vulnerable children. In 2007 the service-learning project involved 48 participants (24 UNZA students and 24 SJSU students).

Since its inception, the programme has helped the students make meaningful contributions to the communities through application of their knowledge gained at university to mitigate the problems they identify in the communities. In all these three editions of the service learning programme, there was an undercurrent of the importance of service learning increasing the students' appreciation of people working together to achieve a common purpose regardless of their cultural background. As postulated in the double loop learning theory proposed by Argyris (1976), service learning can be said to help in changing underlying values and assumptions. Argyris and Schon (1974) argue that changes in values, behaviour, leadership and helping others, are all part of, and informed by, the actors' theory of action. This in a way leads to increased effectiveness in decision-making and better acceptance of failures and mistakes.

The following were the benefits identified by the students who were involved in the programme (Report on 2006 service learning project):

increased knowledge in one's programme of study;
exposure to real and practical issues outside class in the real world;
applying the theoretical knowledge gained at the university to solving real-life issues in the communities;
an increased level of understanding one's career as theory is coupled with practice in addition to academic content, students learn a range of valuable practical skills including: problem solving, organising, collaborating, project management, research, dealing with obstacles and setbacks;
development of character virtues and interpersonal habits such as respect, responsibility, empathy, co-operation, citizenship, initiative, and persistence.

These benefits highlight the impact of such programmes on the learning experience and personal development of students. All of these improve self-efficacy, defined by Bandura (1994) as, ' ... people's beliefs about their capabilities to produce designated levels of performance that exercise influence over events that affect their lives. Self-efficacy beliefs determine how people feel, think, motivate themselves and behave.' Therefore, positive self-efficacy will motivate students to engage and participate more effectively in a global setting.

Implementation of these projects, however, has resulted in a number of challenges that deserve special attention. The majority of the project participants are final-year students. Upon graduation, therefore, what they started may not be accorded the required consistent follow-ups. The funding of the projects has been mainly through finance raised by way of writing project proposals to institutions outside the university. It is, however, envisaged that with appropriate management strategies, service learning is likely to continue being a driving force of internationalisation at UNZA.

Impact at National and International Levels

The student-led initiatives discussed above do have an impact at both national and international levels. The results of the change in the curriculum initiated by students would lead to a more multi-disciplinary approach to the field of clinical neuropsychology. Local ideas have been incorporated into an international field of study that has produced graduates who are of local relevance and have an international understanding of the field in which they are operating. It has also brought a curriculum that has national ownership and is able to be recognised as developed nationally with the understanding of the national issues. The new framework initiated will afford other counties to reframe their curriculum through input from the students taking that course. It shows that including students is a useful method of undertaking the curriculum, as the personal experiences of students provide a deeper understanding to the area of study. Additionally, the student-led review process has helped in opening up other research areas that are understood locally with the application of international methods and tools. This helps bridge the research gap and incorporates a cross-cultural element to the young field of clinical neuropsychology.

Zambia, like most countries, is not an island and there are a lot of foreign mining and construction firms operating in the country and these in many instances bring expatriate workers who have to work with local employees. Because of this, it would be best for graduates to be prepared for such interaction with people from other cultures, and therefore being involved in service learning activities would be to the advantage of the students. Some graduates find themselves working in the service industry, like hotels and airlines, and undoubtedly this industry demands that one not only is a team worker but also can work collaboratively with others from different cultures as well as being able to understand and serve international and local clients without discrimination based on culture. It is therefore imperative to appreciate that internationalisation in higher education helps in integrating an international and intercultural dimension to learning and teaching. The need for preparing graduates to work in an increasingly international society, combined with the demand from employers for employees who can manage international markets, cannot be overemphasised.

Conclusion

Evaluation of the case studies presented in this paper found that students learnt a range of valuable practical skills such as problem solving, organising, collaborating, project management, research; and these skills will be an asset to them in understanding cultural differences and in dealing with a global environment. Such initiatives, therefore, have great impact at both national and international levels in creating student leaders who are able to meet with the challenges of a global village. But it is important to be aware that the sustainability of these initiatives is largely dependent on the commitment of top management at the University, improved infrastructure and commitment of staff and students.

A metaphor which seems particularly appropriate for universities engaging students as change agents is the metaphor of flux and transformation. This metaphor embraces the concept that everything is systemically interdependent. The environment is a part of every learning situation in the same way, and the university seeking to innovate through student-led initiatives leading to internationalisation minimises the boundaries between and among disciplines; between administration and staff; between staff and students; and between their learning environment and community. In such situations the challenge would be to manage the change and be willing to give room for innovations to take forward the internationalisation of higher education.

References

Argyris, C. (1976). *Increasing leadership effectiveness* (pp. 16–18). New York, NY: Wiley.

Argyris, C., & Schon, D. (1974). *Theory in practice*. San Francisco, CA: Jossey-Bass.

Bandura, A. (1994). Self-efficacy. *Encyclopaedia of human behaviour, 4*, 71–81.

Dunne, E. (2012). *Students engaging as change agents*. Retrieved from http://www.reading.ac.uk/web/FILES/cdotl/Presentation_READING2012.pdf. Accessed on 3 January 2013.

K-12 service-learning standards for quality practice. (2008). Retrieved from http://www.nylc.org/k-12-service-learning-standards-quality-practice. Accessed on 3 January 2013.

Leask, B. (2001). Bridging the gap: Internationalising university curricula. *Journal of Studies in International Education, 5*(2), 100–115.

Serpell, R. (2007). Bridging between orthodox western higher educational practices and an African sociocultural context. *Comparative Education, 43*(1), 23–51.

UNZA Service-Learning Club. (2006). *University of Zambia – San Jose State University Service Learning Project*. Lusaka: University of Zambia, Psychology Department, unpublished, limited circulation document.

Yang, R. (2002). University internationalisation: Its meanings, rationales and implications. *Intercultural Education, 13*(1), 81–95.

SECTION 4
TRENDS AND
INTERNATIONALISATION

Chapter 4.1

Editors' Introduction to Section 4

Internationalisation is now a very familiar phenomenon. It has matured and evolved since the early days of Going Global in 2004. We can now trace trends and patterns.

In this section the authors explore some very different trends and characteristics of internationalisation, and enable the reader to understand its impact and predict the future directions we might see.

Hans de Wit challenges the reader to rethink the concept of internationalisation because, he points out, we often attribute far too much significance to the concept. It is, he reminds us, a term which means all too often little more than 'international education'. It does not sufficiently represent the full range of phenomena which belong to the changes — nor has it moved sufficiently far away from a Western, neo-colonial concept. And the whole discourse is dominated by a very small group of stakeholders, with too little attention being paid to the programmes concerned, and too little to the outputs of internationalisation. De Wit charges us to pay more attention to the values and ethics of the practice, and the relationship between the global and the local.

This challenge to rethink what internationalisation means is echoed in Eva Egron-Polak's paper, where she leads us away from our obsession with the definition of internationalisation to the purposes, actions and impacts of the process. Rethinking internationalisation enables us to focus on the goals and purposes of the process, and to move away from the endless debates about definitions to a much more constructive focus on the benefits and impacts.

Going Global: Identifying Trends and Drivers of International Education
Copyright © 2013 by Emerald Group Publishing Limited
All rights of reproduction in any form reserved
ISBN: 978-1-78190-575-3

On a different level, Michael Carrier looks at the role of English in international higher education, and explores how far it is a facilitator, and how far a barrier in the global academy.

Wendy Purcell's paper examines the post-disruption marketplace for education by comparing it with case studies from other sectors such as telecommunications and fashion in particular. She leads the reader to an understanding that higher education needs to learn from the other sectors; that clarity of purpose, innovation and partnership, as well as boldness and responsiveness alongside commitment to their original heritage and values are vital to sustained success.

Abe Harraf's paper goes more deeply into the new economic situation, and points to the importance of higher education institutions taking the opportunity in the current economic context to become agile, proactive and responsive as well as globally active. In this way, they will ensure their survival.

Ingo Rollwagen highlights the importance of developing the approaches to knowledge production in order to play a strong and more prominent role in the world knowledge economy. Being more self-assured and assertive about this will enable academics to go global, and to 'shape the emerging knowledge world order in a more fair and equitable way'.

The paper written by Chiao-Ling Chien then gets under the surface of the British Council's analysis of higher education trends and opportunities in *The shape of things to come* (British Council, 2012). By unpicking the data presented, Chien shows us how the pictures of student behaviour illustrated are more complex — and therefore much richer — than one might otherwise think.

The final paper in this section is one which was commissioned by the British Council for Going Global and its related forums. It is unusual in this book in its length and detail, and is accompanied by a comprehensive resource list which the reader can find in the last chapter. Against the backdrop of a rethinking of internationalisation presented by the other papers in this section, Louise Morley explores international trends in women's leadership in higher education. She identifies common trends and patterns, particularly in relation to key enablers and major obstructions, considering explanatory frameworks for women's under-representation in senior positions in the global academy. We present it to you in a form which is almost the full original length, in order that the reader has a chance to understand the comprehensive research picture presented by Morley.

The trends and patterns evident in features of the internationalisation of higher education, and in the very understandings we have of that pheno-menon, are due re-examination. They are imbued with greater complexity than we have, perhaps, considered thus far. The picture which emerges is richer and far more challenging for us all.

Chapter 4.2

Rethinking the Concept of Internationalisation ☆

Hans de Wit

Attention to the international dimension of higher education is increasingly visible in international, national and institutional agendas. A broadly accepted and widely used definition of internationalisation is the one by Jane Knight: 'the process of integrating an international, intercultural or global dimension into the purpose, functions or delivery of post-secondary education' — a definition she describes as intentionally neutral, not incorporating activities, rationales or outcomes, and which builds on an earlier, more institutionally based definition dating from 1995 (Knight, 2008, p. 21). It is this mindset shift to considering 'internationalisation' as a process, as opposed to the product-oriented notion of 'international education', dominant before the 1990s, which largely explains the change in terminology, although a change in practice has not necessarily followed.

The notion of 'internationalisation of higher education' dates from the 1990s. Although traditional ideas of 'international education' existed earlier, this was usually reflected in international activity which was related either to mobility, for example study abroad, exchanges, international student recruitment or faculty mobility, or to curriculum areas, such as multicultural education, international studies, peace education or area studies. These

☆ *This contribution is based on a presentation given at the British Council's Going Global conference in London, 14 March 2012, as part of the IAU session 'Rethinking internationalisation — who benefits and who is at risk?'*

Going Global: Identifying Trends and Drivers of International Education
Copyright © 2013 by Emerald Group Publishing Limited
All rights of reproduction in any form reserved
ISBN: 978-1-78190-575-3

terms described activities or disciplines as elements of international education (and later internationalisation), and in many cases were used, and still are, as a synonym for the overall term. International education distinguished itself from comparative education by its applied character (De Wit, 2002, p. 105). It is this applied character, and the related notions of practice and policy implementation, that dominated the discourse on international education before and even into the 1990s. Several factors, such as the fall of the Iron Curtain, the European unification process and the increased globalisation of our economies and societies, played a role in this transfer from a fragmented and marginal notion of 'international education' to a more integrated, one could say 'comprehensive' concept of internationalisation.

However, the times have been changing since the early 1990s. Brandenburg and de Wit, in their essay with the provocative title 'The end of internationalization' (2011) state:

> Over the last two decades, the concept of the internationalization of higher education is moved from the fringe of institutional interest to the very core. In the late 1970s up to the mid-1980s, activities that can be described as internationalization were usually neither named that way nor carried high prestige and were rather isolated and unrelated. [...] New components were added to its multidimensional body in the past two decades, moving from simple exchange of students to the big business of recruitment, and from activities impacting on an incredibly small elite group to a mass phenomenon.' (pp. 15–16)

In their view, it is time for a critical reflection on the changing concept of internationalisation.

One result of the increasing attention to internationalisation is the inclination to come up with alternatives to the Knight definition and other terminology, such as 'comprehensive', 'mainstream' or 'deep' internationalisation (De Wit, 2011a). These attempts reflect the evolution of the concept itself. A process of 'rethinking internationalisation' is taking place in response to the changing higher education environment and its international dimensions in the global knowledge economy. In a follow-up article in 2012, Brandenburg and de Wit advocate in this process 'a re-orientation towards outcomes and impacts and away from a purely input and output approach. Instead of bragging about the number of students going abroad and reception of international fee paying students, the number of courses in English and the abstract claim of making students global citizens, we want to focus on learning outcomes.' (2012).

The notion that it is time to rethink internationalisation is in the air. The International Association of Universities (IAU, 2012a) has started a process to rethink the internationalisation process and practices and to develop an action plan on how to position internationalisation and its underlying values in the current global knowledge society (http://www.iau-aiu.net). The process has resulted in a document 'Affirming Academic Values in Internationalization of Higher Education: A Call for Action' (IAU, 2012b).

More than a radical change of its concept, in my opinion, we have to go back to its original meaning and foundation, and understand which contextual factors are influencing the original concept and which require further fine-tuning.

While the discourse seems to suggest a move towards a process-oriented, comprehensive internationalisation, as for instance that outlined in the NAFSA report by John Hudzik — *Comprehensive Internationalization: from Concept to Action* (Hudzik, 2011) — a largely activity-oriented or even instrumental approach still seems to predominate. Major myths and misconceptions about what internationalisation actually means can be the result, as demonstrated in two articles in *International Higher Education* (De Wit, 2011b; Knight, 2011). As Jones and De Wit state, it would not be difficult to add more myths and misconceptions to the ones mentioned by Knight or De Wit. 'The relevance of addressing them lies in the need to clarify what is meant by the internationalization of higher education, what it does not mean, and the new directions it needs to take.' (Jones & De Wit, 2012).

Why Rethinking the Concept of Internationalisation?

If indeed internationalisation is still such a relatively young concept, why is there then a need for rethinking? I see eight main reasons.

In the first place, the discourse of internationalisation does not seem to meet always the reality, in which internationalisation is still more a synonym of international education, in other words a summing up of fragmented and rather unrelated terms, than a comprehensive process and concept. In that respect one has to consider the John Hudzik's NAFSA paper more as a wake-up call than as the introduction of a new concept. In my view, comprehensive internationalisation is a tautology: internationalisation only means internationalisation if it is comprehensive; if the term were used in a non-comprehensive way, then it would be more like the old-fashioned term 'international education'.

Second, the further development of globalisation, the increase of commodification in higher education, and of the notion of a global knowledge society and economy have also resulted in a new range of forms, providers and products – such as branch campuses, franchises and trade in education services. And as a consequence new, sometimes even conflicting dimensions, views and elements are emerging in the discourse of internationalisation.

Also, the international higher education context is rapidly changing. While until recently 'internationalisation' and 'international education' were predominantly a Western phenomenon, in which developing countries only played a reactive role, the emerging economies and the higher education community in other parts of the world are now altering the landscape of internationalisation. Moving away from a Western, neocolonial concept, as several educators perceive 'internationalisation', it has to incorporate these emerging other views.

Fourth, the discourse on internationalisation is dominated too much by a small group of stakeholders: higher education leaders, governments and international bodies. Other stakeholders, such as the professional field and in particular the faculty and the student voice, are far less heard, and so the discourse is insufficiently influenced by those who should stand to be most affected by it.

Related to the previous point, too much of the discourse is oriented to national and institutional levels, with little attention to the programme level: research, the curriculum, and the teaching and learning process, which should be more at the core of internationalisation, as expressed by movements such as Internationalization at Home.

Sixth, internationalisation is too much input/output focused: a quantitative approach on numbers instead of an outcome-based approach. Seventh, too little attention has been given to the norms, values or ethics of internationalisation practice. The approach has been too pragmatically oriented to reaching targets, without a debate on the potential risks and ethical consequences. The recent debates on the use of agents in the United States, the problems with diploma fraud and lack of quality assurance on cross-border delivery all illustrate the need for more attention to the ethics and values of internationalisation.

A last point that influences the need for rethinking of internationalisation is the increased awareness that the notion of internationalisation is not only the relationship between nations but even more the relationship between cultures and between the global and the local.

These eight points are rationales for rethinking internationalisation. The overarching reason is that we consider the internationalisation of higher education too much as a goal in itself instead of as a means to an end. Internationalisation is no more or less than a way to enhance the quality of education and research. That objective is forgotten in striving for quantitative goals. The rethinking exercise initiated by IAU, more than an attempt to redefine the still-young concept of internationalisation, is a call for action to bring the core values and objectives of internationalisation back to the forefront.

References

Brandenburg, U., & De Wit, H. (2011). The end of internationalization. *International Higher Education* (62), pp. 15–16. Boston, MA: Boston College Center for International Higher Education.

Brandenburg, U., & De Wit, H. (2012). Getting internationalisation back on track. *IAU Horizons, 17*(3), *18*(1), 17–18. Paris: International Association of Universities.

De Wit, H. (2002). *Internationalization of higher education in the United States of America and Europe: A historical, comparative, and conceptual analysis.* Westport, CT: Greenwood Press.

De Wit, H. (2011a). Naming internationalisation will not revive it. *University World News*, no. 0194, 23 October.

De Wit, H. (2011b). Internationalization misconceptions. *International Higher Education 64*, pp. 6–7. Boston, MA: Boston College Center for International Higher Education.

Hudzik, J. (2011). *Comprehensive internationalization.* Retrieved from http://www. nafsa.org/uploadedFiles/NAFSA_Home/Resource_Library_Assets/Publications_ Library/2011_Comprehen_Internationalization.pdf. Accessed on 18 September 2012. Washington, DC: NAFSA.

International Association of Universities. (2012a). Focus, rethinking internationalization. *IAU Horizons, 17*(3), *18*(1). Paris: International Association of Universities). Retrieved from http://www.iau-aiu.net/sites/all/files/IAU_Horizons_ Vol17_3_18_1_EN.pdf. Accessed on 18 September 2012.

International Association of Universities. (2012b). *Affirming academic values in internationalization of higher education: A call for action.* Paris: International Association of Universities. Retrieved from http://www.iau-aiu.net

Jones, E., & De Wit, H. (2012). Globalization of internationalization: Thematic and regional reflections on a traditional concept. *AUDEM: The International Journal of Higher Education and Democracy, 3*(3), 35–54. State University of New York Press.

Knight, J. (2008). *Higher education in turmoil. The changing world of internationalization.* Rotterdam: Sense Publishers.

Knight, J. (2011). Five myths about internationalization. *International Higher Education* (64), pp. 14–15. Boston, MA: Boston College Center for International Higher Education.

Chapter 4.3

Rethinking the Internationalisation of Higher Education: Sharing the Benefits, Avoiding the Adverse Impacts

Eva Egron-Polak

In the Afterword to the most recent Global Survey Report on internationalisation of higher education, published by the International Association of Universities in 2010, the continued usefulness of the most commonly used definition of internationalisation, developed by Dr. Jane Knight, is questioned. The value of using this standard and well-known descriptive definition, which sees internationalisation of higher education as 'a process of integrating an international, intercultural and/or global dimension to the purpose, functions (teaching, research service) and delivery of higher education' (Knight, 2006), is undeniable, yet it also has some limitations. A shared vocabulary and a clear conceptual framework are needed to arrive at a minimum of understanding in any discussion. This definition, due to its neutral and comprehensive nature, has become that shared platform for discussing the process. In recent years, however, this broad and all-encompassing definition has begun to fall short as an analytical tool to aid understanding the various and numerous trends and developments in internationalisation. At issue though, in this critique, is less the definition of internationalisation, but rather the purposes, actions and impacts of the process which have evolved and continue to evolve and which, at times, appear to have little to do with the way the process is commonly described and defined.

Going Global: Identifying Trends and Drivers of International Education
Copyright © 2013 by Emerald Group Publishing Limited
All rights of reproduction in any form reserved
ISBN: 978-1-78190-575-3

As the scope, intensity and diversity of its activities have grown exponentially, internationalisation has attracted more and more attention from policy makers and higher education leaders. There is practically no university that would today deny being keen to become more 'international' or make references to the international context. The majority of institutional mission statements mention that their university wishes to be measured against international standards, that it prepares students for success in the global economy, or that it is open to the world, or they include any number of other similar references to internationalisation.

The Roots of Rethinking Internationalisation

In recent years, the perceptions of internationalisation have ceased to be uniformly positive even among those most fervent promoters of the benefits of this process. As one higher education leader has recently stated: 'so much of this debate on internationalization is constructed on romanticised terms as if it is simply an unqualified positive development. But is this really true?' (Habib, 2012). The changing nature of internationalisation has brought about sceptics and critics and, most importantly, a more focused examination of the diversity of meanings and practices that are now all bundled up under this conceptual umbrella.

This questioning of the meaning, the underlying assumptions, the strategies and the impacts of internationalisation have come to be known as a process of 'rethinking internationalisation' in which the IAU is taking a leadership role. Starting in India, at a Global Meeting of Associations of Universities in 2011, the IAU organised a discussion of the current understanding of internationalisation of higher education in different regions of the world. At this meeting, participants were invited to question why perceptions were different in terms of values, benefits and risks and challenged to consider what could be done to address the concerns or to bridge the differences.

Numerous articles and blogs have now been devoted to the 'rethinking of internationalisation' by scholars and practitioners alike. Among these, some used provocative titles to draw attention to this questioning. For example Dr. Knight's brief article entitled 'Five Myths About Internationalization' (2011), the blog 'Has Internationalization Lost its Way?' and 'The End of Internationalization' both by Uwe Brandenburg and Hans de Wit (2011a, 2011b) are just a small sample. These articles and various presentations and debates at conferences echoed what IAU was uncovering through its research on internationalisation at the global level — not everything about this process is perceived as having a positive impact.

Evidence-based Concerns

Since 2003, IAU has been conducting and publishing global surveys on internationalisation of higher education. These surveys, though the samples on which the reports are based remain small, are unique in their global reach and offer a valuable resource for institutional leaders, scholars and policy makers. The third and most recent survey, published by IAU in 2012 (Egron-Polak & Hudson, 2010), was based on responses to a questionnaire from 745 institutions of higher education in 115 countries.

The findings of these global surveys are numerous. Even highlighting just a few results can serve to illustrate the timeliness of the 'rethinking' process. First of all, internationalisation as a policy in higher education institutional reform and planning has been rising in importance over the past decade. The IAU Global Survey shows (Figure 1) that it is no longer a marginal focus of

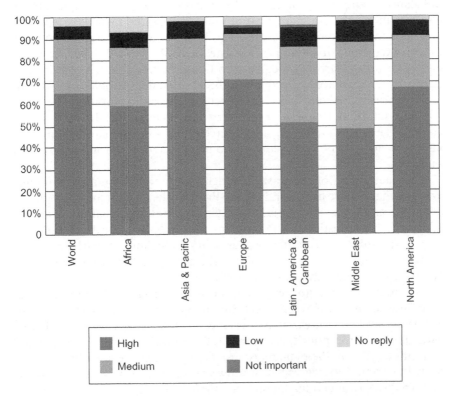

Figure 1: Importance of internationalisation. *Source*: IAU 3rd Global Survey; N = 745.

interest of a few solitary individuals, but has become central for many higher education institutions worldwide.

As well as corroborating this finding about the importance of the policy for institutions, the survey results indicate that internationalisation is now a responsibility of senior academics within the higher education institutions. The majority of the respondents indicate that it is the vice-president or the deputy vice-chancellor who is responsible of this area. As internationalisation moves from the margin to the core mission of the institution its full integration into the senior governance levels of the university is a clear sign of its importance for the overall academic endeavour.

Another finding that merits mention when justifying or explaining why a critical examination of internationalisation trends is warranted concerns the continued and persistent importance that mobility, and in particular, student mobility, plays in internationalisation policies. In fact, for many, mobility is synonymous with internationalisation. Yet, from all accounts, student mobility continues to remain relatively limited and highly unbalanced worldwide. The 2010 IAU Survey shows, for example, that in 66 per cent of the responding institutions, international students represent less than five per cent of the total enrolment at the undergraduate level, though exceptions, for example in Australia or the United States, certainly exist. This rather narrowly focused view of internationalisation constitutes a particular area in need of rethinking because student mobility is also the most expensive, labour-intensive aspect of internationalisation that may not find sufficient resources in a climate of budget cuts. It may, on the contrary, exacerbate the negative perceptions of internationalisation if international student fee revenues become even more central to university budgets.

The questioning of the ways in which internationalisation is unfolding arises perhaps most importantly from the divergent views and perceptions about the rationales, the benefits and the risks of internationalisation among higher education institutions in different world regions. Furthermore, there is a trend towards a rather 'exclusionary' selection of partners which manifests itself mostly, but not only, in the geographic priorities selected by HEIs for their international collaborations.

The main reasons for engaging in the internationalisation process, according to the most recent IAU Survey, are shown in Figure 2. At the aggregate level, it is clear that focusing on preparing students and their curriculum is a top priority as is, in the third place, the pursuit of prestige and status. When these findings are disaggregated regionally, we note fairly important differences which draw the line between HEIs from highly industrialised regions and those from the developing parts of the world. For institutions in Africa, for example, the most important reason for internationalisation is the building up of research capacity and the

Rationales for internationalization	World	Africa	Asia & Pacific	Europe	Latin – America & Caribbean	Middle East	North America
Improve student preparedeness	30%	19%	31%	27%	39%	22%	39%
Internationalize curriculum	17%	15%	17%	16%	18%	16%	17%
Enhance international profile	15%	13%	14%	20%	6%	17%	9%
Strengthen research and K. production	14%	24%	15%	13%	16%	22%	8%
Broaden an diversify source of students	9%	8%	7%	10%	4%	5%	17%

Figure 2: Trends and regional perspectives: divergent views on rationales.
Source: IAU 3rd Global Survey.

production of knowledge. The focus on students is present, but at a much lower level of importance. These different interests in pursuing internationalisation must be considered and addressed in the collaborative efforts being pursued if all participating institutions are to share the benefits.

Furthermore, the pursuit of reputation and prestige (second top rationale for European universities) as a key rationale for internationalisation is also to be given serious consideration. Prestige is often equated with positioning in international rankings and this may mean that many institutions in Latin America, Africa, the Middle East and elsewhere are less likely to be seen as valuable potential partners. Finally, when universities in certain regions, such as North America, state that diversification of source of students is why they internationalise, the implications for the brain drain must be borne in mind, as the attractiveness of these universities remains high and the demand for access to higher education in many developing nations still outpaces the capacity of local institution.

A second area of divergence concerns the perception of risk. There is a fairly strong consensus around the positive nature of the process of internationalisation, yet this 'romantic' view is being challenged, as we saw earlier. The general consistency of the findings in all three IAU Global Surveys with regard to perceptions of risk has, at the aggregate level, crystallised mainly around the following risks: commercialisation or commodification of higher education, the brain drain and the increase in numbers of degree mills or poor-quality providers (see Figure 3). These findings show, however, that there is a difference in magnitude of this perception of risks, with unsurprisingly, the brain drain being the top

Risks of internationalization	World	Africa	Asia & Pacific	Europe	Latin - America & Caribbean	Middle East	North America
Commodification of education programmes	12%	8%	16%	9%	12%	11%	13%
Brain drain	10%	16%	8%	10%	17%	12%	6%
Increase in number of foreign degree mills	9%	6%	11%	7%	12%	6%	7%
Over-emphasis on internationalization	8%	14%	8%	8%	8%	15%	7%
Greater competition among HEIs	8%	6%	11%	8%	4%	4%	6%
Elitism in acess to int'l. education opportunities	7%	9%	4%	6%	11%	4%	7%
Loss of cultural identity	7%	11%	9%	6%	5%	17%	2%
Too much focus on recruitment of fee paying int'l. students	7%	6%	4%	7%	4%	3%	13%
None	6%	1%	5%	7%	3%	6%	11%
Overuse of English as a medium of instruction	5%	1%	3%	6%	5%	5%	5%
Homogenization of curriculum	4%	4%	3%	6%	5%	3%	1%
Growing gaps among HEIs	4%	2%	6%	4%	3%	5%	1%
Growing gaps amongst country and regions	3%	2%	2%	4%	2%	6%	3%
No reply	12%	12%	8%	14%	7%	3%	18%

KEY:
■ 1st   ■ 2nd   ■ 3rd

Figure 3: Risks of internationalisation.

preoccupation in Africa, Latin America and the Caribbean and, somewhat more surprisingly, in Europe. At the same time, the risk of commercialisation of higher education is not even among the top three concerns in Africa or in the Middle East, most likely because the private higher education sector is seen as an essential response to the demand for access to higher education. These differences clearly underline the need to see internationalisation in context, rather than as a phenomenon that can be pursued or applied in the same way everywhere.

Also striking in these findings about risk is the high level of respondents who chose not to respond to this question. The majority of those who did not reply were in Europe and North America, where the response indicating that the process carried no risk was also quite frequent. The institutions that least frequently replied that internationalisation carried no risk were in Africa (one per cent) and in Latin America and the Caribbean (three per cent). As the adverse effects of internationalisation are frequently mentioned by leaders of higher education, and anecdotal references are very often made about the uneven level of the field on which internationalisation is developing, this divergence of views and the persistence of some of the risks provide strong impetus for continuous and careful analysis of internationalisation, rather than taking the positive nature of the process as a given.

The geographic priorities in the internationalisation policies of higher education institutions are also a cause for rethinking internationalisation because of the potential negative effects, and also for the opportunities that they can bring. Figure 4 shows clearly the importance of intra-regional co-operation in internationalisation, and the importance that Europe has gained as a top-priority region in other parts of the world. It is noteworthy

Priority Area \ HEI Region	Africa	Asia and Pacific	Europe	Latin - America and Caribbean	Middle East	North America
Africa	1st					
Asia and Pacific	3rd	1st	2nd			1st
Europe	2nd	2nd	1st	1st	1st	3rd
Latin - America and Caribbean				2nd		
Middle East					2nd	
North America		3rd		3rd	2nd	
No geografic priority			3rd		3rd	2nd

Figure 4: Geographic priority in internationalisation policy. *Source*: IAU 3rd Global Survey.

that three of the world's regions place their own region above all others in their internationalisation policies.

A more disturbing message comes through in Figure 4, when it is noted that Africa, the Middle East and Latin America and the Caribbean are not identified among the top three priority regions by institutions anywhere else. Such geographic targeting, when coupled with the earlier-noted finding that reputation and prestige-seeking are among the top reasons for internationalisation, leads to the conclusion that internationalisation is potentially becoming highly elitist and narrowly focused. For a process that is about opening up to the world, this is not a positive trend, and though it may be highly desirable to strengthen intra-regional networks and South–South collaboration, it is imperative to promote a more inclusive view of internationalisation, one that excludes no regions, and especially not leaving out some of the most dynamic and most populated regions of the world.

In short, there are sufficient and important evidence-based reasons to engage in a careful rethinking of internationalisation.

Where is the Rethinking of Internationalisation Leading?

Wherever internationalisation policy leads or, however, the process is recalibrated it must be a result of an inclusive and collaborative reflection that integrates as many perspectives as possible. This has been the approach adopted by the IAU working with an international ad-hoc Expert Group that came together almost spontaneously after the initial meeting in India, mentioned earlier. This group provided much expert input into a new statement of the IAU entitled *Affirming Academic Values in Internationalization of Higher Education: A Call for Action*, which strives to anchor the internationalisation processes more deeply in the pursuit of academic purposes and to articulate the values that the process should fully embrace.

The Call for Action underlines some of the essential reasons for recentring internationalisation on academic purposes and values and for finding a balanced combination for pursuing multiple goals, including those driven by economic necessity. It offers a brief analysis of the forces that have or are steering this highly dynamic process, the influences of tradition, colonial history, local context and other numerous factors, though these tend to be overshadowed in the present era by globalisation, which is the most important influence shaping university development, including internationalisation.

Though citing the numerous benefits of internationalisation, the Call for Action also articulates some of the adverse effects that internationalisation can bring to higher education institutions and whole systems. The fundamental point of the Call for Action is to urge universities to take care and control of this process. It reminds higher education institutions of the basic values and principles that govern all higher education and research and encourages the institutions to assume their full responsibility to shape and reshape the trajectory that internationalisation takes in the future.

Preparations and deliberations on the IAU Call for Action served as the backdrop for the Going Global 2012 debate that IAU helped to co-ordinate and which took place in at the Going Global 2012 Conference in London in March 2012. Here too, the voices were multiple as participants, organised in different working groups, tackled some of the key questions in the internationalisation of higher education. These discussions were organised around six topics.

Starting with the concept of internationalisation itself, one group debated to what extent there was a shared understanding of internationalisation among the stakeholders and between different parts of the world. A second group discussed which drivers of internationalisation were the most important in shaping the process and how these differed among regions and over time. Given the centrality of student mobility in internationalisation, its place in the process in the years to come, the nature of mobility that was most effective, the manner in which various disciplines incorporated mobility and the notions of equitable access to mobility opportunities were the topics discussed by the third group. A fourth working group came together in order to deliberate on the global responsibility of higher education institutions as they engage in internationalisation. Trying to identify and spell out the role that universities should, could or do play to narrow economic gaps among people, or how they help achieve the Millennium Development Goals set by the UN, was among the topics broached in this group. Internationalisation is often cited as a means to improving the quality of higher education. It is also seen at times as a catalyst for reform of higher education by bringing an opportunity for institutions to learn from one another, to compare and contrast practices. The fifth group engaged with this topic, focusing on the Bologna Process as one example and trying to identify other examples where internationalisation has been a catalyst for positive change, rather than a driver of homogenisation at institutional and system level, as has been at times underlined.

Though internationalisation is a means rather than a goal in itself, it is fairly legitimate to ask the question 'What does or what would an internationalised university look like?' Answering this question was the task assigned to the last working group, which reflected on this question from the perspective of the curriculum as well as by looking at expectations for each of the main actors within an HEI, including students, staff, faculty members and the leadership.

End Note Instead of a Conclusion

To say that these debates were and continue to be rich would be an understatement. The interest in the debate on internationalisation at the Going Global 2012 Conference and in the IAU Call for Action demonstrates that it is a reflection worth having. Internationalisation of higher education is a complex process and can touch on some of the dimensions of education that academics hold dearest. Among these are the specific cultural heritage of the higher education institutions, the socialising role they play for the future leaders of our societies and also the more universal values, including academic freedom and institutional autonomy.

Internationalisation creates linkages and networks among institutions including, at times, those that do not share the same views or that do not benefit from the same rights as other institutions enjoy and almost take for granted. The uneven playing field on which partnerships are often built certainly necessitates care and sensitivity in order to ensure that the geopolitical asymmetries do not spill over into higher education and research collaborations. Such linkages, among partners from vastly different contexts but who share in the purpose of higher education and research, represent or offer perhaps the greatest potential in an increasingly globalised world. Recognising that the very difference of perspectives may offer the greatest terrain for mutual learning and for shared enrichment should be second nature to those who engage actively in the internationalisation of their institutions.

The rethinking of internationalisation is an ongoing conversation in which participants must view the process of internationalisation neither as an unqualified positive, nor as an instrument of domination or homo-genisation. While it is not neutral, the identification of the goals and purposes of internationalisation rests within the policy domain of the higher education institutions. Being clear about the goals and the expected impacts is an essential start and endpoint in this process.

References

Brandenburg, U., & De Wit, H. (2011a). Has international education lost its way, worldwise. *The Chronicle of Higher Education, 15*(November).

Brandenburg, U., & De Wit, H. (2011b). The end of internationalization. *International Higher Education, 62*(Winter). Boston, MA: Boston College.

Egron-Polak, E., & Hudson, R. (2010). *Internationalization of higher education: Global trends, regional perspectives — The IAU 3rd Global Survey Report.* International Association of Universities [IAU], Paris.

Habib, A. (2012). Building partnerships in an unequal world, worldwise. *The Chronicle of Higher Education, 13*(June).

International Association of Universities (IAU). (2012). *Affirming academic values in internationalization of higher education: A call for action.* Retrieved from http://www.iau-aiu.net/content/policy-statements-0

Knight, J. (2006). Crossborder education: An analytical framework for program and provider mobility. In J. Smart & B. Tierney (Eds.), *Higher education handbook of theory and practice.* Dordecht: Springer.

Knight, J. (2011), Five myths about internationalization. *International Higher Education, 62*(Winter). Boston, MA: Boston College.

Chapter 4.4

The Future of English in International Higher Education

Michael Carrier

The Importance of Competence in English for the Individual and the Economy in a Globalised World

This paper examines the main issues and challenges that policy makers and tertiary sector institutions face as they respond to increasing demand for English.

It is clear that English is no longer only *a* world language, but it is *the* world language of business, international relations and the academy. This situation may change in the future and English as a lingua franca may go the way of Latin as a lingua franca, but this is the global reality we need to work with at the moment.

Drivers for English

It is important for us to understand the key drivers for people learning English and adding English proficiency development in their educational and professional aspirations.

It is clear from studies that learners are looking to improve their access to education, employment and opportunity through English as a life skill, focusing on:

- improving access to education;
- increasing employability;

Going Global: Identifying Trends and Drivers of International Education
Copyright © 2013 by Emerald Group Publishing Limited
All rights of reproduction in any form reserved
ISBN: 978-1-78190-575-3

- facilitating international mobility;
- unlocking development opportunities and accessing crucial information;
- acting as an impartial language in context where other languages would be unacceptable.

English as Facilitator — or Barrier?

Cultural Imperialism?

There are some who see English teaching as a form of cultural imperialism, especially when delivered in the developing world. But it is clear that the perception of English in developing countries has completely moved away from its colonial links and is seen more as a life skill that enables people to provide education and mobility opportunities:

> It is definitely unhelpful for Africa and other developing areas to continue viewing English or any other international language the language of colonialism or imperialism. In spite of their historical association with colonial rule and the fact that they have limited the development of indigenous languages, the former colonial languages are useful now in several ways. (Negash, in Coleman, 2011, p. 178)

Undermining Local Languages?

English language competence does not exist in a vacuum. We live in a multilingual world, and the relationship between English and other languages needs to be clearly understood and addressed.

The fact that English is a global lingua franca does not have to mean that it becomes a dominant language that undermines the use of other languages, but it is clear that in order to avoid damaging consequences, government and educational institutions need to set clear language policies that outline the outcomes they wish to achieve.

For example selecting the age at which English is introduced as a foreign language into primary or secondary education systems must be debated carefully. Research, such as Janet Enever's EU project on Early Language learning (ELLIE), has shown that the introduction of English in the early years of schooling can have mixed effects, especially if English is introduced as a medium of instruction, rather than merely as another school subject, at too early a stage, when mother tongue literacy has not yet been fully established. This can undermine the use of local languages as a medium of instruction and even disturb literacy levels — thus it is suggested that only the mother tongue be used as the medium of instruction until learners are successfully literate.

Rwanda presents an indicative case study. The government of Rwanda decided to switch its official language from French (itself an L2 for most learners, not an L1) to English and attempted to introduce English as a medium of instruction from grade 1 of primary school. Academic advisers were able to persuade the government to move to a more gradual introduction of English so that the first years of primary school could be taught in the mother tongue, supporting L1 literacy development.

English as a Medium of Instruction (EMI)

A similar caveat applies in higher education settings as well. The decision to teach some or all of the undergraduate and postgraduate courses in English, as opposed to the language of the country, is not a decision that should be taken lightly. The introduction of EMI — English as a medium of instruction — at university level will have both positive and challenging consequences.

The positive results will be that the institution finds it easier to attract foreign students from anglophone countries or from countries where students have high English competence. This can be a great benefit both from a financial perspective (higher fee income) and from a cultural perspective (bringing a multicultural learning environment to enrich the educational opportunities of the students from that particular country).

The challenging consequences may include a fall in enrolments from local students, who may have the academic credentials for the course but not the English language competence — or the competence but not the confidence required — to participate in the course. This is both a financial and a political loss for the home institution.

One solution is to ensure that a commitment to EMI requires a parallel commitment to teaching the local language to incoming students and insisting on certain standards that must be met for graduation, thus supporting a multilingual community.

This is especially important in countries using a less-widely used language or a language that is under some existential pressure and the institution should ensure that the introduction of EMI is a *support* for multilingualism, not an *abdication* of multilingualism.

Employability

The belief that English proficiency can assist in employability is borne out by the research carried out by Euromonitor (2011) on behalf of the British Council, firstly in sub-Saharan Africa and secondly in Middle East and North Africa.

This research, inspired by the work of Francois Grin in Europe, used quantitative data analysis to demonstrate conclusively that English language proficiency brought major economic benefits both to the individual and to the wider society.

These findings included the discovery that the average salary gap of someone who can speak English at intermediate level as opposed to someone who does not is approximately 20 per cent, with a further uplift as much as 40 per cent for those with advanced English skills (Euromonitor 2011, p. 31 & passim).

In addition, it was shown that countries with higher degrees of English language proficiency in their population attracted higher amounts of foreign direct investment to the country.

This research showed clearly that employers value English language skills, and the sub-Saharan Africa results showed that for example:

- over 50 per cent of companies interviewed said that their workforce was required to speak English
- 72 per cent of all companies interviewed stated that employees with English language skills advance quicker within companies
- 67 per cent of these companies also said that English is beneficial for company growth

The Role of English in Higher Education — and the Challenges

21st-Century Skills

The learning of English at higher education level first needs to be set into the context of 21st-century skills. In many parts of the world there is a movement — especially among multinational employers — to try to influence educational systems to produce young people with skills that are more relevant to the professional employment needs of the 21st century.

Major employers such as Cisco, Oracle, Intel and Microsoft have sponsored research and workshops in trying to identify what those 21st-century skills are.

Fadel and Trilling (2009) show that employers need young people with new ways of thinking and working, new technical and informational literacy skills and new levels of cultural sensitivity and intercultural competence including a focus on critical thinking, collaborative working and data literacy.

Fadel omitted to include English language skills as one of these seven core skills, but it is clear that English plays a role in delivering these 21st-century skills and is in itself one of them — it is difficult for global professionals to operate in their field without some English skill to allow them to access global research and knowledge.

Thus, in preparing students both for *entering* higher education and for *exiting* it with competences that are relevant to 21st-century employers, HE institutions need to take on board the idea that helping students to gain global English language competence is a part of their broader educational remit.

Higher Education English Context

As a result of the development in demand for English in the last 20 years the English language has established itself as vital in the academic world, becoming a necessary communication tool for students, researchers and academics.

In addition, 30 per cent of students in higher education aim to continue their studies abroad, especially in English-speaking countries, such as the UK, United States and Australia.

But there are serious challenges concerning the quality of English skills students bring to the university, how their English is extended while at university and how university programmes prepare students for future employment.

An increasing number of universities are upgrading the English courses they offer as they see a need for students to graduate with English proficiency as well as their academic achievements, in order to prepare them for a globalised world which uses English as a lingua franca.

In addition, more and more universities are offering their graduate and even undergraduate courses using English as a medium of instruction, in order both to attract students from other countries and also to better prepare their own national students. This puts further pressure on the English competence required of new undergraduates.

How can we improve the standards of English for new undergraduates, in order to facilitate their access to the highest quality tertiary education?

Pre-HE — When and How Should English be Taught before University?

First we must look at the early years of English learning — at primary and/ or secondary levels — which should be producing university-ready students with high levels of English (at least B2/C1 on the Common European Framework (CEFR)), suitable for international study and interaction.

How this can be achieved must be the subject of another paper, but it is clear that in most countries a major challenge is the availability of highly qualified and linguistically competent teachers in the primary and secondary teaching workforce. There is currently a shortage in many countries, and certainly a shortage of teachers who are themselves at B2/C1 proficiency level.

A further factor is the nature of examinations and assessment of English language learning at the secondary level, which often has a negative backwash effect on teaching style and learning motivation which can reduce levels of communicative competence by the end of secondary school.

Simply put, if the secondary exit assessments are focused on reading and writing at the expense of speaking (as is often the case), then the result will be university undergraduates who have theoretical knowledge but low performance in oral fluency in English.

In my view, the nature and quality of secondary school language teaching is much more important than the current fascination with teaching English in primary schools globally. Although it is a truism that younger learners in primary school find it easy to learn a new language, especially orally, thanks to their language acquisition device (if Chomsky is still correct), it is also true that this is not necessarily a benefit that can be always measured or perceived in the linguistic competence of students exiting secondary education.

Some studies have shown that learners who started the language at primary school did not achieve better results at 18 than those who only studied the language at secondary school. It is quite possible that the language gains made by age 11 are then lost on transfer to secondary school if the secondary education does not continue on from the same point but requires many students to go back to the beginning of their language learning process, as is often the case.

More research is needed in this area, to provide evidence as to the efficacy of primary language education at raising levels at 18.

In any event, higher education institutions cannot afford to be uninterested in the prior language learning careers of their potential students. Universities should be researching the best approaches to developing English language competence that will contribute to tertiary level success, and should be lobbying governments to raise the standards of English language competence at the point of entry to higher education.

Pre-Entry — What Level of English Should Be Required for Entry to University?

It has been argued that there is sometimes insufficient linguistic rigour applied in university entry testing policy, especially in oral performance. The testing instruments may be appropriate, and students may achieve the required level, but it seems that some still have linguistic problems which will have a negative impact on their education (and the education of others in their class peer-group).

It is not enough for universities to rely upon external testing, but they must have their own internal progress monitoring systems that allow the competences of the students to be brought up to speed as fast as possible after entry to the university course.

There can be particular problems with pronunciation and students' phonological skills, for example, which are often glossed over. A student may be brilliant academically, but if the rest of the class cannot understand their contribution to the seminar discussion, then not only will everyone lose academically, but also students will likely have negative feelings of social and academic isolation. It is not a favour to the student to gloss over the fact that their pronunciation is a barrier to communication.

There should be clear assessment criteria which focus on intelligibility and class participation issues, with the right support resources and mechanisms to assist students who have these difficulties.

Post-Entry — What is the Role of Higher Education Institutions in Developing English Language Proficiency?

Students should be assessed in all four skills in a diagnostic manner that allows them to see where they need to make improvements, and how the university can assist them with classes, self-access study, open educational resources, twinning with other students, technological resources, etc., in order to help them bring all four skills up to the required level.

As well as pre-sessional support, and significant in-sessional support, there should be regular self- testing and formalised assessment of all four skills until students have achieved C1 in all four skills and this can be certificated.

Most institutions offer support for the development of skills in English for Academic Purposes (EAP), as opposed to general proficiency, but it is not always clear whether there is a set standard that should be reached either at pre-sessional stage or by the end of the first semester or year.

It would be highly advisable to define a set of academic English competences (along the lines of the CEFR itself) to inform the teaching and learning of EAP and thus ensure that all students had reached an appropriate starting level in English.

Exiting Higher Education

Towards the end of the course of study, an extra focus on the English required for future research or future employment ought to be introduced in addition, in order to assist the student in developing in advance the competences they will need on graduation.

It would be helpful if universities could also specify a clear *exit* level of proficiency which they expect from students on English medium courses. In other words it should not be possible to graduate from an English medium course without C1 competence at least, across all four skills.

Some colleagues may disagree with this because they feel it is not their place to comment on the English language proficiency of students whose academic proficiency in their chosen subject may be excellent.

However, it can be argued that a more holistic view of students' achievements would be advisable, and in the same way that pastoral care is provided, linguistic care should be provided, and with clear quality and assessment criteria so that exit levels can be guaranteed.

Conclusion

English opens doors; it creates new opportunities, providing access to education, to new types of employment, to mobility. Having English skills means you can have access to the world — to the world's knowledge, much of which is in English and not translated. Thus, English language proficiency is not just nice to have — it is vital and life-changing.

For many students, however, reaching the required level of English for higher education is a challenging aspiration. In the developing and emerging economies, there is a shortage of good teachers of English, students do not have reliable or affordable access to the Internet — there are many obstacles.

In addressing these obstacles, in partnerships between governmental, HE and corporate stakeholders, we need to ensure English becomes a facilitator for higher education, not a barrier to students outside elite groups.

To achieve this, we first need to build a high-performing primary and secondary sectors — and this will require a greater investment in teacher training and development. This will also require that governments modify traditional forms of exam assessment to include spoken assessment so that there is a clear incentive to teach and learn communicatively, avoiding the backwash effect of grammar-based exams on classroom teaching.

Beyond the secondary level of education, it is clear that if we wish to assist students in reaching their academic as well as personal goals, we need more rigorous standards of English language proficiency — before, during and after their university entrance.

In the tertiary context, this means that we need to be more proactive in providing in-sessional language support which is no longer merely optional but holds students to clear objective criteria in terms of achievement and certificates their achievement to at least C1 level. This would include a clearer focus on phonological skills and writing skills, with a clear commitment to high levels of performance commensurate with external expectations.

Overall, we need strategies to create multilingual graduates who are competent in their own language, in English for global professional purposes, and preferably in a third language to give them a competitive advantage, and who have developed the intercultural skills and 21st-century work skills that will equip graduates for global employment.

References

Euromonitor. (2011). *Benefits of the English language for individuals and societies — quantitative indicators from Cameroon, Nigeria, Rwanda, Bangladesh and Pakistan.* London: Euromonitor.

Fadel, C., & Trilling, B. (2009). *21st Century skills.* San Francisco, CA: Jossey-Bass.

Negash, N. (2011). English language in Africa: An impediment or a contributor to development? In H. Coleman (Ed.), *Dreams & realities: English for the developing world* (pp. 161–183). London: British Council.

Chapter 4.5

Success in a Post-Disruption Marketplace: Lessons from Other Sectors

Wendy Purcell

Globally, higher education (HE) is undergoing a period of rapid change, given its correlation with economic recovery and positive societal impact. Many nations with long-established HE sectors, including the UK, are implementing policies to open up delivery to new providers, accommodate student choice and meet increased demand while managing public subsidy. Other nations developing at pace, such as China and India, are investing heavily in tertiary education such that in-country delivery is growing in both capacity and quality (OECD, 2011). In turn, internationalisation strategies in developed markets are responding by moving further up the value chain, for example from undergraduate to graduate programmes, and are connecting with other providers globally through consortia and networks.

The British Council identifies a number of key trends in international higher education. These include a change in international student mobility flows, the emergence of new models of global HE partnerships, changing patterns in research output and international distribution and an increase in commercial research activities by HE institutions as a reaction to decreased public investment in research (British Council, 2012). The established character of the global higher education market is being challenged by significant investment and growth in other nations. Across the world, tertiary enrolments in 2009 reached 170 million (British Council, 2012), and by 2020 it is estimated that China will have educated more university graduates than the United States and European Union countries combined (Universities UK, 2011). Other challengers to a traditionally 'Western-centric' view of higher

Going Global: Identifying Trends and Drivers of International Education
Copyright © 2013 by Emerald Group Publishing Limited
All rights of reproduction in any form reserved
ISBN: 978-1-78190-575-3

education are emerging economies investing heavily in tertiary education. For example there are significant increases in the numbers of tertiary enrolments in Brazil (6.2 million), Indonesia (4.9 million), Iran (3.4 million) and South Korea (3.3 million).

However, this is not simply a matter of increasing student numbers; there are changes to the balance of academic excellence across the world too. The scale of this change is demonstrated in the latest *Times Higher Education* (2012a) World University Rankings , where a number of Western universities were displaced from the top 100 by new entrants from emerging economies including Brazil and Turkey, and with Japan now having five institutions in the top 100. Chinese universities are also climbing in reputation, for example Tsinghua University, up to 30th from 35th, and Peking University rising to 38th from 43rd. We see this trajectory particularly powerfully in the most recent league of the top 100 global universities under 50 years old (Times Higher Education, 2012a, 2012b).

Overall, recessionary pressures, increased demand and the policy instruments used in response to these present a significant level of disruption and present a number of challenges for established HE institutions. Early considerations include pricing academic programmes and commoditisation of delivery. However, there are more considered responses that include communicating and articulating the brand promise, expressing the nature of the student experience, student support and the return on their investment and building communities of practice of appropriate critical mass to sustain world-class research.

For some this period has been described as a 'perfect storm'. This is perhaps somewhat disingenuous, but it does perhaps convey the fact that opportunities for innovation emerge from situations characterised by high levels of ambiguity. Looking to other sectors outside HE that have already emerged successfully from a disruptive change in their established market, there are insights relevant for HE institutions and their leaders. This paper is framed within the context of the English higher education sector, an established and mature sector, but one which is undergoing significant and disruptive regulatory, financial and market reforms. Indeed, many of the issues set out later will, by the nature of the topic of disruption to established marketplaces, be more relevant to more mature higher education landscapes internationally. However, the key points raised and questions asked will also have resonances across the HE sector given its hyper-connectedness.

Market Disruption

Market disruption can occur at a number of different levels, affecting players in various markets to different extents. The Harvard academic

Clayton Christensen first coined the term '*disruptive innovation*' to 'describe a process by which a product or service takes root initially in simple applications at the bottom of a market and then relentlessly moves "up market", eventually displacing established competitors' (2012). A distinct advantage of disruptive innovations for consumers is that in commercial marketplaces it often allows a new demographic of consumers access to a product or service that was historically only accessible to consumers with a lot of money or skill. Christensen (2012) states that:

> Disruptive businesses are often able to respond quickly to subtle changes in consumer demand, as they have lower gross margins, smaller target markets, and simpler products and services that may not appear as attractive as existing solutions when compared against traditional performance metrics.

While disruption in an established market or sector can cause instability for those being disrupted, it can also clearly be a key driver of new innovation, growth and success. Those organisations that can be agile and adapt their existing products or service to changes being driven by disruptors can emerge as leaders in the newly created market landscape.

Case Studies: Success in a Post-disruption Marketplace

In periods of rapid change, such as those currently taking place, it is easy for the HE community to focus inwards rather than outwards and on short-term issues rather than their long-term vision. However, the present disruptive changes within higher education are nothing new when considered globally and across all sectors. There is a wealth of evidence and experience across a range of sectors that disruption of a marketplace does not necessarily imply the worst for established providers within that marketplace.

In their book *Bold: How to be brave in business and win* (2011) Smith and Milligan present a number of case studies from globally successful businesses within markets that are currently experiencing or have recently experienced significant disruption. It is argued that universities can draw a number of pertinent lessons from several of these case studies, of which two key examples are cited in the following sections.

Case Study: O2

For the telecommunications company O2, formerly BT Cellnet, the mobile business of British Telecommunications, a major disruptive influence was a deregulation of the sector which enabled a number of new disruptive businesses to start up. At the same time as this deregulation, a number of new technologies were emerging, and this became a crucial focus for many of O2's competitors. This led to a shift in consumer behaviour focusing on obtaining the latest technology at the best price, and therefore an increasing commoditisation of the sector.

O2, however, believed that they could differentiate themselves in this commoditised market by focusing on the experience they provided as opposed to the technology they used (as cited in Smith & Milligan, 2011). O2 also later partnered with Apple in an exclusive deal to launch the iPhone in the UK, reflecting the importance of a partnership approach to innovation.

O2's success shows that a focus on the customer experience is vital. This is relevant to HE, and discussions about the student experience also serve to reinforce the importance of partnership. We are seeing this already in the sector as HE institutions focus on enriching the student journey and engage the student voice in shaping their experience.

Case Study: Burberry

The fashion company Burberry was established in 1856 and has a long history, evolving from a company providing trench coats for the military in the First World War to a cutting-edge international fashion and clothing design brand.

Market disruption for Burberry took the form of the recent global recession, causing in 2009 the biggest decline in luxury sales in many years. However, Burberry took the bold decision to remain true to the heritage of their established brand, increasing its investment in brand-building activity and seeking to explore new horizons in making it contemporary. This, combined with a focus on reducing costs within their supply chain, ultimately led to Burberry gaining increased profits in 2010, despite challenging market conditions.

Christopher Bailey, Burberry's Chief Creative Officer, stated that for Burberry, 'our heritage is our foundation, but we continue to grow and develop' (as cited in Smith & Milligan, 2011). Burberry worked to engage customers with the brand in new ways, embracing technology and online opportunities and these innovations underpin the long-term sustainability of the business. For Burberry, 'Being bold is about believing in your brand and your instinct' (as cited in Smith & Milligan, 2011).

For HE, the Burberry case reveals that a focus on distinctiveness and sustaining the brand promise are essential components of success in response to disruption. Indeed, we are already seeing HE institutions refresh their brand image, more fully articulate their unique academic offers and aggressively market them.

Hybrid Value Chains

Another model for success in a marketplace experiencing disruption is a new model of collaboration known as hybrid value chains (HVC). This model sees established, larger businesses working closely with traditionally 'disruptive' organisations, often social enterprises or small- to medium-sized businesses (SMEs). Drayton and Budinich (2010) state that:

> The power of such partnerships lies in the complementary strengths of the participants: Businesses offer scale, expertise in manufacturing and operations, and financing. Social entrepreneurs and organizations contribute lower costs, strong social networks, and deep insights into customers and communities.

In higher education, we have long seen institutions' move to divest themselves of operations not related to their core educational purpose, bringing in commercial partners to deliver services such as catering or accommodation. However, we can anticipate this going further in the future in response to disruptive forces, for example the establishment of social enterprises to deliver services at community level. Established HE institutions could benefit from such HVC activities through arrangements such as validation services for new market entrants, while emergent providers can offer programme innovation more responsive to market needs.

The Leading, Governing and Managing Enterprising Universities Project

The Leading, Governing and Managing Enterprising Universities project, led by Plymouth University, in partnership with colleagues at Teesside University, was one of the Higher Education Funding Council for England's (HEFCE) flagship Leading Transformational Change projects, designed to better understand the distinctiveness strategies being pursued in the sector.

Drawing on an analysis of the mission statements and in-depth case reviews of English universities, the study revealed that HE institutions in the UK are already starting to aggressively pursue differentiation strategies along key axes, in particular research, enterprise and learning.

Increasingly we are seeing a move out of the crowded space of 'sameness' in institutional mission to a more open space of clarity around the academic experience on offer. Alongside traditionally specialist or 'boutique' institutions (such as arts or veterinary colleges) a number of 'clusters' of institutions with a clearer focus on what might be considered traditional higher education pillars — teaching and research — are evident. Furthermore, there is an emergence of a newer type of cluster that is founded upon business-facing and/or 'enterprise principles'.

Kim and Mauborgne (2005) propose a metaphor of red and blue oceans to describe this situation. In this model of the market, red oceans represent the known market space. Here, industry boundaries are well defined and the rules of the game are known. Businesses (in this case, universities) attempt to outperform their rivals, in an effort to increase their share of a product or service demand. In this case, competition is 'vertical,' as competition for reputational advantage, measured by proxy through various ranking systems, becomes cut-throat and turns the ocean 'bloody'.

The blue ocean analogy offers an alternative, 'horizontal' means of differentiation in moving to occupy different or 'new' market spaces in calmer waters – the 'blue ocean'. This strategy can support long-term institutional sustainability and innovation, but it is not without risks, particularly if it is built upon a form of differentiation that the market does not support or that is not in accord with an institution's heritage and values. However, well-conceived differentiation strategies that are derived from the university's own sense of identity, values, context and place, whether founded on an ethos of enterprise or indeed other distinctive academic focus, can help institutions to connect deeply with the society they serve and help the sector move away from inward looking.

Conclusions — Lessons for Global Higher Education

HE institutions have much to learn from other sectors that have already experienced dramatic changes as they move to articulate their positioning and response. Success in post-disruption marketplaces appears to be enabled by clarity of purpose, innovation and partnership. Boldness and the ability to respond quickly to the market while remaining true to their heritage and values are also essential to sustained success.

The experience and success of O2 show that the user experience of an organisation within an increasingly commoditised sector is a vital aspect of its distinctiveness and therefore its success. For higher education, which is arguably becoming increasingly consumer-driven in a number of established higher education systems (for example the United States and the UK, with increasing tuition-fee levels), this supports a need for a strong focus on the student experience. This will likely translate into graduates who are strong ambassadors for the institution, vested in its future success and more likely to continue support it as a donor or through other means. The Burberry's branding was recognised as a crucial part of its success and one that, through innovation, could be made contemporary for new customers through technology and innovation. HE institutions can draw upon their own values as communities of practice and make them visible as a key part of articulating their distinctiveness to potential students and other major stakeholders.

To thrive, institutions need to have a powerful sense of their own identity and purpose such that they can engage with confidence with other organisations and also respond in a timely manner to new requirements with agility.

Internationally many countries have only recently begun to invest significantly in higher education, but the lessons from the case studies presented here may still be applied. New providers must take the opportunity to develop their unique identity from the outset, as without differentiation, universities within emerging HE sectors may quickly find themselves struggling to articulate their offer in a potentially saturated market. New universities do not remain new for long, and so they too must be on the lookout for disruptive entrants to their marketplace as they evolve.

But as global population movement becomes more free-flowing and institutions become increasingly interconnected, we can begin to see higher education as one international network instead of separate national systems. This presents opportunities for HE institutions to build on the hybrid value chain model, with institutions in established HE systems working with newer institutions in countries with relatively young HE systems. The benefits of such a system for collaborative research and the student experience would be clear, but such a system would also help to improve the responsiveness of the sector to changing global markets thanks to shared intelligence, and enhance quality as established institutions share best practice with their newer partner institutions.

In the future global higher education landscape, the winners will be those that focus on their core strengths, develop their distinctiveness and are innovative and bold in facing the future in a post-disruption market space by looking to new models and partnerships.

References

British Council. (2012). *The shape of things to come: Higher education global trends and emerging opportunities to 2020*. London, UK: British Council.

Christensen, C. M. (2012). Disruptive innovation. In M. Soegaard & R. F. Dam (Eds.), *Encyclopedia of human-computer interaction*. Aarhus: The Interaction-Design.org Foundation. Retrieved from http://www.interaction-design.org/encyclopedia/disruptive_innovation.html. Accessed on 4 July 2012.

Drayton, B., & Budinich, V. (2010). *A new alliance for global change. Harvard Business Review Magazine*, September. Harvard University. Retrieved from http://hbr.org/2010/09/a-new-alliance-for-global-change/ar/1. Accessed 30 June 2012.

Kim, W. C., & Mauborgne, R. (2005). *Blue ocean strategy: How to create uncontested market space and make competition irrelevant*. Boston, USA: Harvard Business Press.

OECD. (2011). *Education at a glance 2011: OECD indicators*. London: OECD Publishing.

Smith, S., & Milligan, A. (2011). *Bold: How to be brave in business and win*. London, UK: Kogan Page Ltd.

Times Higher Education. (2012a). *Times Higher Education World University rankings 2011–12*. London, UK: TSL Education Ltd.

Times Higher Education. (2012b). *The* 100 under 50. London, UK: TSL Education Ltd.

Universities UK. (2011). *Driving economic growth*. London, UK: TSL Education Ltd.

Chapter 4.6

Strategic Implications of the New Economy in Regard to Higher Education

Abe Harraf

Higher education has been caught in a paradoxical tangle in recent years. On one hand, the necessary resources to sustain academic quality and improve the educational experiences of students have been drastically trimmed, while on the other, public expectation for a higher rate of graduation, an improved completion rate, and access to a greater number of students has dealt a significant challenge that will require open-minded and adaptable strategies. However, the higher education industry, particularly the public one, has historically been less agile and, according to many observers, resistant to change. Furthermore, the academic world has been inherently adverse to entrepreneurship and does not embrace change comfortably. Meanwhile, the entrepreneurial, for-profit institutions that have emerged in the last decade or two have taken advantage of the lack of agility and higher degree of red tape and regulations that inherently exist in traditional higher education institutions. The newcomers and their thirst for competitive posture to grab a sizeable market share, particularly in off-site and online delivery of courses and degree programmes, have fundamentally altered the once stable and comfortable higher education industry.

The higher cost structure of traditional institutions, coupled with their full-scale student services, tends to alter their competitive position with their non-traditional competitors. What complicates the matter further is the traditional institutions' lack of culture of agility and entrepreneurship that exacerbates their failure to react to the changing dynamic of the higher education industry. Another external force that inhibits the public higher

Going Global: Identifying Trends and Drivers of International Education
Copyright © 2013 by Emerald Group Publishing Limited
All rights of reproduction in any form reserved
ISBN: 978-1-78190-575-3

education institutions from effectively competing is the scrutiny and regulations that are being enforced by legislators and states' higher education authorities. Although most public institutions no longer rely totally on public funds for their operational expenditure, the degree of regulation has not diminished. Rather, in most states the pressure and oversight have escalated as further governmental constraints and limitations are levied on them.

Higher Education at the Crossroads

The challenges encountered by traditional higher education institutions require striking a balance between equally important priorities. These priorities, though equally imperative, must be decided upon if higher education institutions are to strive for financial solvency and operational sustainability. Foremost among them are the balance between cost and quality, stability and change, tradition and innovation, access and retention, credit-bearing education and training, exclusive provider and partnership, education and support service, market niche segmentation and one-size-fits-all strategy, and last but not least between providing collegiate education exclusively and expanding the students' educational horizon beyond the borders of their home state or country's culture. While these priorities are equally vital to the sustainability of the institutions and their operations, addressing the challenge of identifying the most strategic route that is consistent with the mission of the institution for the most part remains unsettled.

The 'new normal' is going to force the institutions to become more open and less parochial in delivering collegiate education. The deregulated market of the higher education industry, where entry to the market is uncontested, necessitates openness to partnerships and alliances. These partnerships should undoubtedly extend to worldwide providers of collegiate education and encourage institutions across the globe to develop practices that promote collaboration and resource sharing. Such collaborative moves by global institutions not only assist them in their cost minimisation strategies but also directly benefit their students. The international experience that could be gained by seamless and transfer-friendly practices by partner institutions across the globe unquestionably enriches the breadth and depth of their collegiate education.

In addition to making hard choices about how to compete, higher education institutions must engage in intentional cultural transformation. Competitive forces stemming from new entrants and providers of substitute services, coupled with the buying power that students and their families are exerting, necessitate a fundamental cultural shift on the part of the institutions. All stakeholders of the institutions, including the administration, faculty, staff and governing boards, must realise that they need to support a common goal of altering the established culture from mostly rigid and adverse to change to one that embraces change and risk-taking practices.

In recognition of the need for a cultural overhaul, institutional stakeholders must take into consideration that the higher education market has become a very congested one, ranging from traditional institutions to corporate, for-profit, and online 'universities'. No longer can short-term solutions overcome the fundamental paradigm shift that institutions must navigate through. 'After centuries of excellence and decades of cyclical recessions, higher education has developed some bad habits. When facing budget shortfalls, colleges and universities have not always adequately addressed underlying cost drivers and have instead pursued short-term solutions' (Lumina Foundation, 2010).

Strategies for the 'New Normal'

The 'new normal' and the resulting challenges that confront higher education institutions and their leadership require employing sound and timely strategies that could not only help in weathering the current turbulent economic times but also sustain the institution for the long haul. The necessary cultural shift that could alter the traditional model of managing higher education institutions should emphasise intentional multi-pronged strategies that address cost, quality, innovation, agility, entrepreneurship and partnership. At the core of these sweeping changes, designing the seamless transfer of credits and joint degree programmes between domestic and global institutions must be given utmost priority. A distributive model of delivering a degree programme where institutions across the globe can collaborate and share their resources could undoubtedly enrich the educational experience of students and lessen the cost of delivering the same degree programme exclusively.

Similarly, outsourcing non-core activities and processes to trim the cost of managing an educational enterprise, coupled with embracing technology as a medium of educational delivery could reduce the inflationary pressure of the escalating cost of higher education tuition. Adapting to the use of web-based instructional models where online course delivery and use of social media could markedly adjust the cost structure in favour of institutions. Demand for competitive and reduced tuition fees is increasing as students and their families are becoming much more sophisticated in searching for discounted tuition, when institutions are vying for increased enrolment by offering various financial and in-kind aids to lure students. Moreover, embracing technology in delivering courses and degree programmes is not only cost-effective but it is in concert with the technologically inclined and savvy students and their expectations.

Using technology to deliver 2 + 2 degree programmes, where half of the students' experience could include attending another institution offers a viable alternative to physically bound and financially strapped students, who otherwise could not expand their educational breadth by taking advantage of in-person attendance. Providing such an experience with international institutions provides even further richness to the preparation of students for entering an increasingly global marketplace.

Designing innovative strategies where cost effectiveness is coupled with enriching the educational experience of students to become global citizens could assist institutions in strategically positioning themselves for a permanently altered landscape of the higher education industry.

Strategic Issues to Consider

The ability of higher education institutions to adjust their strategies to operate within an environment of shrinking resources, higher expectations and renewed scrutiny will determine how well they can compete and garner adequate support from their key stakeholders. Strategic issues that leadership of the institutions and their governing boards should consider are how to transform their institution into one of agility and responsiveness. They should contemplate how they can drive their institutions to embrace partnerships with other institutions on course and degree programme delivery, particularly the foreign ones. 'To prepare our students for this changing world, to enhance and advance discovery, to carry out our mission of engagement, and to maintain our competitive edge, our colleges and universities must make global competency and international involvement, in its many different forms, important components of their strategic plans, policies and practices' (National Association of State Universities and Land-Grant Colleges, 2007). They should espouse the importance of embracing a borderless world by internationalising their curriculum through the inclusion of foreign languages, area and country studies, study abroad, joint degree programmes, faculty and student exchanges, training their students in cultural appreciation, global insight, and embracing diversity.

Equally important is to ensure that outsourcing, alliances and partnerships do not erode their institutional identity and sense of distinctiveness. Rather, it is very plausible that striking strategic relationships with global institutions that fit with the culture of both institutions could indeed generate distinction and differentiate them from their competitors. Developing unique and value-added partnerships, particularly with reputable foreign institutions, could also afford partner institutions a significant advantage, resulting in reducing the price sensitivity of students, enabling the institutions to exert tuition power over their competitors.

Conclusion

Higher education institutions should view the economic crisis as an opportunity to transform their institutions into agile, proactive and responsive entities with expanding global reach. However, their response to the 'new normal' in higher education funding and internationalisation has been contrary to their strategic interest. In its most recent global survey report on the internationalisation of higher education, the International Association of Universities, among its many findings, reports that 'The economic crisis is having a marked impact on internationalization, with lack of funding seen by HEIs worldwide as the most important internal and external barrier to internationalization' (International Association of Universities, 2010). While the study underscores the strategic importance of the institutional leaders, the economic conditions, and consequent shrinking of resources force them to trim their internationalisation pursuits. 'Internationalization is seen as more central to institution's future planning, and is of greater and growing importance to HEI leaders, than ever before' (International Association of Universities, 2010). Building strategic alliances and partnerships to simultaneously share costs and prepare their students for a global world is an intentional strategy that tends to afford the institutions an opportunity to fend off competition and sustain their operations in the ever-changing funding landscape.

References

International Association of Universities. (2010). *Internationalization of higher education: Global trend regional perspectives – the IAU 3rd Global survey report.* Paris, France: International Association of Universities.
Lumina Foundation. (2010). *Navigating the new normal.* Indianapolis, Indiana: Lumina Foundation.
National Association of State Universities and Land-Grant Colleges. (2007). *A national action agenda for internationalizing higher education.* Washington DC: National Association of State Universities and Land-Grant Colleges.

Chapter 4.7

Building Bricks of a New Knowledge World Order? Implications of the Knowledge Revolution for Building Winning Strategies in Higher Education

Ingo Rollwagen

The Predictability of the Future and the Relevance of Foresight

Structural changes are occurring in business activities in general as well as in research, (higher) education and learning.[1] For every higher education institution, business organisation — whether transnational large company or SME — or governmental body, the question of how to respond to the emerging challenges caused by structural changes is one of the most important issues. Faced with these tremendous, fast-moving changes, decision makers require strategic foresight. Given the complexity and the dynamics of highly interwoven systems, future developments cannot be predicted. But planning can help decision makers to learn more about the

---

1. In a recent scenario study of the European Commission projecting economic growth, the redistribution of economic power at the world level is impressive in all scenarios. While in 2010 the EU accounts for 29 per cent of the world GDP, with the United States at 26 per cent, Japan at 9 per cent and China at 8 per cent, in one scenario ('Nobody cares'), by 2030 the United States overtakes the EU (23 and 22 per cent respectively), while China and India double their share (18 and 5 per cent respectively in 2030), and Japan remains constant at 7 per cent of the world economy (European Commission, 2011, p. 14).

Going Global: Identifying Trends and Drivers of International Education
Copyright © 2013 by Emerald Group Publishing Limited
All rights of reproduction in any form reserved
ISBN: 978-1-78190-575-3

present, to validate information, to construct certain frames of reference and to reflect upon their own position and potential of agency given certain possibility spaces (Miller, 2007). In that vein, this paper looks at developments based on and informed by qualitative and quantitative data. This view does not claim to fully cover all developments. It is meant as an inspiration and information to encourage decision makers to think about the implications and thus shape the future as it unfolds.

Revisiting Structural Changes and the Emerging Knowledge Economy

More Knowledge Is Produced by Increasing Investment...

Discussions on future structural, technological, economic and societal transformations are ongoing. In this structural change,[2] the huge investments that have been made — and will be made — by several developed, emerging market economies — particularly Asian nations,[3] are fuelling the global race for excellence and the emergence of the global knowledge economy (Rollwagen & Renkin, 2012). There is a more competitive attitude among different nations and players in the worldwide production of knowledge. In this race, the developed countries remain heavyweights in terms of investment in research and development. The United States invests by far the most in research and development: the total spent in 2007 was US$397 billion. In Japan, investment totalled US$214 billion and in Germany some US$63 billion in the same year. By comparison, R&D spending in the much-discussed BRIC countries remains low: US$42 billion in China, US$11 billion in Brazil and US$7 billion in Russia. However, their percentage increase in spending on R&D has rocketed, especially in China: up 615 per cent since 1996. Brazil's increase is 110 per cent; India's 156 per cent and Russia's 106 per cent since 1966, suggesting that the BRICs are also banking on growth through knowledge production (Rollwagen & Renkin, 2012, p. 4).

---

2. For an overview of dynamics in structural change please refer to 'DBR's dynamics map' (Deutsche Bank Research, 2007).
3. Global R&D expenditure almost doubled in real terms from 1993 to 2009 (OECD, 2011, 2012; Rollwagen, & Renkin 2012).

...*By More (Highly) Educated People*

The dynamics of the number of highly educated people and researchers worldwide provide another facet of the emerging knowledge world order. As the UNESCO Science Report of 2010 shows, the number of researchers worldwide has been steadily increasing since 2000. Although developed countries still account for the majority of researchers (with slightly over 60 per cent of the world's share), some developing countries — especially China — have also been starting to structure their knowledge bases more thoroughly by investing in researchers (UNESCO, 2011).[4] Apart from choosing research as a field of occupation, a growing number of individuals worldwide are engaging more actively in increasing their competencies by, for example, learning to live and work in a culture other than their own. International student mobility figures show that more people set out to study and engage in knowledge-intensive activities (British Council, 2012) than at the beginning of the new century. We are thus at the beginning of a new era of globalisation, in which more and more highly educated people are moving around the globe, adding up to the phenomenon often referred to as 'brain circulation' (UNESCO, 2011, p. 7).

...*And More Diverse Players*

Scrutinising these developments further in order to catch a glimpse of the future knowledge world order, another pattern is evident: An increasing number of strategically oriented global and local actors — governments and multinational companies increasingly also from emerging markets,[5] public research organisations (PROs) and integrated education (technology) providers — shape the things to come. They not only produce knowledge on a large scale,[6] but they have also been intensifying the codification activities of knowledge: they have been getting more active in filing for patents, industrial designs and copyrights in recent

---

4. China is on the verge of overtaking both the United States and the EU in terms of sheer numbers of researchers. These three giants each represent about 20 per cent of the world's stock of researchers (UNESCO, 2011, p. 6).
5. The trend to more private players from emerging markets shows in the number of Global Fortune 500 companies from emerging markets: while in 2005, only 16 Chinese companies have made it up there, in 2011, there were 61 Chinese companies in the Global Fortune 500 index.
6. The output of especially China but also South Korea of scientific publications has been growing at an enormous pace in the last years (OECD, 2011; UNESCO, 2011).

years.[7] China in particular is producing more patents, having increased its share of global patent filings from 0.3 per cent to 3.5 per cent between 1996 and 2007. Between 1996 and 2007 India increased its share of global patent filings from 0.1 per cent to 0.7 per cent, and Brazil from 0.1 per cent to 0.3 per cent. However, despite the growth in the BRIC countries, the industrial nations remain undisputed leaders in their role as innovation drivers: in 2007, 28 per cent of all global patent applications filed were from the United States, 17 per cent from Japan and 15 per cent from Germany (Rollwagen & Renkin, 2012, p. 4).

Looking more closely at patents, in order to identify the most relevant players, it becomes apparent that higher education institutions and PROs have been starting to play a more prominent role in the emerging global knowledge economy. Fulfilling their mission to do both basic and applied research and to educate, they account for a substantial share of total R&D spending (WIPO, 2011, p. 140). When it comes to patenting activity, there has been a marked increase in patent applications by universities and PROs — both in absolute terms and as a share of total patents filed (WIPO, 2011, p. 147). Since 1979, the number of international patent applications filed by universities and PROs has been steadily increasing. The new knowledge world order is thus increasingly also being shaped at the moment by PROs and research-intensive universities, who are successfully combining knowledge production, research and education with application and product-oriented work.[8]

More Collaborative Knowledge Production on the Basis of Advanced IT

More players are collaborating intensely, intra-regionally and internationally to produce knowledge. The co-operation between different firms and between firms and the public sector is increasing: international and domestic co-authorship is on the rise, R&D outsourcing is increasing (also to PROs), as is the number of patent co-inventors (WIPO, 2011, pp. 44–45). Studies show that with advances in information and communication technologies, we are entering a phase of more structured global collaboration based on global production and innovation networks (Ernst, 2005, 2009). As the

---

7. Taking a longer view, data from the World Intellectual Property Organization shows that the demand for patents alone has risen from 800,000 applications worldwide in the early 1980s to 1.8 million in 2009 (WIPO, 2012, pp. 8–9).
8. An example of this trend is the German Fraunhofer Gesellschaft.

knowledge economy gains ground, partners from different sectors and countries co-operate and learn from each other in the search for the most attractive products for their clients. In this way different players can make use of more advanced information and communication technologies, making knowledge of existing patents more accessible, and facilitating discussion and more structured forms of collaboration on products — co-designing, co-engineering and co-working. As a result, a larger number of players can interact on a 'glocal' — global and local — basis, enabled by web-based forms of communication.

More Glocally Distributed Knowledge Production

Looking more closely at this interaction in global production and innovation networks, and at the regional distribution of patent applications, the emerging global knowledge economy can be seen to be even more locally based than before. This means that the existing hot spots of knowledge production (OECD, 2012), which have been important in the past, will be important centres in the years to come as the knowledge economy develops. But as in every great transformation, new centres of glocal production of knowledge and value-creation can also be seen. For example, from 1999 to 2009 the Chinese Shenzhen/Guangdong region has now undisputedly become one of the centres of knowledge production and knowledge-based business activities in China (WIPO, 2011). There are a number of different examples of new centres and 'hubs' of knowledge production, education and business activity throughout the world.[9] These centres are prospering because higher education institutions, with the help of regional govern-ments, are pioneering new ideas and integrating them into their unique profiles as players in global production and innovation networks, thus getting more closely associated with other centres of knowledge- and value-creation all over the world.

More Project-Based Knowledge Production

Trying to better understand the pattern of more glocal and collaborative knowledge production and value-creation and looking at how PROs or

---

9. One of the prominent examples of the 'hub'-strategy is Singapore, which has been developing flagship institutions especially in biotech based on strong (also financial) commitment of Singaporean government and private players (Royal Society, 2011).

research-intensive universities operate, it is seen that the knowledge economy is based on the project-economy approaches of several players — higher education institutions, PROs, companies, governments and municipalities, public and private organisations and even societal players (Rollwagen, 2010).[10] On the basis of more intense partnerships and project-based collaboration these players are able to share resources (e.g. using cloud-based services; co-financed by partners from industry) and thus shape developments.

More Complex, Specialised, Hybrid Knowledge Production

This project-based form of knowledge production is also gaining ground in the emerging knowledge economy because products and service solutions are getting more complex and knowledge-intensive. As data from the OECD shows, along with changes in the global manufacturing, the share of service activities necessary for manufacturing has increased in recent years. In 2008, services-related employees accounted for about 35 per cent of employees in manufacturing in the OECD area (OECD, 2012). This is a clear indication that today complex technological products can be characterised as technological configurations made up of different techno-logical and service components. These technological configurations, like integrated smart grids or home solutions can only result from project-based collaboration. As in the case of the different demonstration projects of smart home solutions in Germany (Karlsruhe, Aachen, Berlin) or the Netherlands (Eindhoven), private sector players, together with govern-ments and higher education and PROs, work together to provide single components, services or research to be able to co-create service solutions that are attractive for customers. Due to increasing knowledge-intensity in nearly all fields of manufacturing, production and services, the focus is on producing specialised knowledge which can then be combined and applied to provide complex, technological, hybrid products, smart manufacturing and services that are easy-to-use for different customer groups. This trend towards more intensive products is also reflected in the increasing number of international registrations for industrial designs through the Hague system (WIPO, 2011, p. 54).

---

10. As one indication for the increasing orientations of higher education institutions on 'project-economy approaches', analyses show that the share of third-party funds has become an important pillar of higher education institutions' financial base, sometimes accounting for over 25 per cent of resources (Rollwagen, 2010).

More Marketable Knowledge (As Direct Value Creation)

But it is not only the relevance of knowledge for creating and marketing new products that is increasing. More refined statistical data on services trade also shows that knowledge slowly but surely is becoming marketable. In financial terms, international royalties and licensing fee receipts increased from US$2.8 billion in 1970 to US$27 billion in 1990, and to approximately US$180 billion in 2009 — outpacing growth in global GDP (WIPO, 2012, pp. 60–65). Other statistics also show that some countries are profiting from knowledge as a marketable commodity. Germany, for example, has developed from an importer of knowledge to an exporter of knowledge, whereas other nations, building their own position in the knowledge economy, like the Republic of South Korea, are still net importers of knowledge (United Nations Service Trade Statistics Database, 2010), although they are world-leaders in other matters, for example in the production of displays as in South Korea.

A Revolution in Knowledge — Implications for the Knowledge World Order

Taking these different trends into account, we are definitely seeing the emergence of a new 'knowledge world order', which will still be structured not only by today's leading science nations but also be increasingly by other nations, PROs and integrated education providers. Today the United States leads the world in research, producing 20 per cent of the world's authorship of research papers, and the United Kingdom, Japan, Germany and France also command strong positions. However, the traditional scientific leaders are gradually losing their 'share' of published articles. Meanwhile, China and India are gaining ground as are South Korea, Brazil, Turkey, Iran, South-East Asian nations such as Singapore, Thailand and Malaysia, and European nations such as Austria, Greece and Portugal (Royal Society, 2011, p. 16). Whether these nations capitalise on their knowledge remains to be seen, but countries like China, India, Indonesia and the Philippines (McArthur, 2012) and also South Africa, Singapore, Turkey, Malaysia, Brazil, Qatar and others will profit much more from the advances in the information technology infrastructures that are increasing student mobility, enhanced brain circulation and the online provision of educational modules and knowledge.

Taking into account the global race for excellence and skilled labour, different players and alliances (based on strategic cross-border partnering of prestigious players and strategic hubs), the new knowledge world order will also be characterised by an era of international collaboration between colleges and universities (IIE, 2012, p. xxii) and more, new centres[11] with global knowledge- and value-creation networks (McKinsey Global Institute, 2012) and clusters as hubs of invention and/or production. These new centres and networks will compete rather fiercely on the basis of different frameworks for financing and codifying knowledge and platforms for computing data (Royal Society, 2011).

In the new knowledge world order, PROs, higher education institutions or dedicated knowledge providers will compete primarily on the basis of designing and marketing complex knowledge products (e.g. commented and detailed patent databases, construction plans in (electrical) engineering or developer tools) and providing more pervasive (educational) content on various platforms. For example, the Open University already successfully uses electronic platforms to disseminate knowledge and educational modules internationally, blending local and online/virtual learning experiences for young and adult learners.[12] This pervasive content will be nurtured by mobile researchers, experts and students working together from different regions and cities in different institutional contexts, co-financed by several players all over the world.

Winning Strategies in the New Knowledge World-Order: Understanding Knowledge and the Power of Projects

In this new knowledge world order those players, cities and regions that are able to adequately transform knowledge into new (knowledge) products, solutions and brands for local and global markets will thrive. In international education particularly, the competition for personalised knowledge products, or so-called flexible, competence-based, learning solutions, will intensify in the wake of new generations of learners being internationally very mobile and being used to pursuing electronic infrastructures for accessing (educational) content of interest.

Against the background of more pronounced brain circulation and more international student mobility, focused in some hubs and centres of activity around the globe, higher education organisations will have to redefine their information technology, regional and global strategies.

---

11. As the Royal Society report shows, in most countries there is a degree of concentration of research activity in particular places (Royal Society, 2011).

12. In the case of Open University the platform being used is itunesU with more than 50 million downloads of course materials in only three years (from 2009 to 2012).

By defining and planning projects and programmes with other (private and public sector) players, higher education institutions can be in the vanguard of the emerging knowledge economy. Using the potential of advanced information and communication technologies for the next generations of students to deliver smart, personalised combinations of lectures, seminars, self-learning and immersive educational experiences on the basis of modified learning management systems (Quillen, 2012) and to enable students who want to improve their skills, will be key to succeeding in the intensifying global knowledge-based competition for higher education institutions, private sector players and regions.

The new knowledge world order will also mean going beyond the establishment of international branch campuses (Lawton & Katsomitros, 2012) and joint- and dual-degree programmes (IIE, 2011). With the number of students enrolled in higher education around the globe forecast to more than double — to 262 million — by 2025 and the number of students seeking study abroad possibly rising to 8 million — nearly three times more than today (Davis & Mackintosh, 2012), collaborative ways of designing curricula will become more prominent. Building education and knowledge products and brands in certain regions seems to be mostly adequate, following the examples of other pioneering organisations (IIE, 2012). Developing and experimenting with technologies together with private sector players to provide local solutions to water, energy, food, housing and mobility challenges as well as solutions in distance-, electronic and blended learning hold great potential.

To succeed in the new knowledge world order, higher education institutions will have to design sound project and partnering[13] strategies and manage the complex relationship between partners, providers (of technology, customer knowledge) and governments. In this context, governments and organisations in developed countries will have to increasingly co-operate on a bi-, tri- and multilateral basis with aspiring institutions (like the research-intensive universities founded in the last 50 years in other developed countries and emerging markets, as well as the new multinational companies). Of utmost importance in this is the design of new frameworks to support and fund these initiatives to pave the way for more people to attain higher education and increase their individual capabilities.

Working on sustainable social business models which incorporate public and private players and which are based on new forms of impact investments and new forms of knowledge transfer and export specialisation

---

13. For an overview of different advice and case studies on how to manage international partnerships see Institute of International Education (2012).

may help to spur science-to-business activities in many world regions. In this vein, setting up more internationally, nationally and regionally integrated explorative development and implementation projects especially for 'mega-cities', in line with more integrative regional and structural policy of certain political actors like the European Union, triggered in collaboration with other states, seems to be important.

Accompanying that, most PROs and higher education institutions also need to work more thoroughly on overarching intellectual property management strategies. With the new knowledge order being structured by often-competing regulatory frameworks for granting intellectual property rights and by an increasing relevance of revenues from licensing fees in the future, knowledge and education players have to rethink their standardisation strategies. Apart from protecting their ideational impulses on the basis of patents, copyrights and industrial designs, co-designing and co-working with companies on industry standards and technical norms may help knowledge-intensive players to succeed in the future. Patenting and standardisation are two sides of the same coin. With knowledge and property rights becoming a commodity and being traded on the basis of several platforms and research findings commissioned by public actors being put under an 'open access' regime, PROs and research-intensive universities will have to think about ways to protect and commercialise their knowledge-validation activities in a subtle way. Working on standards and technical norms for future smart energy solutions thus holds the potential to help sound technical solutions to succeed, and so for partially public-funded players to provide a valid contribution to technological progress in society.

With the intensifying competition for skilled labour and prospective talented students, the challenge for research and knowledge-intensive organisations also lies in enriching the perspectives for their scientists, faculty and employees. Being faced with more competition, other emerging players, more structured brain circulation and the mobility of highly qualified people, talent development, the support of promoters in university and hiring leading experts from outside higher education and research institutions seem to be the key to success.

In conclusion, being more open — yet structured — in financing and managing knowledge-based projects and partnerships, with an increasing number of heterogeneous actors worldwide, managing intellectual property, design and branding as well as the provision of knowledge products and educational modules based on electronic platforms (more integrated information technology infrastructure management) with more talent development for would-be scientists seem to be the order of the day to go global and to be able to shape the emerging knowledge world order in a more fair and equitable way.

References

British Council. (2012). *The shape of things to come: Higher education global trends and emerging opportunities to 2020* (J. Ball & J. Ilieva, Eds.). Retrieved from http:// ihe.britishcouncil.org/educationintelligence/shape-of-things-to-come. Accessed on 30 June 2012.

Davis, D., & Mackintosh, B. (2012). *Making a difference: Australian International Education.* Sydney: University of New South Wales Press.

Deutsche Bank Research. (2007). *Germany 2020 — New challenges for a land on expedition* (J. Hofmann, I. Rollwagen, & S. Schneider, Eds.). Retrieved from www.dbresearch.de. Accessed on 30 June 2012.

Ernst, D. (2005). The new mobility of knowledge: Digital information systems and global flagship networks. In R. Latham & S. Sassen (Eds.), *Digital formations: IT and new architectures in the global realm* (pp. 89–114). Princeton, NJ: Princeton University Press.

Ernst, D. (2009). A new geography of knowledge in the electronics industry? Asia's role in global innovation networks. *Policy Studies, 54,* Retrieved from www.east westcenter.org/fileadmin/stored/pdfs/ps054_2.pdf. Accessed on 30 June 2012.

European Commission. (2011). *Global Europe 2050: Report summary.* Brussels: European Commission. Retrieved from http://ec.europa.eu/research/social-sciences/ fwl-experts-groups_en.html. Accessed on 15 August 2012.

Institute of International Education. (2011). *Joint and double degree programs in the global context. Report on an international survey* (D. Obst, M. Kuder, & C. Banks, Eds.). Paris: Institute of International Education.

Institute of International Education. (2012). *Developing strategic international partnerships. Models for initiating and sustaining innovative institutional linkages* (S. Buck Sutton & D. Obst, Eds.). Paris: Institute of International Education.

Lawton, W., & Katsomitros, A. (2012). *International branch campuses: Data and developments.* London: The Observatory on Borderless Higher Education.

McArthur, J. (2012). From physical BRICS to digital CHIIPs. Retrieved from www.brookings.edu. Accessed on 30 June 2012.

McKinsey Global Institute. (2012). *Urban world: Cities and the rise of the consuming class* (R. Dobbs, Ed.). Retrieved from http://www.mckinsey.com/insights/mgi. Accessed on 1 August 2012.

Miller, R. (2007). Futures literacy: A hybrid strategic scenario method. *Futures, 39*(4), 341–362.

OECD. (2011). *OECD science, technology and industry outlook 2010.* Paris: OECD.

OECD. (2012). *OECD science, technology and industry scoreboard 2011: Innovation and growth in knowledge economies.* Paris: OECD.

Quillen, I. (2012, 13 June). New companies seek competitive edge in LMS market. *Education Week, 5*(3), 4, 32, 34, 36. Retrieved from www.edweek.org. Accessed on 30 June 2012.

Rollwagen, I. (2010). Project economy approaches for higher education: Diversifying the revenue base of German universities. *Higher education management and policy, 22*(3). (Paris).

Rollwagen, I., & Renkin, T. (2012). *The global race for excellence and skilled labor. A status report*. Deutsche Bank Research. Frankfurt. Retrieved from www.dbresearch.de. Accessed on 30 June 2012.

The Royal Society. (2011). *Knowledge, networks and nations: Global scientific collaboration in the 21st century*. RS Policy document 03/11. London.

UNESCO. (2011). *UNESCO science report 2010: The current status of science around the world* (S. Schneegans, Ed.). Paris: United Nations Educational Scientific and Cultural Organization. Retrieved from www.unesco.org. Accessed on 30 June 2012.

United Nations Service Trade Statistics Database. (2010). *Trade in other royalties and license fees*. Available from United Nations Service Trade Statistics Database under 'selected services'. Retrieved from https://unstats.un.org/unsd/servicetrade/default.aspx

World Intellectual Property Organization. (2011). *Patent applications by region*. Available from WIPO Statistics Database. Retrieved from www.wipo.org

World Intellectual Property Organization (2012). *World intellectual property report 2011: The changing face of innovation*. Geneva: WIPO Economics & Statistics Series.

Chapter 4.8

Responses to the British Council's *The Shape of Things to Come: Higher Education Global Trends and Emerging Opportunities to 2020*

Chiao-Ling Chien

Globalisation has influenced the higher education sector profoundly. The way that different types of actors respond to globalisation has evolved so fast, it is difficult to forecast the shape of future higher education by reviewing past performance and settings. That said, several widespread trends have been identified, of which some will likely continue and even intensify. These trends include the mobility of people, programmes and institutions; the rising prominence of research capacity and collaborative research; and interconnected higher education sector globally and regionally (e.g. see Altbach, Reisberg, & Rumbley, 2009; Dale & Robertson, 2002; de Wit, 2008b; Marginson, 2006; Salmi, 2012; Schofer & Meyer, 2005).

The British Council's newly released report, titled *The Shape of Things to Come: Higher Education Global Trends and Emerging Opportunities to 2020* is informative on emerging trends in higher education. Specifically, the report identifies opportunities for international educators to engage in three aspects: direct student recruitment; transnational education; and research co-operation. It sheds some light on the future shape of the tertiary education sector and its growing international dimension.

This paper serves two purposes: one is to respond to the British Council's international student forecast and opportunities for global engagement; the

Going Global: Identifying Trends and Drivers of International Education
Copyright © 2013 by Emerald Group Publishing Limited
All rights of reproduction in any form reserved
ISBN: 978-1-78190-575-3

other is to provide information about the state of international data collection on student mobility and data quality. In responding to findings disclosed in that report, I further elaborate on the notion of opportunities by asking: 'Whose opportunities and towards what ends?'; 'Who will be key actors in cross-border higher education?'; and 'How do we know where these opportunities and changes are taking place?'

I will begin by identifying and critically analysing some assumptions in the British Council's methodology in student forecast. Then, I continue to examine a shift in student subject choices and demand, and discuss factors that are overlooked in the British Council's report, followed by analysing data issues and concluding remarks.

Changing Dynamics and the Challenges of Student Mobility

Before addressing the assumptions in the British Council's report, it is worth noting that emerging developments in cross-border higher education present a challenge to measuring student mobility. Students nowadays have various options to access overseas higher education. For instance, partnerships between institutions allow students to take courses from two or more universities across nations (e.g. joint and dual degree programmes). Moreover, other than traditional hot spots (e.g. the United States and Western European countries) of overseas education, students now have a wide range of destinations (e.g. Australia, Canada, China, Dubai, Malaysia or Singapore). In addition, without travelling abroad, students can obtain a degree from foreign universities' international branch campuses that are set up in students' home countries.

Heterogeneity in Student Mobility

Cross-border student mobility is more complex and nuanced than often acknowledged. For example, not all students study abroad to obtain a diploma in their host institutions (i.e. degree mobility[1]). A large number of students study abroad in the framework of ongoing studies at the home institution for the purpose of gaining academic credits from the host

---

1. Diploma/degree mobility aims at the acquisition of a degree or certificate in the country of destination, and programmes principally last a period of at least one year (UOE, 2012).

institution (i.e. credit mobility[2]) (Teichler, Ferencz, Wächter, Rumbley, & Bürger, 2011). Because policy implications for different types of mobility vary, it is important to clarify these two distinct groups within international student population.

Given the absence of credit mobility statistics gathered at the international level, the British Council's analysis is limited to degree mobility. The British Council assumes that the key determinants of demand for overseas tertiary education will be: the tertiary age (18–22) population, a combination of economic factors (including national economic growth, GDP per capita and household income) and domestic higher education capacity. Its analysis builds on aggregate administrative data on tertiary enrolment in each country, inbound and outbound degree mobile students, mainly coming from joint data collection by the UNESCO Institute for Statistics (UIS), Organisation for Economic Co-operation and Development (OECD) and the Statistical Office of the European Communities (Eurostat) (hereafter called UOE).

Expansion of Secondary Education Drives Demand for Tertiary Education

Demand for tertiary education in the next decade is more likely to be driven by the growth of secondary graduates (Schofer & Meyer, 2005) than by the 18- to 22-year-old population; the latter is analysed as a key determinant in the British Council's model. This argument is logically true because limited secondary graduates (i.e. appropriate candidates for higher education) would constrain tertiary demand, even in countries with a large 18- to 22-year-old population.

Besides secondary education, Schofer and Meyer (2005) found that countries with strong links to the international system yield faster expansion of higher education. This phenomenon is relevant to the role of international or regional non-governmental organisations in educational development, which will be discussed shortly.

A Shift in Subject Choice and Demand by International Students

Shifting patterns in subject choice may well affect demand in ways that are not included in the British Council's forecasting model. UNESCO statistics

---

2. Credit mobility aims at getting credits. After the mobility phase, students return to their home institutions to complete their studies. This kind of mobility usually involves a period abroad of less than one year (Teichler et al., 2011).

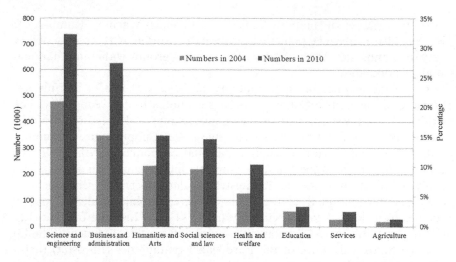

Figure 1: Number and distribution of internationally mobile students by field of study, 2004 and 2010. *Note:* Data analysis is based on 35 OECD countries and EU counties where such information is collected. *Source:* UNESCO Institute for Statistics database.

show that international students in business and administration programmes[3] represented the largest group among international students worldwide (26 per cent) in 2010. Two broad fields — science and engineering[4] — also attracted a high number of international students (30 per cent). By contrast, relatively small numbers of international students studied in education, services and agriculture fields (see Figure 1). When comparing to 2004,[5] there has been a notable increase in international students in certain fields: business and administration, health, science and engineering, and social sciences.[6]

A shift in subject choices by international students comes from the interaction of push and pull forces. These forces can be understood by using science and engineering programmes as an example. Currently, over

---

3. Business and Administration is actually a sub-category of Social Science, Business and Law, which is one of the eight broad fields of education classified by the International Standard Classification of Education 1997 (UNESCO-UIS, 2012b).
4. Science includes the following sub-fields: life sciences, physical sciences, mathematics and statistics, and computing. Engineering includes the following sub-fields: engineering and engineering trades, manufacturing and processing, and architecture and building.
5. Since 2004, UOE has started to gather information on international students by field and type of educational programmes.
6. See the difference in the length of bars for 2004 and 2010 (Figure 1).

738,000 international students worldwide are enrolled in science and engineering programmes (and this group of students will likely to grow in the next decade). On the one hand, high-quality science and technology education at the tertiary level requires well-equipped laboratories, modern libraries and qualified professors and researchers which constitute the minimum requirements of a scientific infrastructure. With scarce funds in developing countries, such investment is difficult. Consequently, the unmet demand for university science and engineering education in students' home countries may stimulate students to study abroad.

On the other hand, the increasing demand for science and engineering education appears to be embraced by host countries or institutions that look for students to fill university places. For instance, Europe's aging population and a shortage of students, especially in the sciences, contribute to a strong trend for European countries to admit students from developing countries who cannot be absorbed by institutions at home (de Wit, 2008a).

Whose Opportunities, Towards What Ends?

Universities' motivation behind their global engagement matters to the outcomes of international higher education. The example of increasing demand for science and engineering education signals opportunities for direct recruitment. However, before universities formulate international strategies, it is worth asking 'whose opportunities and towards what ends?' 'Is the goal for competition for talents, revenue generation, campus diversity to enhance intercultural and international competence, or capacity building?' Many European countries' foreign policies are aligned with the goals of capacity-building activities within the higher education sector in developing countries (Altbach et al., 2009). Currently, a subject that needs immediate attention from the broader international community is teacher training programmes for capacity building. According to UNESCO, 58 countries face a moderate or severe shortage of teachers in primary education, which represents an important barrier to the achievement of the goal of universal primary education by 2015 (UNESCO-UIS, 2012a). Assisting countries to find solutions to teacher shortage problems can be one relevant opportunity for global engagement.

Identifying Actors in the Global Arena

When looking for opportunities for global engagement, it is important to identify key actors in the global arena of higher education. Nation states, analysed in the British Council's report, are certainly key actors because their legal framework (e.g. student visa) and policies on education and research and development (R&D) play a role in internationalising higher education. However, the British Council does not take into account that regional organisations and universities with global ambitions are getting increasingly influential in promoting mobility and international partnership, and in redirecting the movement of international students.

Regional Organisations

Regional organisations are increasingly shaping globally structured agendas for education and leading to a convergence of education systems or policies within their own regions (Dale & Robertson, 2002). One clear example is the Bologna Process and Lisbon Strategy initiated by the European Union (EU) in creating European Higher Education Area, aiming to ensure more comparable, compatible and coherent systems of higher education in Europe (de Wit, 2008a). The concept of regional focus in Europe seems to become 'the key point of reference for regionalization efforts' to other parts of the world (Altbach et al., 2009, p. 28). In sub-Saharan Africa, for instance, the Southern Africa Development Community (SADC) included student and staff mobility in its 1997 *Protocol on Education and Training*. SADC specifically recommended that higher education institutions in its member states reserve at least five per cent of their admissions for students from other SADC countries. SADC's efforts are reflected in a high percentage of SADC mobile students staying within their own region (50 per cent) (Chien & Chiteng, 2011). Similarly, Southeast Asian countries' Regional Centre for Higher Education and Development (SEAMEO RIHED), and the Latin American and Caribbean Higher Education Area (ENLACES) initiatives are both moving towards regional integration (Altbach et al., 2009).

   A recent empirical study adopting a network analysis found that indeed intra-regional student mobility has increased, and that there is a strong connection between regional ties (i.e. nation-states' membership in international governmental organisations) and growth in student flows (Shields, Forthcoming, 2013). Figure 2 shows the proportions of mobile students who study within their region of origin.

Universities

The competition for international students between universities, another key actor in the global arena, is no less than that between countries. Particularly,

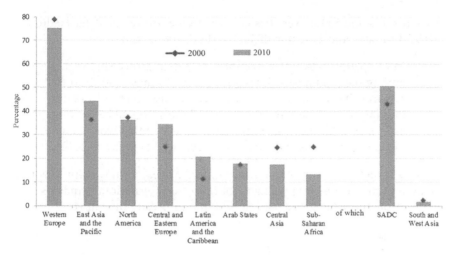

Figure 2: Percentage of internationally mobile students who studied in countries within their region of origin, 2000 and 2010. *Note:* Internationally mobile students not specified by country of origin are excluded. They account 13 per cent of the estimated global figure (3.6 million) in 2010. Countries that host large numbers of mobile students yet did not specify students' country of origin include China (host 2.0 per cent of total mobile students globally), Egypt (1.4 per cent), Singapore (1.4 per cent), United Arab Emirates (1 per cent) and Lebanon (0.9 per cent). *Source:* UNESCO Institute for Statistics.

the rankings of universities worldwide has fuelled competition between universities and provided high-achieving institutions opportunities to outdo local competitors and move up the national hierarchy through global initiatives (Marginson & McBurnie, 2004). The ability to attract, recruit and retain excellent academics (e.g. students, researchers and faculty) is identified as a key factor in becoming a top research university (Hazelkorn, 2008; Salmi, 2012). Therefore, competition between universities may affect student mobility.

Heterogeneity within countries is also relevant to institutional status. For instance, many universities in Asia are eager to become, and some of them have attained, world-class university status (Salmi, 2012). The Global Research Benchmarking System (GRBS)[7] highlights niche research

---

7. www.researchbenchmarking.org

strengths of some 500 universities in Asia Pacific. Professor Peter Haddawy, GRBS Founder and Director of UNU-IIST, commented that:

> Many people may not know that Universiti Sains Malaysia is among the top universities worldwide in Biomass and Biofuels research. This kind of information can be useful to universities looking for partners for research collaboration since looking at only the big flagship universities in a country would miss out on some focused centers of excellence. (Haddawy, 2012)

Indeed, high-achieving universities appear appealing to institutions that seek international research partners, but also to international students who desire to pursue a higher education diploma in prestigious universities.

Data Demand, Availability and Quality

There is considerable data demand to capture new developments in cross-border higher education with empirical evidence. In most cases, developments have evolved at a much faster pace than data collection (Teichler et al., 2011). Currently, other than the mobility of tertiary students and doctorate holders, data on the mobility of academic staff, educational programmes and institutions have not been gathered at the international level.

Statistical data on student mobility comes from three data collection instruments: UOE Data Collection, WEI Data Collection and Questionnaire on Statistics of Tertiary Education; the first involves a joint effort among three organisations: UIS, OECD and Eurostat; whereas the latter two are administered by the UIS. The strengths of this dataset include worldwide coverage and measurement of both inbound and outbound mobility. According to the latest data available in the UIS database, 160 out of 210 survey participating countries (or territories) reported inbound international student hosted; these countries' tertiary education sectors represented 95 per cent of global tertiary enrolment.

Based on inbound statistics reported by host countries, the UIS estimates the number of outbound students from a given country by summing the numbers of mobile students from the same country of origin in all host countries. Generally, outbound mobility statistics are less likely to be maintained by the home country because students who travel abroad do not necessarily report to national governments, particularly those who fund their study abroad through personal and family funds.

The dataset on student mobility has limitations, however. Firstly, the current data collection framework heavily relies on data reported by host countries, and because not all host countries specify international students' country of origin, the number of outbound mobile students from a given country is underestimated. Additionally, current UOE and UIS data collection includes degree mobility but excludes credit mobility, which may pose a question about cross-national comparability.

The exclusion of credit mobility in the current UOE data collection has caused some confusion as to whether a shift in student mobility from the West to the East (e.g. Asia) has emerged, but is not recorded in current international statistics, as speculated in the British Council's report. In fact, it is a matter of definition and coverage. For instance, Chinese national statistics show some 265,000 international students in China in 2010, regardless of type of mobility, duration of study and academic level (IIE, 2012). Meanwhile, the Chinese Ministry of Education reported to the UIS that it hosted around 71,700 degree-seeking international students, representing 25 per cent of total international students in China. This example illustrates a large discrepancy between these two types of mobility statistics. Relevant agencies have taken some initiatives to improve the coverage and quality of data on internationally mobile students.

The UIS, OECD and Eurostat continue to work jointly to develop a methodology for cross-national comparative data collection. UOE partners have introduced new initiatives to respond to emerging data demand related to student mobility, including the following.

- A pilot survey on credit mobility has been conducted across European Union Member States, given increased interest in credit mobility.
- A new International Standard Classification of Education (ISCED) has been adopted by the UNESCO General Conference in 2011, to better reflect the tertiary education structure that is found around the world (associate, bachelor, master and doctorate) but also has been more recently introduced across Europe following the Bologna Process in 1999. The newly adopted ISCED 2011 allows disaggregating data between bachelor and master, which are currently lumped together. The first international data collections based on the new ISCED will begin in 2014.
- UOE partners have worked a uniform operational definition of inter-nationally mobile students (usual residence or the country of prior education) to measure genuine mobility[8] and increase cross-national comparability. Importantly, they continue to work with countries to ensure they follow the definition and instruction when reporting data.

---

8. Physically crossing national borders for the purpose of schooling.

Conclusion

The British Council's analysis confirms the upward trend in the demand for tertiary education globally and identifies 'markets' for international students in the next decade. To translate its analytical results into opportunities for global engagement, we need to take a step further. By looking beyond the aggregate numbers, we learn that international students' subject choices have shifted, and such information provides universities with initial directions for formulating their ongoing direct recruitment or international partnership strategies. Besides assessing student demand, we need to keep an awareness of the increasing influence that regional organisations and emerging universities have on redirecting international students' destinations for schooling.

Opportunities for global engagement go to countries, higher education institutions and marketing teams who know their strengths and the changes in the external environment, and to those who can best address the needs of their clients: students. To assist these stakeholders in capturing new trends in the rapidly changing world of cross-border higher education, the UIS and its data collection partners need to continue to 'catch up' on gathering relevant, timely data and developing indicators.

Acknowledgements

I would like to acknowledge and extend my gratitude to Robin Shields for his valuable comments and constructive suggestions throughout this paper. I also appreciate feedback and help from my colleagues: Sheena Bell, Samuel Kutnick and Said O.A. Voffal.

The author is responsible for the choice and the presentation of the facts contained in this paper and for the opinions expressed therein, which are not necessarily those of UNESCO and do not commit represent the Organization.

References

Altbach, P. G., Reisberg, L., & Rumbley, L. E. (2009). *Trends in global higher education: Tracking an academic revolution.* Paris: UNESCO.

Chien, C-L., & Chiteng, F. (2011). New patterns in student mobility in the Southern Africa development community. In P. Kotecha (Ed.), *Building regional higher education capacity through academic mobility* (pp. 4–22). Johannesburg: SAURA.

Dale, R., & Robertson, S. (2002). The varying effects of regional organizations as subjects of globalization of education. *Comparative Education Review*, 46(1), 10–36.

de Wit, H. (2008a). International student circulation in the context of the Bologna Process and the Lisbon Strategy. In H. de Wit, P. Agarwal, M. E. Said, M. Sehoole & M. Sirozi (Eds.), *The dynamics of international student circulation in a global context* (pp. 168–198). Rotterdam, The Netherlands: Sense Publishers.

de Wit, H. (2008b). The internationalization of higher education in a global context. In H. de Wit, P. Agarwal, M. E. Said, M. Sehoole & M. Sirozi (Eds.), *The dynamics of international student circulation in a global context* (pp. 1–14). Rotterdam, The Netherlands: Sense Publishers.

Haddawy, P. (2012). *Email correspondence on GRBS results and coverage.*

Hazelkorn, E. (2008). Higher education rankings and the global 'battle for talent'. In R. Bhandari & S. Laughlin (Eds.), *Higher education on the move: New developments in global mobility* (pp. 79–92). New York, NY: The Institute of International Education.

Institute of International Education (IIE). (2012, 14 June). *Fast facts: China.* Retrieved from www.iie.org/Services/Project-Atlas/China

Marginson, S. (2006). Dynamics of national and global competition in higher education. *Higher education, 52,* 1–39.

Marginson, S., & McBurnie, G. (2004). Cross-border post-secondary education in the Asia-Pacific region. In OECD (Ed.), *Internationalisation and trade in higher education: Opportunities and challenges* (pp. 137–204). Paris: OECD.

Salmi, J. (2012). The road to academic excellence: Lessons of experience. In P. G. Altbach & J. Salmi (Eds.), *The road to academic excellence: The making of world-class research universities* (pp. 323–347). Washington, DC: World Bank.

Schofer, E., & Meyer, J. W. (2005). The world-wide expansion of higher education in the twentieth century. *American Sociology Review, 70*(6), 898–920.

Shields, R. (Forthcoming, 2013). Globalization and international student mobility: A network analysis. *Comparative Education Review.*

Teichler, U., Ferencz, I., Wächter, B., Rumbley, L., & Bürger, S. (2011). *Study on mapping mobility in European higher education: Volume I: Overview and trends.* Brussels: European Commission.

UNESCO-UIS. (2012a). *The global demand for primary teachers — 2011 update (Information sheet No. 6).* Retrieved from www.uis.unesco.org/Education/Documents/IS6-2011-Teachers-EN6.pdf Accessed on 12 June 2012.

UNESCO-UIS. (2012b). *The International Standard Classification of Education (ISCED) 1997.* Retrieved from www.uis.unesco.org/Library/Documents/isced97-en.pdf. Accessed on 12 June 2012.

UNESCO-UIS, OECD & Eurostat (UOE). (2012). *UOE Data collection on education systems manual volume1: Concepts, definitions and classifications.* Paris: UOE. Retrieved from www.uis.unesco.org/UISQuestionnaires. Accessed on 12 June 2012.

Chapter 4.9

International Trends in Women's Leadership in Higher Education

Louise Morley

This paper provides a brief introduction to the issue of women's participation as leaders in higher education (HE). The research objectives are to capture international trends in women's participation in higher education (HE) leadership across a range of countries, aiming to identify:

- key enablers facilitating women's leadership across high-, middle- and low-income countries;
- major factors obstructing women's leadership across high-, middle- and low-income countries;
- patterns related to women's leadership emerging across countries.

The methodology involves a meta-analysis and literature review of research that captures trends and issues. It also considers selected explanatory frameworks for women's under-representation in leadership positions in the global academy.

Feminising the Academy?

Gender equality legislation and policy initiatives, changes in socio-economic gender relations, aspirations and global expansion of higher opportunities have all contributed to increasing numbers of women undergraduate students globally (Leathwood & Read, 2009; Morley, 2011). As estimated

Going Global: Identifying Trends and Drivers of International Education
Copyright © 2013 by Emerald Group Publishing Limited
All rights of reproduction in any form reserved
ISBN: 978-1-78190-575-3

138 million students enrol in tertiary education each year, 45 million more than in 1999 (UNESCO, 2009). Female enrolment ratios now exceed those of men in two out of every three countries with data, and the number of women enrolled in tertiary institutions has grown almost twice as fast as that of men since 1970 (UNESCO, 2010). The Global Gender Parity Index of 1.08 means that there are now slightly more women undergraduates than men enrolled in higher education worldwide. Globally, the number of female students rose six-fold from 10.8 to 77.4 million between 1970 and 2008 (UNESCO, 2010). There are disciplinary and regional variations. In many countries, women comprise 60–75 per cent of graduates in health, welfare and education (UNESCO, 2009). Globally, men predominate in science, technology, engineering and mathematics (STEM) and manufacturing and construction (OECD, 2008).

As Tables 1 and 2 indicate, high rates of women's participation in higher education are yet to translate into proportional representation in the labour market or access to leadership and decision-making positions (OECD, 2010). From the limited statistical data on the topic (e.g. Blandford, Brill, Neave, & Roberts, 2011; Lund, 1998; She Figures, 2003, 2006, 2009; Singh, 2002, 2008), it appears that a global gender gap remains in leadership of higher education. She Figures (2009) reported that throughout the 27 countries in the European Union (EU), 13 per cent of institutions in the HE sector were headed by women. Only 9 per cent of universities that award PhD degrees were headed by women. The highest shares of female rectors (vice-chancellors) were recorded in Sweden, Iceland, Norway, Finland and Israel. In contrast, in Denmark, Cyprus, Lithuania, Luxembourg and Hungary, no single university was headed by a woman when She Figures reported in 2009. Women's proportion of rectors was also very low (7 per cent at most) in Romania, Austria, Slovakia, Italy, the Netherlands, the Czech Republic, Belgium and Germany. This under-representation reflects not only continued inequalities between men and women, but also missed opportunities for women to contribute to solving the most pressing problems facing humankind and the future of universities. There is a business case, for example skills wastage; a social justice case, for example removing exclusionary structures, processes and practices; and a cognitive error case, for example gender bias in knowledge, technology and innovation and in the recognition of leadership potential (EC, 2011).

Absent Leaders

The pattern of male prevalence in senior leadership positions is visible in countries with diverse policies and legislation for gender equality. In the

Table 1: Women professors and heads of higher education institutions 1997–2003.

No.	Region/country	1997		1998		1999		2000		2001		2002		2003	
		P	H	P	H	P	H	P	H	P	H	P	H	P	H
	Region														
1	EU[b]	—	—	—	—	13[a]	—	15.2[a]	—	—	—	16[a]	—	15[a]	—
2	Americas	—	—	—	—	—	—	—	—	—	—	—	—	—	—
3	Sub-Saharan Africa	—	—	—	—	—	—	10[e]	—	—	—	—	—	—	—
4	Asia	—	—	—	—	—	—	—	—	—	—	—	—	—	—
5	Australasia	4.5[k]	—	—	—	—	—	—	—	—	—	—	—	—	—
6	Commonwealth	9.9[j]	8.3[a]	9.9	6.9[c]	—	—	13.1[m]	9[m]	—	—	—	—	—	—
	Country														
1	Australia	9.4	14.8	9.4	—	15.4[h]	—	3.1[h]	—	3.3[h]	—	3.5[h]	—	3.6[h]	—
2	Austria	—	—	—	—	—	—	6.2[a]	—	—	—	9[a]	—	—	—
3	Canada	11.8	15.7	—	—	—	—	—	—	—	—	—	—	—	—
4	Ghana	10	—	10.5	—	—	—	15[d]	—	—	—	—	—	14[d]	—
5	India	10.5	—	—	—	—	—	18	—	—	—	—	—	—	—
6	Nigeria	5	—	—	—	—	—	15[d]	—	12[d]	—	23[d]	—	23[d]	—
7	Norway	—	—	—	—	7	—	13.3[a]	—	10	—	16[a]	—	13	—
8	South Africa	8	—	8	—	—	—	74	—	—	—	—	—	—	—
9	Sweden	—	—	—	—	—	—	13.8[a]	—	—	—	14[a]	—	—	—
10	Tanzania	8.6	—	—	—	—	—	—	—	—	—	8[d]	—	—	—
11	The Netherlands	—	—	—	—	5	—	6.3[a]	—	—	—	8[a]	—	8[d]	—
12	Uganda	16.7	—	—	—	—	—	—	—	—	—	—	—	—	—
13	UK	8.6	6.7	—	—	13	—	12.6[a]	—	—	—	15[a]	—	—	—
14	USA	19.8	—	—	19.3	20.8	—	—	—	22.7	21.1	—	—	23.7	—

P, professors; H, heads of institutions, for example vice-chancellors, rectors, presidents.

[a]Grade A women (European Commission, 2003, 2006, 2009).

[b]EU 15 till 2004; EU 25 2004–2007; EU 27 2007 onwards. Data from 1999 to 2003 have included EU 25 statistics in this table. Figure for 2000 refers to EU 15 (European Commission, 2003, 2006, 2009).

[c]Vice-chancellor. Other senior management positions: 13.9 per cent of registrars, 8.4 per cent deputy vice-chancellors, 3.2 per cent of pro-vice-chancellors and 8.5 per cent deans of faculties (UNESCO, 2002).

[d]University of Ghana, University of Ibadan (and Bayero only for 2008 figure for Nigeria), University of Stellenbosch, University of Dar es Salaam, University of Makerere, respectively (Tettey, 2008).

[e]figure approximated for Africa (Tettey, 2010).

[f]All HE institutions. Doctoral universities: 19.2 per cent; MA universities: 28.7 per cent; BA universities: 31.3 per cent; associate degree universities: 47.1 per cent (West & Curtis, 2006).

[g]Deans, as compared to 23 per cent in 2006 women presidents of universities (Curtis, 2011).

[h]'Above senior lecturer' positions (Universities Australia).

[i]University of Witwatersrand (Tettey, 2010).

[j]Only for professors (P) & executive heads (H). Deans 4 per cent in 1997 (Lund, 1998).

[k]Australasia referred to as South Pacific (UNESCO, 2002).

[l]Peterson (2011).

[m]Singh (2002).

[n]Singh (2008).

[o]Blandford et al. (2011).

Table 2: Women professors and heads of higher education institutions 2004–2010.

No.	Region/country	2004		2005		2006		2007		2008		2009		2010	
		P	H	P	H	P	H	P	H	P	H	P	H	P	H
	Region														
1	EU[b]	15.3[a]	–	–	–	18[a]	–	19[a]	9	–	–	–	–	–	–
2	Americas	–	–	–	–	–	–	–	–	–	–	–	–	–	–
3	Sub-Saharan Africa	–	–	–	–	–	–	–	–	–	–	–	–	–	–
4	Asia	–	–	–	–	–	–	–	–	–	–	–	–	–	–
5	Australasia	–	–	–	–	–	–	–	–	–	–	–	–	–	–
6	Commonwealth	–	–	–	–	15.3[n]	9.8[n]	–	–	–	–	–	–	–	–
	Country														
1	Australia	3.8[h]	–	4.1[h]	–	4.5[h]	24	4.3[h]	–	4.4[h]	–	4.7[h]	–	4.9[h]	–
2	Austria	9.4[a]	–	–	–	–	–	14[a]	–	–	–	–	–	–	–
3	Canada	–	–	–	–	–	15.7	–	–	–	–	–	–	–	–
4	Ghana	7[d]	–	18[d]	–	7[d]	–	7[d]	–	10[d]	–	–	–	–	–
5	India	–	–	–	–	–	9.3	–	–	–	–	–	–	–	–
6	Nigeria	24[d]	–	15[d]	–	–	–	–	–	16[d]	–	–	–	–	–
7	Norway	15.7[a]	–	14	–	–	–	18[a]	–	–	–	20	–	–	–
8	South Africa	–	–	–	42.3[i]	–	0	19[d]	–	–	–	–	–	–	–
9	Sweden	16.1[a]	–	–	–	8[d]	–	18[a]	–	–	–	–	–	–	43[l]
10	Tanzania	7[d]	–	9[d]	–	–	–	10[d]	–	–	–	–	–	–	–
11	The Netherlands	9.4[a]	–	–	–	–	–	11[a]	–	–	–	–	–	–	–
12	Uganda	6.1[d]	–	–	–	–	–	–	–	12[d]	–	–	–	–	–
13	UK	15.9[a]	–	–	–	16	–	17[a]	–	22[o]	–	15.7[o]	–	19.8[o]	–
14	USA	–	–	25.1	–	24[f]	23	26.5	36[g]	–	–	28	–	–	14[o]

P, professors; H, heads of institutions, for example vice-chancellors, rectors, presidents.

[a]Grade A women (European Commission, 2003, 2006, 2009).

[b]EU 15 till 2004; EU 25 2004–2007; EU 27 2007 onwards. Data from 1999 to 2003 have included EU 25 statistics in this table. Figure for 2000 refers to EU 15 (European Commission, 2003, 2006, 2009).

[c]Vice-chancellor. Other senior management positions: 13.9 per cent of registrars, 8.4 per cent deputy vice-chancellors, 3.2 per cent of pro-vice-chancellors and 8.5 per cent deans of faculties (UNESCO, 2002).

[d]University of Ghana, University of Ibadan (and Bayero only for 2008 figure for Nigeria), University of Stellenbosch, University of Dar es Salaam, University of Makerere, respectively (Tettey, 2008).

[e]figure approximated for Africa (Tettey, 2010).

[f]All HE institutions. Doctoral universities: 19.2 per cent; MA universities: 28.7 per cent; BA universities: 31.3 per cent; associate degree universities: 47.1 per cent (West & Curtis, 2006).

[g]Deans, as compared to 23 per cent in 2006 women presidents of universities (Curtis, 2011).

[h]‘Above senior lecturer’ positions (Universities Australia).

[i]University of Witwatersrand (Tettey, 2010).

[j]Only for professors (P) & executive heads (H). Deans 4 per cent in 1997 (Lund, 1998).

[k]Australasia referred to as South Pacific (UNESCO, 2002).

[l]Peterson (2011).

[m]Singh (2002).

[n]Singh (2008).

[o]Blandford et al. (2011).

UK, in 2009–2010, women were 44 per cent of all academics. Of staff in professorial roles males (80.9 per cent) were in higher proportion than females (19.1 per cent). Men comprised 55.7 per cent of academic staff in non-manager roles and 72.0 per cent of academic staff in senior management roles (Blandford et al., 2011). This is by no means unusual. In the EU, She Figures (2009) noted how women's academic careers remain characterised by strong vertical segregation. The proportion of female students (55 per cent) and graduates (59 per cent) in the EU exceeds that of male students, but women represent only 18 per cent of grade A (professorial) academic staff. In 70 per cent of Commonwealth countries, *all* universities were led by men in 2007 (Garland, 2008; Singh, 2008).

Sixteen years ago, Davies (1996) observed that women were entering adjunct roles, but not attaining the most senior positions in organisations. While the reform of higher education has created new middle managerial positions including quality assurance, innovation, community engagement and marketing managers (Deem, 2003; Fitzgerald & Wilkinson, 2010; Morley, 2003; Noble & Moore, 2006), many women find themselves in the 'velvet ghettos' of communication, finance, human resource management (Guillaume & Pochic, 2009) or languishing in what was described by the late Joan Eveline as the 'ivory basement' (2004). In some locations, there has been a feminisation of lower level managerial positions in higher education. In Australia, for example, women constitute 40 per cent of the pro-vice-chancellors but only 18 per cent of the vice-chancellors (Bagilhole & White, 2011).

Women's absence from senior leadership is a recurrent theme in studies in the Global North (Bagilhole & White, 2011; Blackmore & Sachs, 2001, 2007; Elg & Jonnergård, 2010; Husu, 2000). It has also emerged as a theme in studies from the Global South in the past two decades for example from Ghana (Ohene, 2010; Prah, 2002); Kenya (Kanake, 1997; Onsongo, 2004); Nigeria (Adadevoh, 2001; Odejide, 2007; Odejide, Akanji, & Odekunle, 2006; Pereira, 2007); Pakistan (Rab, 2010; Shah, 2001); South Africa (Dunne & Sayed, 2007; Shackleton, Riordan, & Simonis, 2006); and Sri Lanka (Gunawardena & Lekamge, 2002; Gunawardena, Rasanayagam, Leitan, Bulumulle, & Abeyasekera-Van Dort, 2006).

It seems as if there are at least three major questions:

1. How to interrupt cycles and structures of disadvantage and discrimination and support women who wish to enter senior leadership?
2. How to make senior leadership more attractive to a wider range of candidates?
3. How to re-invigorate thinking about women in leadership to address contemporary global challenges in HE?

Lack of women in senior positions means that women are under-represented across all-decision-making fora, including committees, boards, recruitment panels and the executive. This means that currently the expertise and skills of a significant part of the HE workforce are being under-utilised.

What Impedes Women's Entry in HE Leadership?

Research studies from the Global South and the Global North are attempting to offer explanatory frameworks for women's absence from HE Leadership. Common themes include:

- the gendered division of labour;
- gender bias and misrecognition;
- management and masculinity;
- greedy organisations.

The Gendered Division of Labour

Leadership is often perceived to be at odds with the demands of motherhood, domestic responsibilities and work/life balance. Lynch (2010) suggested that the academy is constructed as a 'carefree zone' that assumes that academics have no relations other than to their profession. The senior manager is constructed as a zero-load worker, devoid of familial and care responsibilities (Grummell, Devine, & Lynch, 2009a). Runte and Mills (2004) claimed that as it is women who invariably 'navigate between parental and employee roles, it is women only who pay the "toll" for crossing the boundary between work and family' (p. 240).

The sense that women academics are caught between two greedy institutions — the extended family and the university — is a theme in research from Australia (Currie, Thiele, & Harris, 2002; Probert, 2005), Ghana (Adu-Yeboah & Dzama Forde, 2011; Tsikata, 2007), Ireland (Devine, Grummell, & Lynch, 2011; Russell, O'Connell, & McGinty, 2009), Kenya (Kamau, 2006; Onsongo, 2004), South Africa (Dosekun, 2007; Moultrie & De la Rey, 2004), South Korea (Kim, Yoon, & McLean, 2010), the South Pacific (Thaman & Pillay, 1993), Tanzania (Bhalalusesa, 1998) and the UK (Raddon, 2002). In Morley et al.'s (2006) Commonwealth study, management was perceived in all five countries as incompatible with women's responsibilities in the private domain.

A dominant view is that time expended on role performance in one domain depletes time available for the demands of the other domains

(Runte & Mills, 2004). Research has indicated that given the moral imperative on women to care for children, the sick and elderly, women have a form of negative equity in the workplace (Guillaume & Pochic, 2009; Lynch, Baker, & Lyons, 2009; O'Brien, 2007). Bardoel, Drago, Cooper, and Colbeck (2011) used the term 'bias avoidance' to describe how individuals feel that they have to minimise or hide extended family commitments to achieve career success.

While the gendering of primary care responsibilities is a major consideration, it does not account for why some women who are single and child-free are also absent from senior HE leadership positions (Currie et al., 2002). Explanations that name the barriers as marriage, housework and childcare fail to challenge essentialist and heterosexist assumptions that all women live in nuclear families and that, within those families, women do and will continue to take total responsibility for domestic arrangements. Such assumptions are problematic as they reinforce the traditional binary system of gender roles and ignore differences between women, for example in relation to differing cultural and social capital relating to social class, age, sexualities and ethnicities. They also overlook changing relations between women and men. Modern forms of gender identity are more multifaceted, fluid and varied than they were a couple of decades ago (Billing, 2011). Furthermore, increased global competitive pressure has intensified working hours for all employees regardless of their identities (Brennan, Locke, & Naidoo, 2007; Fanghanel & Trowler, 2008; Kagan, 2008; Mercer, 2009).

Gender Bias and Misrecognition

How the leadership role is constructed determines the selection process in so far as particular qualities are normalised and prioritised (Grummell, Devine, & Lynch, 2009b; Smit, 2006). Gender bias has been theorised in terms of the dominant group 'cloning' themselves and appointing in their own image in order to minimise risk (Gronn & Lacey, 2006). This is often unintentional. Husu (2000) argued that bias is more likely to occur if assessments are based on obscure criteria and the evaluation process is kept confidential. Rees (2010, p. 25) argued that transparency in the appointment process can benefit women, as opposed to decisions taken behind closed doors. One example of accountability and transparency is Sweden which had 43 per cent of women vice-chancellors in 2010. There is a statutory requirement for public universities to provide gender statistics on students, doctoral students, teachers and professors, deans and heads of departments (Peterson, 2011).

However, Van den Brink, Benschop, and Jansen's (2010) study of 13 universities in the Netherlands revealed a range of casual discriminatory practices in the appointment of professors that eluded formal protocols and objective criteria. The local logic of the institution and the organisational status quo are often informally invoked to determine who would be a comfortable fit (Grummell et al., 2009b; Pullen & Simpson, 2009). Women can still be perceived as 'risky' appointments to senior positions (Ibarra, Carter, & Silva, 2010).

Bias can exist at different stages of academic life, with women's skills and competencies misrecognised. Leaders need to have also demonstrated excellence in publishing and research (Deem, 2003; Fletcher, Boden, Kent, & Tinson, 2007). Women account for only 29 per cent of the world's researchers (UNESCO, 2010). Rees (2011) identified that gender bias exists in judgements of excellence — even by peers. Hence the importance of reviewing research resource allocation processes (Wenneras & Wold, 1997). The Swedish Research Council, in 2010, identified goals for achieving gender equality that included achieving and maintaining equal gender distribution in evaluation panels; ensuring that the percentages of female and male applicants for grants correspond to the percentages of women and men among the potential group of applicants for research grants, and ensuring that women and men have the same success rates and receive the same average size of grants, taking into account the nature of the research and the type of grant (EC, 2011).

Management and Masculinity

It has been hypothesised that a good leader is defined according to normative masculinity (Binns & Kerfoot, 2011), with maleness seen as a resource and femaleness as a form of negative equity. Fitzgerald (2011) believed that the focus on productivity, competitiveness, hierarchy, strategy and the inalienable logic of the market renders senior HE management a masculine domain. Femaleness is often perceived as irreconcilable with intellectual and managerial authority — a theme explored in Pakistan by Shah (2001) and Smit in South Africa (2006), and theorised by scholars in the Global North including Eagly, Makhijani, and Klonsky (1992) and Valian (1999). These views suggest that woman managers challenge a gender stereotype. The concept of social cognition suggests that we 'think gender' and that we have deeply embedded notions of gender-appropriate behaviour and roles. When we think 'manager', we think 'male' (Sinclair, 2001).

A conventional view is that the skills, competencies and dispositions deemed essential to leadership including assertiveness, autonomy and authority are embedded in socially constructed definitions of masculinity (Knights & Kerfoot, 2004). In Sri Lanka, Morley et al. (2006) found that leadership was perceived as demanding, aggressive, authoritarian and more fitting for males. Odejide (2003) reported how, in Nigeria, male leaders were preferred as they were thought to be more suited to dealing with student unrest. The imperative for tough, detached and even ruthless decision-making led Devine et al. (2011) to argue that masculinity is not equated with caring in the way that femininity is, so men can practise careless masculinity without moral disapproval (Seidler, 2007). This has implications for how women construct their leadership identities. In masculinised organisational cultures women leaders can sometimes find that they are the organisational 'other' and must manage their otherness in order to succeed (Probert, 2005). This incongruence can involve minimising their gender difference in order to be treated equally to men (Bailyn, 2003). Managing identity, discrimination and other people's negativity can be an additional affective workload which deters women from applying for highly visible senior positions (Kram & McCollom Hampton, 2003; Morley, 1999).

Some literature suggests that women and men have innately different managerial dispositions. This approach is highly problematic as it essentialises male and female characteristics and posits that some women's highly developed skills, for example in communication, are innate (Billing & Alvesson, 2000). Binns and Kerfoot (2011) discussed the 'female advantage' literature (Helgesen, 1990; Rosener, 1990), which claimed the existence of superior female leadership traits such as empathy and relationality. The gendering of leadership styles and skills is a theme in some Commonwealth Literature (Morley, Sorhaindo, & Burke, 2005), with views that increased numbers of woman managers will render the organisation more gender sensitive (Gill, 2000; Lamptey, 1992; Manya, 2000; Tete-Mensah, 1999). It is erroneous to imply that women lead differently and such propositions create binds for women who do not 'fit' the gender script. Muhr (2011) critiqued the dualism of leadership as masculine or feminine. Billing (2011) recommended more sophisticated frames of analysis and asked in what sense do work practices and norms still reflect the life situations and interests of men (p. 300). The Margaret Thatcher syndrome highlights that gender sensitivity is more significant in leading change than the biological sex of post holders (Itzin, 1985).

Greedy Organisations

Leadership is experienced as an all-consuming activity. Devine et al. (2011) claimed that 'Effective senior management required relentless commitment to the strategic goals of the organization and an implicit assumption of their 24/7 availability to their management roles.' Fitzgerald (2011) described leadership as exhausting, with unrelenting bureaucratic demands and institutional pressures. Universities' leadership involves multiple, complex tasks and responsibilities including management of staff, strategy, finances and resources, operational planning, policy development, quality assurance processes, improving student outcomes and engaging with community and the professions/industry (Currie et al., 2002). Women HE managers in Woodward's UK study (2007) reported 'unmanageably large workloads' (p. 11). These observations have led to leadership being described as 'greedy work' (Currie et al., 2002; Gronn & Lacey, 2006). Devine et al. (2011), in their Irish study, discussed leaders requiring 'an elastic self' in the context of new managerial reforms of higher education, and 'a relentless pursuit of working goals without boundaries in time, space energy or emotion' (p. 632). Stress, well-being, work/life balance and sustainability are concerns in academic life (Barrett & Barrett, 2007; Edwards, Van Laar, Easton, & Kinman, 2009; Kinman, Jones, & Kinman, 2006; Kinman et al., 2008). HE leaders are under increasing pressure to succeed in competitive, performative audit and austerity cultures (Lynch, 2006; Morley, 2003).

Concluding Comments

It would be misleading to construct women as victims in all-powerful patriarchal organisations of knowledge production. Women are entering leadership positions and are being creative and innovative (Bagilhole & White, 2011). However, the global literature suggests that women and men in higher education are largely placed differently, with differential access to leadership, and hence to influencing meanings, discourses and practices (Marshall, 2007). While numbers have increased in some countries, for example Sweden, it is indisputable that women are under-represented in senior leadership positions internationally. It is still relevant to call for power itself to be theorised and to seek ways to 'lessen the power of the male order, rather than to 'join the ranks' (Squires, 1999, pp. 117–118). Gender in HE leadership is about more than focussing on women's under-representation. The gendered world of HE affects the very nature of knowledge production itself (Calás & Smircich, 2009; EC, 2011; Wickramasinghe, 2009). Discussions often rely on unproblematic notions of polarised gender identities — in both the public and professional domains. Gender is treated as a demographic variable, rather than something that is in continual production, such as via processes of knowledge production and distribution, opportunity structures and social relations in higher education.

Metaphors abound: of entrapment, such as 'glass ceilings'; waste, 'leaky pipelines'; and victimhood, 'ivory basements'. Ironically, while much of the literature describes male norms, it often reproduces female norms and overlooks differences in age, ethnicities, sexualities and cultural and social class locations. The literature overflows with normative assumptions about childcare, innate, benign female dispositions and aspirations. There is scant coverage of success stories of women accessing authority and facilitating change. Nor is there much consideration of the ambivalence or pleasures that many women experience in higher education — either by becoming leaders or by making positive choices not to (Hey & Leathwood, 2009). It seems that we require a re-invigorated and re-textured vocabulary and expanded lexicon to focus on the leadership values and challenges that lie ahead for HE, such as sustainability, social inclusion and creating knowledge for a rapidly changing world — one in which gender relations are also in flux.

Women *are* entering HE leadership, albeit in low numbers. We need to build on this momentum to envision what type of sustainable and gender-sensitive leadership is required for the university of the future (Morley, 2011). Counting more women into posts is important, but representational space cannot be the only goal for gender equality (Bonner, 2005; Neale & Özkanli, 2010). It is the gendered world itself that represents the problem, not simply the exclusion of women or the existence of the male norm (Butler, 2004; Verloo & Lombardo, 2007). Leadership roles appear to be so over-extended that they represent a type of virility test. We need to ask how leadership practices can become more sustainable, with concerns about well-being as well as competitive advantage in the global arena.

References

Adadevoh, I. O. (2001). Feminism, professionalism and educational leadership: An approach to capacity building in Nigerian universities. *Social Science Academy of Nigeria: The Nigerian Social Scientist, 4*(2), 16–22.

Adu-Yeboah, C., & Dzama Forde, L. (2011). Returning to study in higher education in Ghana: Experiences of mature undergraduate women. *Research in Comparative and International Education, 6*(4), 400–414.

Bagilhole, B., & White, K. (Eds.). (2011). *Gender, power and management: A cross-cultural analysis of higher education.* London: Palgrave Macmillan.

Bailyn, L. (2003). Academic careers and gender equity: Lessons learned from MIT. *Gender Work & Organization, 10*(2), 137–153.

Bardoel, E. A., Drago, R., Cooper, B., & Colbeck, C. (2011). Bias avoidance: Cross-cultural differences in the US and Australian academies. *Gender, Work and Organization, 18,* e157–e179. Accessed on 21 February 2012.

Barrett, L., & Barrett, P. (2007). Current practice in the allocation of academic workloads. *Higher Education Quarterly, 61*, 461–478.

Bhalalusesa, E. (1998). Women's career and professional development: Experiences and challenges. *Gender and Education, 10*(1), 21–33.

Billing, Y. (2011). Are women in management victims of the phantom of the male norm? *Gender, Work and Organization, 18*(3), 298–317.

Billing, Y. D., & Alvesson, M. (2000). Questioning the notion of feminine leadership. A critical perspective on the gender labelling of leadership. *Gender, Work & Organization, 7*(3), 144–157.

Binns, J., & Kerfoot, D. (Eds.). (2011). Editorial: Engendering leadership: Dedicated to the spirit and the scholarship of the late Joan Eveline*Gender, Work and Organization, 18*(3), 257–262.

Blackmore, J., & Sachs, J. (2001). Women leaders in the restructured and internationalised university. In A. Brooks & A. Mackinnon (Eds.), *Gender and the restructured university* (pp. 45–66). Buckingham: Open University Press.

Blackmore, J., & Sachs, J. (2007). *Performing and reforming leaders: Gender, educational restructuring and organizational change*. New York, NY: State of New York Press.

Blandford, E., Brill, C., Neave, S., & Roberts, A. (2011). *Equality in higher education: Statistical report 2011*. London: Equality Challenge Unit.

Bonner, F. B. (2005). Gender diversity in higher education: 'The women are fine, but the men are not?' In W. R. Allen, M. Bonous-Hammarth & R. T. Teranishi (Eds.), *Higher education in a global society: Achieving diversity, equity and excellence. Advances in education in diverse communities: Research, policy, and praxis* (Vol. 5, pp. 159–180). Bingley, UK: Emerald Group Publishing Limited.

Brennan, J., Locke, W., & Naidoo, R. (2007). United Kingdom: An increasingly differentiated profession. In W. Locke, U. Teichler, (Eds.), *The changing conditions for academic work and career in selected countries* (163–176). Werkstattberichte series. Kassel: International Centre for Higher Education Research.

Butler, J. (2004). *Undoing gender*. London: Routledge.

Calás, M. B., & Smircich, L. (2009). Feminist perspectives on gender in organizational research: What is and is yet to be. In D. Buchanan & A. Bryman (Eds.), *Handbook of organizational research methods* (pp. 246–269). London: Sage.

Council for Higher Education. (2011). *Women in South African higher education*. Retrieved from http://www.che.ac.za/heinsa/whe/. Accessed on 18 May 2012.

Currie, J., Thiele, B., & Harris, P. (2002). *Gendered universities in globalized economies: Power, careers and sacrifices*. Lexington: Lexington Books.

Curtis, J. W. (2011). Persistent inequity: Gender and ACADEMIC Employment. Paper of the American Association of University Professors, prepared for 'New Voices in Pay Equity', 11 April. Retrieved from http://www.aauw.org/learn/research/upload/NewVoicesPayEquity_JohnCurtis.pdf. Accessed on 18 May 2012.

Davies, C. (1996). The sociology of professions and the profession of gender. *Sociology, 30*, 661–678.

Deem, R. (2003). Gender, organizational cultures and the practices of manager academics in UK universities. *Gender, Work & Organization, 10*(2), 239–259.

Devine, D., Grummell, B., & Lynch, K. (2011). Crafting the elastic self? Gender and identities in senior appointments in Irish education. *Gender, Work and Organization, 18*(6), 631–649.

Dunne, M., & Sayed, Y. (2007). Access to what? Gender and higher education in Africa. In K. April & M. Shockley (Eds.), *Diversity in Africa. The coming of age of a continent. Education* (pp. 223–237). London: Palgrave.

Eagly, A. H., Makhijani, M. G., & Klonsky, B. G. (1992). Gender and the evaluation of leaders: A meta-analysis. *Psychological Bulletin, 111*(3–22).

Edwards, J., Van Laar, D., Easton, S., & Kinman, G. (2009). The work-related quality of life scale for higher education employees. *Quality in Higher Education, 15*(3), 207–219.

Elg, U., & Jonnergård, K. (2010). Included or excluded? The dual influences of the organisational field and organisational practices on new female academics. *Gender and Education, 22*(2), 209–225.

(EC) European Commission: Directorate-General for Research and Innovation. (2011). *Structural change in research institutions: Enhancing excellence, gender equality and efficiency in research and innovation*. Brussels: European Commission.

Eveline, J. (2004). *Ivory basement leadership: Power and invisibility in the changing university*. Crawley: University of Western Australia Press.

Fanghanel, J., & Trowler, P. (2008). Exploring academic identities and practices in a competitive enhancement context: A UK-based case study. *European Journal of Education, 43*, 301–313.

Fitzgerald, T. (2011). Troubling leadership? Gender, leadership and higher education. Paper presented at the AARE conference, 30 November. Hobart, Australia.

Fitzgerald, T., & Wilkinson, J. (2010). *Travelling towards a mirage? Gender, leadership and higher education*. Brisbane: Post Pressed.

Fletcher, C., Boden, R., Kent, J., & Tinson, J. (2007). Performing women: The gendered dimensions of the UK new research economy. *Gender, Work & Organization, 14*(5), 433–453.

Garland, D. (2008). Where are all the women? *ACU Bulletin*, 163 (February). Retrieved from http://www.acu.ac.uk/member_services/bulletin. Accessed on 30 April 2008.

Gill, S. K. (2000). Asian and global communication skills for women leaders. In S. H. Shahabudin & S. K. Gill (Eds.), *Asian women leaders in higher education* (pp. 93–122). Kuala Lumpa: UNESCO/Universiti Kebangsaan.

Gronn, P., & Lacey, K. (2006). Cloning their own: Aspirant principals and the school-based selection game. *Australian Journal of Education, 50*(2), 102–121.

Grummell, B., Devine, D., & Lynch, K. (2009a). The careless manager: Gender, care and new managerialism in higher education. *Gender and Education, 21*(2), 191–208.

Grummell, B., Devine, D., & Lynch, K. (2009b). Appointing senior managers in education: Homosociability, local logics and authenticity in the selection process. *Educational Management Administration and Leadership, 37*(3), 329–349.

Guillaume, C., & Pochic, S. (2009). What would you sacrifice? Access to top management and the work–life balance. *Gender, Work & Organization, 16*(1), 14–36.

Gunawardena, C., & Lekamge, D. (2002). Men and women in leadership roles: A study of the open university of Sri Lanka. Paper presented at the 8th National Convention on Women's Studies, Colombo.

Gunawardena, C., Rasanayagam, Y., Leitan, T., Bulumulle, K., & Abeyasekera-Van Dort, A. (2006). Quantitative and qualitative dimensions of gender equity in Sri Lankan higher education. *Women's Studies International Forum, 29*(6), 562–571.

Helgesen, S. (1990). *The female advantage: Women's ways of leadership.* New York, NY: Doubleday Currency.

Hey, V., & Leathwood, C. (2009). Passionate attachments: Higher education, policy, knowledge, emotion and social justice. *Higher Education Policy, 22*(1), 101–118.

Husu, L. (2000). Gender discrimination in the promised land of gender equality. *Higher Education in Europe, XXV*(2), 221–228.

Ibarra, H., Carter, N. M., & Silva, C. (2010). Why men still get more promotions than women. *Harvard Business Review, 88*(9), 80–85.

Itzin, C. (1985). Margaret Thatcher is my sister: Counselling on divisions between women. *Women's Studies International Forum, 8*(1), 73–83.

Kagan, C. M. (2008). Pillars of support for wellbeing in the community: The role of the public sector. In J. Haworth (Ed.), *Wellbeing and sustainable living.* Manchester: RIHSC, MMU.

Kamau, N. (2006). Invisibility, silence and absence: A study of the account taken by two Kenyan universities of the effects of HIV and AIDS on senior women staff. *Women's Studies International Forum, 29*(6), 612–619.

Kanake, L. (1997). *Gender disparities among the academic staff in Kenyan universities.* Nairobi: Luceum Educational Consultants.

Kim, N., Yoon, H. J., & McLean, G. N. (2010). Policy efforts to increase women faculty in Korea: Reactions and changes at universities. *Asia Pacific Education Review, 11*(3), 285–299.

Kinman, G., Jones, F., & Kinman, R. (2006). The well-being of the UK academy, 1998–2004. *Quality in Higher Education, 12*(1), 15–27.

Knights, D., & Kerfoot, D. (2004). Between representations and subjectivity: Gender binaries and the politics of organizational transformation. *Gender, Work & Organization, 11*(4), 430–454.

Kram, K., & McCollom Hampton, M. (2003). When women lead: The visibility-vulnerability spiral. In R. Ely, E. G. Foldy & M. Scully (Eds.), *Reader in gender, work and organization* (pp. 211–223). Oxford: Blackwell Publishing.

Lamptey, A. S. (1992). Promoting women's participation in teaching research and management in African universities. In Dakar Regional Office (Ed.), *Higher education in Africa: Trends and challenges for the 21st century* (pp. 77–88). UNESCO Dakar Regional Office.

Leathwood, C., & Read, B. (2009). *Gender and the changing face of higher education: A feminised future?* Maidenhead: McGraw-Hill, Open University Press.

Lund, H. (1998). *A single sex profession? Female staff numbers in commonwealth universities.* London: Commonwealth Higher Education Management Service.

Lynch, K. (2006). Neo-liberalism and marketization: The implications for higher education. *European Educational Research Journal, 5*(5), 1–17.

Lynch, K. (2010). Carelessness: A Hidden Doxa of Higher Education CHEER/ ESRC Seminar Series 'Imagining the University of the Future'. Seminar 2: What are the Disqualified Discourses in the Knowledge Society? Centre for Higher Education and Equity Research (CHEER), University of Sussex. Retrieved from http://www.sussex.ac.uk/education/cheer/esrcseminars/seminar2. Accessed on 5 September 2012.

Lynch, K., Baker, J., & Lyons, M. (2009). *Affective equality: Love, care and injustice.* London: Palgrave Macmillan.

Manya, M. O. (2000). Equal *opportunities policy (gender) a means to increasing the number of female senior managers and decision-makers at the University of Nairobi.* MA dissertation, Institute of Education, University of London.

Marshall, J. (2007). The gendering of leadership in corporate social responsibility. *Journal of Organizational Change Management, 20*(2), 165–181.

Mercer, J. (2009). Junior academic-manager in higher education: An untold story? *International Journal of Educational Management, 23*(4), 348–359.

Morley, L. (1999). *Organising feminisms. The micropolitics of the academy.* Basingstoke: Macmillan Press.

Morley, L. (2003). *Quality and power in higher education.* Buckingham: Open University Press.

Morley, L. (2011). Misogyny posing as measurement: Disrupting the feminisation crisis discourse. *Contemporary Social Science, 6*(2), 163–175.

Morley, L., Gunawardena, C., Kwesiga, J. C., Lihamba, A., Odejide, A., Shackleton, L., & Sorhaindo, A. (2006). *Gender equity in commonwealth higher education: An examination of sustainable interventions in selected commonwealth universities.* London: Department for International Development (DFID).

Morley, L., Sorhaindo, A., & Burke, P.-J. (2005). *Researching women: An annotated bibliography on gender equity in commonwealth countries.* London: Institute of Education.

Moultrie, A., & De la Rey, C. (2004). South African women leaders in higher education. Professional development needs in a changing context. *McGill Journal of Education, 38*(3), 407–420.

Muhr, S. (2011). Caught in the gendered machine: On the masculine and feminine in cyborg leadership. *Gender, Work and Organization, 18*(3), 337–357.

Neale, J., & Özkanlı, O. (2010). Organisational barriers for women in senior management: A comparison of Turkish and New Zealand universities. *Gender and Education, 22*(5), 547–563.

Noble, C., & Moore, S. (2006). Advancing women and leadership in this post feminist, post EEO era. *Women in Management Review, 21*(7), 598–603.

O'Brien, M. (2007). Mothers' emotional care work in education and its moral imperative. *Gender and Education, 19*(2), 159–177.

Odejide, A. (2003). Navigating the seas: Women in higher education in Nigeria. *McGill Journal of Education, 38*(3), 453–468.

Odejide, A. (2007). "What can a woman do?" Being women in a Nigerian university. *Feminist Africa, 8*, 42–59. Retrieved from http://agi.ac.za/sites/agi.ac.za/files/fa_8_feature_article_3_0.pdf. Accessed on 5 September 2012.

Odejide, A., Akanji, B., & Odekunle, K. (2006). Does expansion mean inclusion in Nigerian higher education? *Women's Studies International Forum, 29*(6), 552–561.

OECD (Organisation for Economic Cooperation and Development). (2008). *Tertiary education for the knowledge society.* OECD Thematic Review of Tertiary Education: Synthesis Report.OECD, Paris.

OECD. (2010). *Atlas of gender and development: How social norms affect gender equality in non-OECD countries.* Paris: OECD.

Ohene, I. (2010). *Gender and leadership in higher educational institutions: Exploring perceptions and practices in University of Cape Coast, Ghana.* International EdD thesis, University of Sussex.

Onsongo, J. (2004). *Factors affecting women's participation in University Management in Kenya.* Addis Ababa: Addis, Organisation for Social Science Research in Eastern and Southern Africa.

Pereira, C. (2007). *Gender in the making of the Nigerian university system.* London: James Currey. Retrieved from http://www.foundation%20partnership.org/pubs/nigeria/nigeria_2007.pdf. Accessed on 18 May 2012.

Peterson, H. (2011). 'The Men Next in Line Aren't Interested Anymore'. Academic management as 'women's work'. *GEXcel conference gender paradoxes in academic and scientific organisation(s)*, 11–12 October, Örebro University, Sweden.

Prah, M. (2002). Gender issues in Ghanaian tertiary institutions: Women academics and administrators at Cape Coast University. *Ghana Studies, 5*, 83–122.

Probert, B. (2005). 'I just didn't fit in': Gender and unequal outcomes in academic careers. *Gender, Work & Organization, 12*(1), 50–72.

Pullen, A., & Simpson, R. (2009). Managing difference in feminized work: Men, otherness and social practice. *Human Relations, 62*(2), 561–587.

Rab, M. (2010). *The life stories of successful women academics in Pakistani public sector universities.* EdD thesis, Institute of Education, University of London.

Raddon, A. (2002). Mothers in the academy: Positioned and positioning within discourses of the 'successful academic' and the 'good mother'. *Studies in Higher Education, 27*(4), 387–403.

Rees, T. (2010). In the last three years I've been a Pro Vice Chancellor… . In A.-S. Godfroy-Genin (Ed.), *Women in engineering and technology research* (pp. 21–29). Berlin: Lit Verlag.

Rees, T. (2011). The gendered construction of scientific excellence. *Interdisciplinary Science Reviews, 36*(2), 133–145.

Rosener, J. B. (1990). Ways women lead. *Harvard Business Review, 68*(6), 119–125.

Runte, M., & Mills, A. J. (2004). Paying the toll: A feminist post-structural critique of the discourse bridging work and family. *Culture and Organization, 10*(3), 237–249.

Russell, H., O'Connell, P., & McGinty, F. (2009). The Impact of Flexible Working Arrangements on Work–Life Conflict and Work Pressure in Ireland. *Gender, Work & Organization, 16*(6), 73–97.

Seidler, V. (2007). Masculinities, bodies, and emotional life. *Men and Masculinities, 10*(1), 9–21.

Shackleton, L., Riordan, S., & Simonis, D. (2006). Gender and the transformation agenda in South African higher education. *Women's Studies International Forum, 29*(6), 572–580.

Shah, S. (2001). Tertiary colleges in Pakistan: Gender and equality. *The School Field, XII*(3/4), 49–70.

She Figures. (2003). *Statistics and indicators on gender equality in science.* Brussels: European Commission.

She Figures. (2006). *Statistics and indicators on gender equality in science.* Brussels: European Commission.

She Figures. (2009). *Statistics and indicators on gender equality in science.* Brussels: European Commission.

Sinclair, A. (2001). The body and management pedagogy. *Proceedings of the Gender, Work & Organization conference,* 22–29 June, Keele.

Singh, J. K. S. (2002). *Still a single sex profession? Female staff numbers in commonwealth universities.* London: Association of Commonwealth Universities.

Singh, J. K. S. (2008). *Whispers of change. Female staff numbers in commonwealth universities.* London: Association of Commonwealth Universities.

Smit, P. (2006). *Leadership in South African higher education: A multifaceted conceptualisation.* PhD thesis, Institute of Education, University of London.

Squires, J. (1999). *Gender in political theory.* Cambridge: Polity Press.

Tete-Mensah, W. (1999). *Effective implementation of anti-sexual harassment policies as equal opportunities issue in universities in Ghana.* Unpublished MA thesis, Institute of Education, University of London.

Tettey, W. J. (2008). Comparative analysis of next generation's academic indicators. Paper prepared for the University Leaders' Forum, 22–25 November 2008, Accra, Ghana. Retrieved from http://www.foundation-partnership.org/ulf/resources/ tettey.pdf Accessed 5 September 2012.

Tettey, W. J. (2010). Challenges of developing and retaining the next generation of academics: Deficits in academic staff capacity at African universities. Partnership for Higher Education in Africa. Retrieved from http://www.foundation-partnership.org/pubs/pdf/tettey_deficits.pdf. Accessed on 5 September 2012.

Thaman, K. H., & Pillay, S. (1993). *Women in higher education management in the South Pacific – the case of the University of the South Pacific.* Paris: Commonwealth Secretariat.

Tsikata, D. (2007). Gender, institutional cultures and the career trajectories of faculty of the university of Ghana. *Feminist Africa, 8,* 26–41. Retrieved from http://agi.ac.za/sites/agi.ac.za/files/fa_8_feature_article_2_0.pdf. Accessed on 5 September 2012.

UNESCO. (2002). Women and management in higher education. A practice handbook. *Follow-up to the world conference on higher education,* 5–9 October 1998, Paris. Retrieved from http://www.unesco.org/education/pdf/singh.pdf. Accessed on 6 September 2012.

UNESCO Institute of Statistics. (2009). *Global education digest 2009: Comparing education statistics across the world.* Montreal: UNESCO Institute of Statistics.

UNESCO Institute of Statistics. (2010). *Global education digest 2010: Comparing education statistics across the world (a special focus on gender).* Paris: UNESCO.

Universities Australia. (2012). *Statistics for Staff.* Retrieved from http://www.deewr.gov.au/HigherEducation/Publications/HEStatistics/Publications/Pages/Staff.aspx. Accessed on 26 January 2012.

Universities New Zealand. (2012). *Women in leadership programme.* Retrieved from http://www.universitiesnz.ac.nz/aboutus/sc/hr/women-in-leadership. Accessed on 5 September 2012.

Valian, V. (1999). *Why so slow? The advancement of women.* Boston, MA: MIT Press.

Van den Brink, M., Benschop, Y., & Jansen, W. (2010). Transparency in academic recruitment: A problematic tool for gender equality? *Organization Studies, 31*(12), 1–25.

Verloo, M., & Lombardo, E. (2007). Contested gender equality and policy variety in Europe: Introducing a critical frame analysis approach. In M. Verloo (Ed.), *Multiple meanings of gender equality. A critical frame analysis.* Budapest: Central European University Press.

Wenneras, C., & Wold, A. (1997). Nepotism and sexism in peer review. *Nature, 387*(May), 341–343.

West, M. S., & Curtis, J. W. (2006). *AAUP faculty gender equity indicators 2006.* Washington, DC: American Association of University Professors.

Wickramasinghe, M. (2009). *Feminist research methodology: Making meanings of meaning-making.* London: Routledge.

Woodward, D. (2007). Work-life balancing strategies used by women managers in British 'modern' universities. *Equal Opportunities International, 26*(1), 6–17.

What is Changing in Higher Education

Janet Ilieva, Michael Peak and Kevin Van-Cauter

Conclusion

Throughout this book, we have presented papers which have explored the regional initiative and patterns; institutions; students; and we have looked at some trends. The British Council study The Shape of Things to Come *is an empirical look at past trends and forecasts of the future. In this concluding paper, Janet Ilieva, Michael Peak and Kevin Van-Cauter present the data and the statistics by which we can understand better the patterns the earlier authors have described.* (Editors)

The Shape of Things to Come: Higher Education Global Trends and Emerging Opportunities to 2020[1] studies past trends and forecasts future developments in the higher education landscape. Internationalisation of higher education has become a major preoccupation for universities globally. Universities maintain global relevance through reaching out to home and international students and through the appeal of their research addressing global issues.

While the number of international students has increased more than five times from 800,000 in the mid-1970 s to over 4.1 million in 2010 (OECD,

---

1. The British Council acknowledges the great contribution from Oxford Economics to this study. All data analysis and forecasts have been carried out by Oxford Economics. While there were large teams involved in the production of this study, a special thank you goes to Graeme Harrison, Mike Phillips and Melissa Woods.

Going Global: Identifying Trends and Drivers of International Education
Copyright © 2013 by Emerald Group Publishing Limited
All rights of reproduction in any form reserved
ISBN: 978-1-78190-575-3

2012) the global average outbound mobility ratio (mobile tertiary students divided by total tertiary enrolments) has remained unchanged at about 2 per cent per annum over the same period of time. However, this ratio varies from 50 per cent in Botswana, 30 per cent in Trinidad and Tobago and Mauritius to under 1 per cent for the United Kingdom, the United States, Brazil, Russia and Indonesia, but there has been very little change in this ratio even at country level over the past decades, indicating a fine interplay between 'pull' and 'push' factors, as detailed by earlier research (British Council, 2011).

This study identifies the following significant shifts which will affect the international higher education landscape over the next decade:

- a slowdown in the growth of global student mobility on one hand; and a shift in the balance of international student mobility from West to East on the other;
- an increase in international collaborations in teaching and research;
- further diversification in the income sources for universities.

Changing International Student Mobility

Lower growth rates in diploma-mobile students (as opposed to credit-mobile students) will be predominantly driven by the slowdown of global tertiary enrolments from average 5 per cent annual growth in the previous three decades to 1.4 per cent in the decade to 2020. This is caused by unfavourable demographics in some countries with the largest tertiary education systems, such as Russia, Germany, South Korea and most recently China.

Figure 1 shows the countries forecasted to have the largest changes in their student outflows to the year 2020. Some major sources of internationally mobile students (including China, South Korea, Germany) do not appear on this chart as the student outflows from these countries are not forecast to change significantly.

The shift in the balance of international student mobility from West to East is triggered by the rising economic power of emerging economies, with China, India, Brazil and Russia now in the top 10 largest economies (GDP measured by PPP). Their rising economic strength has been complemented by their more proactive role in the higher education community globally. In addition to the shift in the economic power from West to East and South, data on international student mobility (also including exchanges and TNE) suggests a shift in the balance from West to East and, to a less extent, to South. The previous decade (between 1999 and 2009) has marked an increased international mobility within the world's regions (Chien, 2012). The highest rates are in East Asia where 42 per cent of the international students opt to study in another country in the region. Strong intra-regional

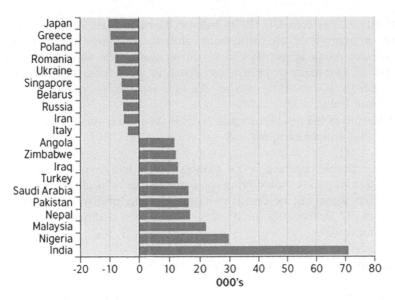

Figure 1: Growth in global outbound mobile tertiary students by origin market (2011–2020). *Source:* Oxford Economics.

mobility is evidenced by the high numbers of Asian students studying in the major Asian countries like Japan, South Korea and China, where they often exceed 80 per cent of the total international student population.

A further boost to international student mobility in Asia stems from governments' commitment in the region to deliver on their international student recruitment targets: collectively, five countries in Asia have ambitions to attract over 1 million new international students by 2020 — China, 500,000 students by 2020; Singapore, 150,000 international students by 2015; Malaysia, 200,000 international students by 2020; and South Korea with 200,000 by 2020.

Growing Prominence of International Teaching and Research Collaborations

The aforementioned shift in the student mobility from West to East is also evidenced by the growing variety and quantity in off-shore operations that are now popular with both local and international students. In addition, Lawton and Katsomitros (2012) project further expansion East in the development of international branch campuses (IBCs). There are 37 additional campuses set to open between 2012 and 2014, and the majority of those, 81 per cent (30 IBCs) will be based in East Asia. In addition, about a quarter of all institutions globally opening branch campuses abroad are Asian universities (nine universities). The authors explain the growth of international branch campuses in Asia with the governments' drive across some of the major Asian countries to establish them as 'education hubs'.

A feature of the newly emerging IBCs is their niche remit. Worton (2012) argues that a niche campus:

> ... should operate as a catalyst for change in research thinking ... It should bring some challenges to local providers, but these will be creative challenges, and precisely because of its deliberately small size, it will never threaten local universities ...

Niche campuses are seeing increasing popularity in Malaysia with more countries set to follow this trend.

Countries with the largest tertiary education systems in the world — China, India and Brazil — have some of most restrictive regulatory frameworks for foreign providers. However, higher education features high on the respective governments' agendas. Local cultural and political contexts will have much greater importance in determining the terms of engagement when delivering transnational education (TNE). While some countries are still cautious about how much freedom to grant to foreign education providers, the only way to access such markets is often in partnership with a local institution, as is the case in Indonesia. The importance of a 'foreign partner' is also argued in Gore (2012).

A good example of a new model of international partners coming together to set up independent joint ventures is the establishment of the first Sino-foreign university, which was set up in 2006 by the University of Liverpool and Xi'an Jiaotong University. A similar model is being used with the setting up of the New York University Shanghai — an independent institution established by New York University and the East China Normal University. These are just two examples; however, it is likely that more models for international partnership will develop in the near future.

Internationalisation of teaching and research are critical objectives for most tertiary institutions. There are a number of motivations for this, including institutional profiling, raising quality standards and global relevance, attracting the best students and staff, generating revenue, and promoting internal diversity.

To justify claims that an institution provides a true international education, and to attract top students from around the world, it is necessary to clearly demonstrate a strong physical global footprint; a sizeable body of international students — 16 per cent of all students in the United Kingdom are from abroad (OECD, 2012) — and lecturers — 25 per cent of UK's lecturers are from outside the United Kingdom (HESA Staff Record 2010/11); a strongly internationalised course content; and a suitable number of opportunities for exchange and overseas study.

The increase in international research collaborations is driven by the growing interconnectedness among academic communities globally. Research produced through international collaboration has significantly higher quality (with citation impact generally accepted as a proxy for quality). The Royal Society (2011) established that the larger the number of collaborating countries, the higher the impact of the respective research (up to 10 collaborating partners). The international research collaboration rate has increased steadily from 25 per cent 12 years ago to over 35 per cent at present. While it is difficult to give an accurate estimate of international collaborations in teaching and research in 2020, the trend is positive.

The Shape of Things to Come finds that for the top 18 countries with highest research output, 80 per cent of their research impact is attributed to their international research collaboration rate, i.e. the higher the international research collaboration rate, the higher the impact of the research output (see Figure 2).

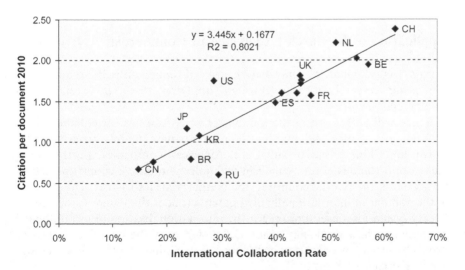

Figure 2: Collaboration rate and citation per document (2010).
Source: Oxford Economics and British Council analysis.

With view of expanding access to research findings, Finch (2012) recommends that publicly funded research should become more openly accessible in future years. Consequently, we expect that there will be fewer barriers to accessibility to UK and European research internationally, and such openness to research findings should positively affect future international research collaborations.

In order to maximise on opportunities in research collaboration, collaborations with institutions from the following countries should be considered:

- high-volume research leaders such as the United States, China, the United Kingdom, Germany, France, Italy, Canada and Australia;
- high average citation impact leaders which, in addition to the United Kingdom and the United States, this group also includes Switzerland, the Netherlands and Denmark. There is a distinct niche sub-group which provides opportunities in smaller, technology-intensive countries such as the Nordic countries, Switzerland and Israel;
- key emerging markets (countries with high research output growth), most notably China and Brazil, but also Malaysia, Iran, Saudi Arabia, India and Qatar.

Marginson (2012) argues that the higher education systems in 49 countries now produce over 1000 journal articles per year. The significance of 1000 articles is that it indicates 'the presence of local research and doctoral capacity'.

Application of Research Excellence in Commercial Activities

Across many countries universities are an under-utilised resource for generating research income through applying research excellence in commercial activities.

There will be growth in the number of opportunities for collaborations between universities and multinational companies, mainly from the US, European, Chinese, Indian and Latin American companies. Furthermore, niche opportunities are presented in technology-intensive countries such as Switzerland, the Nordic countries, the Netherlands and Israel. The increase in the number of internationally filed patents (under the Patent Cooperation Treaty system) is a useful proxy for the internationalisation of technological development in a particular country. Growth over the past five years was driven by just a few countries, including Japan, China, the United States and South Korea.

In addition to engagement in commercial activities, there is an increased private interest in higher education as an investment. The strong performance record of higher education during times of recession and economic downturn when most industries are underperforming has undeniable appeal. The sale of the London-based College of Law to Montagu Private Equity raised a lot of questions about the future of public funding. Robin Middlehurst, Professor of Higher Education at the University of Kingston and the Leadership Foundation for Higher Education, commented:

> ... as public funding goes down, publicly funded institutions will ... look to issue bonds and have some kind of different private financing. It means the beginning of something that hasn't been here up to now. (Swain, 2012)

Conclusion and Discussion

In conclusion, this study captures trends which will shape the international higher education landscape this decade. It has focused only on aspects of international education that lend themselves to robust statistical analysis. However, there are wider influences that need to be taken into consideration. Marginson (2012) draws three future trends in internationalisation of higher education. He sees those being: pluralisation of higher education; growing emphasis on hard-edged indicators measuring internationalisation; and the emergence of mass open online courseware. By pluralisation of higher education Marginson sees less concentration of international students in traditional host study destinations in future. Improved domestic teaching and research capacity across emerging economies increases their appeal for students and researchers. Equally, with internationalisation becoming a preoccupation at government and institutional level, a growing emphasis is being placed on quantitative indicators to measure progress and provide international benchmarking. In addition, technological advances have facilitated the rapid worldwide expansion of mass open online courseware (MOOCs) provided by some of the world's best universities.

De Wit argued at the British Council Going Global conference (2012)[2] that the emerging economies and the higher education communities in other parts of the world are altering the landscape of internationalisation and that there is a shift from the 'Western concept' of internationalisation. The concept of internationalisation is certainly becoming broader and multifaceted. However, there is also a shift in the debate from being over-preoccupied with student recruitment to broader collaborations in

---

2. http://ihe.britishcouncil.org/going-global

teaching and research and the wider impacts of internationalisation. The latter became a focal point in the debate at Going Global 2012 on 'rethinking internationalisation' initiated by the International Association of Universities (IAU), where ethical considerations of the consequences of internationalisation were discussed. IAU published their 'Affirming Academic Values in Internationalisation of Higher Education: Call for Action' (IAU, 2012). This notion is echoed in Knight's (2012) five truths about internationalisation, where she explores some of the risks and unintended negative consequences of internationalisation. In her first truth, Knight writes:

> Internationalization acknowledges and builds on national and regional priorities, policies, and practices.

As such, it should not

> overshadow or erode the importance of local context. Thus, internationalization is intended to complement, harmonize, and extend the local dimension — not to dominate it. (Knight, 2012)

Further research is needed to establish whether there is a paradigm shift taking place in the Western concept of internationalisation of education in the context of rapid evolutionary development in the higher education sector globally. Jones and de Wit (2012), in their paper on globalisation of internationalisation, arrive at eight priorities, the first of which is the 'need to learn from other non-western national and cultural contexts — to understand the full extent of internationalisation as a phenomenon and what we can learn from each other in order to benefit students, employers and nations'.

Postscript

Janet Ilieva, Michael Peak and Kevin Van-Cauter have thus presented a fitting empirically rich round-up of the data which underpinned the collection of papers in this book. We hope the book provides the reader with some understanding of how we have reached this point in the internationalisation of education, and some clarity about how things might evolve.

From Going Global 2012 we have a rich tapestry of analysis, viewpoints and trend-spotting. At Going Global 2013 we will see how far these trends have developed, and we will be able to understand more about the importance, significance and influence of the internationalisation of education. (Editors)

References

British Council. (2011). *Students in motion: Forecasting malaysian student mobility to the US*. British Council. Retrieved from http://ihe.britishcouncil.org/educationin telligence/forecasting-malaysian-student-mobility-us

Chien, C.-L. (2012). *Opportunities for global engagement and the role of UNESCO-UIS*. British Council Going Global Conference, London. Retrieved from http://ihe.britishcouncil.org/going-global

Finch, J. (2012, June). *Accessibility, sustainability, excellence: How to expand access to research publications*. Research Information Network. Retrieved from http://www.researchinfonet.org/wp-content/uploads/2012/06/Finch-Group-report-FINAL-VERSION.pdf

Gore, T. (2012). *Higher education across borders: Models of engagement and lessons from corporate strategy*. The Observatory on Borderless Higher Education Report, April. Retrieved from http://www.obhe.ac.uk/documents/view_details?id = 895

HESA Staff Record 2010/11. Copyright *Higher Education Statistics Agency Limited 2011*.

International Association of Universities. (2012). *Affirming academic values in internationalization of higher education: A call for action*. Retrieved from http://www.iau-aiu.net/sites/all/files/Affirming_Academic_Values_in_Internationalization_of_Higher_Education.pdf

Jones, E., & de Wit, H. (2012). Globalization of internationalization: Thematic and regional reflections on a traditional concept. *AUDEM: The International Journal of Higher Education and Democracy, 3*(1).

Knight, J. (2012). Five truths about internationalization. *International Higher Education, 69*(Fall), 4. The Boston College Center for International Higher Education.

Lawton, W., & Katsomitros, A. (2012). *International branch campuses: Data and developments*. The Observatory on Borderless Higher Education Report, January.

Marginson, S. (2012). *Future paths of international higher education*. European Association for International Education. Retrieved from http://www.eaie.org/blog/future-paths-of-international-higher-education. Accessed on 9 October 2012.

OECD. (2012). *Education at a glance*.

Swain, H. (2012). Could universities be sold off? *The Guardian*, 23 April. Retrieved from http://www.guardian.co.uk/education/2012/apr/23/college-of-law-private-sale?CMP = twt_gu. Accessed on 10 October 2012.

The Royal Society. (2011, March). Knowledge, networks and nations: Global scientific collaborations in the 21st century. Retrieved from http://royalsociety.org/uploadedFiles/Royal_Society_Content/Influencing_Policy/Reports/2011-03-28-Knowledge-networks-nations.pdf

Worton, M. (2012). University College London — Big visions, small overseas campuses. *University World News*, Issue No. 219, 29 April.

About the Authors

Professor Dr Mohd Ismail Abd Aziz is the Director in the Office of International Affairs at Universiti Teknologi Malaysia (UTM). He is currently the Chair of Critical Agenda Project (Internationalisation) for Ministry of Higher Education, Malaysia. He has held various administrative positions in UTM for more than 10 years, ranging from Head of Department for External Programmes, Faculty of Science; Deputy Dean for School of Professional and Continuing Education (SPACE); and Deputy Director for Office of International Affairs. He is an applied mathematician specialising in dynamic optimisation methods and its applications. Besides his own specialisation, his other research interest is internationalisation of higher education, with a focus on policies and operational frameworks in operationalising internationalisation activities in individual institutions. He has a PhD from City University, London, in Control Engineering; an MSc degree (Mathematics of Control Systems) from Loughborough University, UK; and a BSc degree (Applied Mathematics and Computer Science) from University of New South Wales, Australia.

Doria Abdullah is a doctoral candidate from the Perdana School of Science, Technology and Innovation Policy, University of Technology Malaysia (UTM). She assists the Office of International Affairs, UTM in research and consultation projects concerning internationalisation of Malaysian higher education. Her current research examines policies that would enhance study and living experiences of international students in Malaysian higher education institutions.

Professor Dinos Arcoumanis is Deputy Vice-Chancellor, International and Development, and Professor of Mechanical Engineering at City University London. He joined City University London in October 2000 and became Dean of the School of Engineering and Mathematical Sciences in 2001. In July 2006 he was appointed Pro-Vice-Chancellor and in 2008 Deputy Vice-Chancellor. Previous experience includes 20 years in various academic positions at Imperial College. Professor Arcoumanis is a Fellow of the UK Institution of Mechanical Engineers, the International Society of Automotive Engineers and the Royal Academy of Engineering. In 2009 he received an honorary doctorate from St Petersburg State Polytechnic University of Russia and in 2010 an honorary professorship from Tianjin University of China. He holds degrees in Physics (Aristotelian University of Thessaloniki, Greece, 1973) and Engineering (University of California at

Irvine, USA, 1980), a PhD in Mechanical Engineering (Imperial College, London, 1984) and a DSc (Eng) from the University of London.

Dr Graeme Atherton has been in the field of widening access to higher education since 1995. After Philosophy, Politics and Economics at Oxford he completed a doctorate at the University of Liverpool looking at access to higher education for working class adults. He spent five years at Liverpool Hope University as Associate Dean, Widening Participation before managing the Aimhigher Central London Partnership and then becoming Executive Director of the Aimhigher London West Central and North (WECAN) Partnership. Aimhigher, one of the largest projects in the world committed to HE access worked with over 200,000 young people, ended in July 2011. Dr Atherton is now Director of AccessHE, an independent, non-governmental organisation enabling higher education institutions to collaborate in widening access activities in London. He has founded and is Director of a professional organisation for the widening access to HE community in the United Kingdom called NEON (National Education Opportunities Network). Dr Atherton is visiting professor in Higher Education and Social Mobility Practice at London Metropolitan University and has two books scheduled for publication in 2013: *Is 50% enough? Why we need to raise participation in Higher Education and How to Do It* and *How can we make Higher Education Fair?* He has produced over 80 publications and conference papers, and spoken in over 10 countries on widening access including Australia, the United States and Canada.

Gareth Barham started his career in the early 1990s as an industrial design consultant and won a prestigious business award for his services to industry. He went on to be appointed to the position of Product Development Manager at a design-led organisation in the United Kingdom where he worked for a number of years before moving to the Cardiff School of Art and Design at Cardiff Metropolitan University where he is Principal Lecturer in product design and is involved in course delivery and fostering creativity and innovative design practices on both the Bachelors and Masters degree courses. He also delivers professional development workshops for academics in the United Kingdom and internationally (most recently in Brunei, Malaysia and South Korea). He has collaborated with the Welsh Joint Education Committee on issues relating to pedagogical creativity in design and technology teaching in schools. In addition to his teaching, research and consultancy activities, he is the International Development Manager for the Cardiff School of Art and Design. As a product designer, he believes that his systematic thinking and organisational skills have helped to develop strategies for implementing internationalisation theory into the curriculum and his creative skills have helped to overcome resistance that is sometimes associated with change.

Dr Jo Beall joined the British Council and its Executive Board in July 2011 as Director, Education and Society. She was formerly Deputy Vice-Chancellor, University of Cape Town, with responsibility for academic matters, social responsiveness and external relations and the University's internationalisation strategy. A graduate of the London School of Economics, Dr Beall joined its academic staff in the early 1990s, first in the Department of Social Policy and then the Development Studies Institute, which she directed between 2004 and 2007. She has published or co-published numerous books and articles in the areas of gender and social policy, social development, local governance, cities and conflict and state fragility. Her work in the field of international development spans 20 years and has taken her to Africa, Asia and Latin America, with significant periods of research time in Afghanistan, Pakistan, India and South Africa. Her move to the British Council signals her commitment to education and particularly higher education as a force for global, national and individual good. She has been a Fellow of Goodenough College since 2000, currently serves on the Council of the Overseas Development Institute and the British Academy's Area Panel for South Asia and has served the Higher Education Funding Council for England on the 2008 Research Assessment Exercise and on the current Research Excellence Framework's Panel for Anthropology and Development.

Dr Vera Bondarenko is an Associate Professor of the Oil-Gas Practice and Director of the Research Institute for Education Issues at M. Auezov South Kazakhstan State University.

She is a specialist in the field of processes and apparatuses for the chemical and petrochemical industries. Her focus of scientific interest is the intensification of heat-and-mass transfer processes, issues of development and exploitation of oil and gas fields, and quality management system of HELs. She has an international certificate in TQM and a certificate in ISO 9000:2001. She is a recipient of the "Honourable Worker in Education of the Republic of Kazakhstan" and "USSR Inventor" awards.

Vera Bondarenko carries out research on the basis of the national grant "Formation of qualification framework of specialists on the basis of competence approach and outcomes oriented teaching." As a member of the working group of the Ministry of Education and Science, she is involved in the development of criteria of classification for the HEIs of the Republic. She is an expert auditor of the independent Kazakhstan Assurance Quality Agency.

Vera is a graduate of the Kazakh Chemical-Technological Institute in Refrigerating Machines and Apparatuses. She is the author of over 120 published scientific works, among them 12 patents and author's certificates.

Michael Carrier is Head of English Language Innovation, British Council, London. He is also currently serving on the Board of the European Association for Quality Language Services (EAQUALS) organisation as Special Advisor, and is a member of the Board of Oxford University Press's *ELT Journal* and Cambridge University Press's *Language Teaching* journal. He is a Fellow of the Royal Society of Arts, a Member of the Institute of Directors, a Member of the Society of Authors, London, the Editor of the Technology section of Modern English Teacher, and was recently Associate Professor at New School University, New York. Michael Carrier was formerly Executive Director of Eurocentres in Washington, DC and until 2008 CEO of the International House World network of schools. He has been involved in English language training (ELT) for over 30 years as a teacher, trainer, author, school director and network director. He has worked in Germany, Italy, Poland, UK and the United States, and lectured in many other countries worldwide. He has written a number of ELT coursebooks and skills books, including the *Front Page* series, *Business Circles*, *Intermediate Writing Skills* and *Spotlight Readers*. His special field of interest is in e-learning and the application of technology to language leaching.

Dr David X. Cheng is Associate Vice-President responsible for international affairs at City University of Hong Kong. He previously served as Assistant Dean at Columbia College and School of Engineering and Applied Science, Executive Director for international dual degree programmes in the Office of the Provost, and Adjunct Professor at Teachers College, Columbia University. He was also Executive Director of Columbia Global Center in Beijing. He has published extensively in the areas of higher education research and assessment in both English and Chinese.

Chiao-Ling Chien is a researcher and data analyst on tertiary education at the UNESCO Institute for Statistics. She has co-authored UNESCO reports on the subject of academic mobility and higher education, including *Cross-Border Student Mobility: The Changing Global Landscape*, and *Global Education Digest*. She is a doctoral candidate in the Higher Education programme at the University of Minnesota. She is the recipient of fellowships for international and national data policy training awarded by the Association for Institutional Research, the National Science Foundation, and the National Center for Education Statistics in the United States.

Professor Hans de Wit is Director of the Centre for Higher Education Internationalisation of the Università Cattolica Sacro Cuore in Milan and

Professor of Internationalisation of Higher Education at the Centre for Applied Research in Economics and Management (CAREM), School of Economics and Management of the Amsterdam University of Applied Sciences. He is the Co-Editor of the *Journal of Studies in International Education*. He is a visiting professor at the Centre for Academic Practice and Research in Internationalisation of Leeds Metropolitan University, UK.

He has (co-)written several books and articles on international education and is actively involved in assessment and consultancy in international education, for the European Commission, UNESCO, World Bank, IMHE/OECD, NVAO and ESMU. His latest books are: *Sage Handbook on International Higher Education* (co-author), and *Trends, Issues and Challenges in Internationalisation of Higher Education*. He writes a bimonthly blog on internationalisation of higher education for *University World News*.

Hans de Wit is founding member and past president of the European Association for International Education (EAIE). Currently he is Member of the Board of Trustees of World Education Services (New York), Member of the ESL TOEFL Board, Co-Chair of the Special Interest Group Research in International Education of EAIE, and Member of the Consell Assessor de l'Institut Internacional de Postgrau at the Open University of Catalonia.

Eva Egron-Polak is Secretary-General of the International Association of Universities (IAU), an international non-governmental organisation based at UNESCO in Paris, France. Bringing together higher education institutions and associations from every region, the IAU is committed to strengthening higher education worldwide by providing a global forum for leaders, undertaking research and analysis, disseminating information and taking up advocacy positions in the interest of quality higher education being available to all. With substantial experience in international co-operation in higher education, and now as head of the IAU, Eva Egron-Polak is engaged with many of the most pressing issues in current higher education policy debates globally, such as internationalisation, cross-border higher education, higher education for sustainable development, and equitable access to higher education, among others. Before joining the IAU, she was Vice-President, International of the Association of Universities and Colleges of Canada. She was educated in the Czech Republic, Canada and France.

Chandra J. Embuldeniya is the founder and first Vice-Chancellor of Uva-Wellassa University. He is the first person from the private sector to have been invited by the government of Sri Lanka to establish a new university from scratch. He served the university for over six years, developing a new vision and a robust strategy to meet its future needs. Starting with identification of the location, he designed, developed, recruited academic and non-academic staff members, trained them, enrolled students and ensured that they were ready for local and global markets. He developed an effective strategy that caters to contemporary needs locally and globally.

Jelena Gledic is an Assistant Professor of Chinese Studies at the University of Belgrade. She is also a Project Associate for the EU TEMPUS project Reforming Foreign Language Studies in Serbia (REFLESS) and a senior associate at Petnica Science Center in Serbia. She is experienced in designing and implementing both short-term and semester courses and workshops on high-school and university levels, as part of a traditional degree and as extra-curricular activities. She has published several articles on education, as well as in the field of cultural studies, and she regularly participates in relevant conferences and workshops. She holds a Masters degree and is currently a PhD candidate in Cultural Studies at the University of Belgrade.

Tim Gore is Director, Global Networks and Communities for the University of London International Programmes. His main role is to maintain and expand the network of teaching institutions and communities of students and alumni worldwide. Currently this represents over 52,000 students in nearly 190 countries and a network of over 120 independent teaching centers.

He was previously the Director of the Centre for Indian Business, the University of Greenwich and led their award winning international strategy for India. In addition, Tim has worked closely with educationalists, institutions, companies and governments to improve bilateral and multi-lateral educational links in Hong Kong, Singapore, United Arab Emirates, Jordan and India in his earlier role at the British Council. Tim is pursuing a doctorate in business administration (DBAHEM) at the University of Bath focusing on higher education management. He also holds two masters as an applied linguist and in business administration. He speaks Arabic and French. He was awarded an OBE for services to the British Council in June 2008.

Professor Colin B. Grant is Pro-Vice-Chancellor of the University of Bath. He was formerly the inaugural Pro-Vice-Chancellor of International Relations at the University of Surrey (2009–2012). Before this he was Head of the School of Arts, Communication and Humanities there before becoming Dean of International Relations.

He served as inaugural chair of the University Global Partnership Network, which includes the University of Surrey, North Carolina State University and São Paulo University, and has partnership relations with Fapesp and Banco Santander. He also led the South East–India Partnership Network consortium with IISER Pune, India.

Professor Grant was responsible for oversight of the running of the Surrey International Institute-DUFE, a joint academic partnership institution between the University of Surrey and Dongbei University of Finance and Economics (DUFE) in Dalian, China. He was inaugural chair of the University International Relations Committee (2008–2012) and International Advisory Board (2010–2012).

After taking his PhD at Bath in 1993, he was a DAAD/CNPq postdoctoral fellow in the LUMIS-Institut, University of Siegen (Germany), and has devoted his research career to the philosophy of communication, a field in which he has published nine books.

Professor Grant is a fluent writer and speaker of French, German and Portuguese and a learner of Chinese, Spanish and Korean. He is also an alumnus of the Leadership Foundation Top Management Programme.

Dr Julia Haes is a Senior Programme Manager at the Center for International Cooperation at Freie Universität Berlin. She studied business administration at Ludwig-Maximilians University, Munich and California State University San Bernardino, California. Julia completed her PhD studies on university brands at the University of St. Gallen, Switzerland, where she also co-developed and administered the international Executive MBA in Media and Communication, the pioneer of international postgraduate programmes at the university, and set up several Executive Education programmes for multinational corporations. Prior to joining Free University, she worked for an Executive Search firm specialised in the media industry. Julia currently manages various aspects of strategic internationalisation at Freie Universität Berlin, such as the development of strategic partnerships, the development of joint degree programmes and supervises some of Freie Universität's liaison offices.

Dr Abe Harraf is a tenured professor of Management at the Monfort College of Business at the University of Northern Colorado. During 2007–2011, he served as the Provost and Senior Vice-President, leading the academic and student affairs divisions that included enrolment management, academic colleges, Dean of Students, libraries, academic and student support services, sponsored programmes, graduate school, assessment centre, centre for international education and multi-cultural centres. Dr Harraf had budgetary responsibility for the Division of Academic and Student Affairs. He worked closely with the academic Deans and Directors, leading the implementation of the academic plan of the university. Prior to this he served as Provost at the Southern Utah University for five years, and as the Chief Academic Officer at Daytona Beach Campus of Embry Riddle University. He has been instrumental in leading these institutions to gain national rankings for academic programmes and campuses, turning around enrolment declines, and improving student retention and graduation rates. Dr Harraf has consulted with numerous national and international public and private institutions and businesses on strategic management, pricing strategies and customer relations. He received his PhD in Economics from Utah State University and MBA and MEd from Sul Ross State University.

Professor John Hearn is Chief Executive of the Worldwide Universities Network. He is Vice-President (International) of the University of Sydney, responsible for international engagement and internationalisation, and Professor of Physiology (Medical School) at the University of Sydney. He was awarded his PhD from the Australian National University (ANU) and has served for six to seven years each in leading research, teaching and administrative positions at the Universities of Edinburgh, London UCL, Wisconsin, ANU and Sydney. He is a graduate of the Australian Institute of Company Directors. He has published 190 research papers and edited 6 books in reproduction and fertility, stem cell biology and biotechnology. A committed international citizen, he has worked globally in research capacity development, especially in China, India, Thailand, Kenya and Brazil. He is a senior scientific adviser to the World Health Organisation in research for human reproduction, and the Australian Government in higher education, science and international partnerships. He is a Board member of the Australian Nuclear Science and Technology Organisation, and Chairman of the Board of the Sydney Confucius Institute. He is an advisor and board member to OECD for the Programmes on Internationalisation of Higher Education; Innovation, Higher Education and Research for Development; and previously for Bio-economy Futures 2030.

Professor Alex Hughes, as Pro-Vice-Chancellor External, leads the University of Kent's Internationalisation and Student Experience strategies. She is responsible for the University's International and European activities, Information Services, Student Services and the Centre for English and World Languages, as well as Kent's centre in Brussels. Professor Hughes was formerly Pro-Vice-Chancellor for Quality and Students at the University of Birmingham and, before that, she was Head of the School of Humanities and Professor of Twentieth-Century French Literature at the University.

Christine Humfrey is a Special Professor and Management Consultant in International Higher Education. She has spent her career in the university sector and was the founding Director of the International Office at the University of Nottingham. She has researched, published, taught and advised on internationalisation, international marketing and the development of the university sector in the United Kingdom. She has undertaken consultancies for Universities UK, the British Council, the Danish Government and UKCISA, including the project report *TNE and the Student Experience* for the Prime Minister's Initiative for International Education. Christine Humfrey is a Commonwealth Scholarship Commissioner and is advising on several international Masters programmes.

Dr Janet Ilieva is a Senior Education Adviser with the British Council, Hong Kong. Her area of expertise is policy analysis of education systems across the world and their openness to international engagement. Her recent research studies focus on the future shape of internationalisation of higher education and its impact on universities' core activities — university research and teaching. Dr Ilieva has been with the British Council for nine years. She is a member of the advisory group for Project Atlas (a global student mobility think-tank based with the Institute for International Education, USA) and the Association for Studies in International Education (on behalf of the British Council). Janet has 17 years' experience with different education systems across Europe and, most recently, East Asia. She holds a PhD in Macroeconomics. Before joining the British Council, she lectured in Economics at the University of Veliko Turnovo (Bulgaria) and was a guest lecturer at the University of Applied Sciences in Ludwigsburg (Germany) and the University of Calabria (Italy).

James Otieno Jowi is the founding Executive Director and Secretary General of the African Network for Internationalisation of Education (ANIE). He also teaches Comparative and International Education at the School of Education, Moi University, Kenya. He has published on the internationalisation of higher education, especially in Africa, and has also presented conference papers on the subject. His other research interests are in governance, management and leadership in higher education. He was member of the IAU Task Force on the Third Global Survey on Internationalisation of Higher Education. He is also a member of the IAU Ad-hoc Expert Group on Rethinking Internationalisation. He holds a Bachelor of Education and Masters in Linguistics from Moi University (Kenya), a Masters in Comparative and International Education from the University of Oslo, Norway and is finalising doctoral studies in Higher Education Studies at CHEPS, University of Twente, Netherlands.

Professor Kazuo Kitahara served as the Chair of the Science Council of Japan's Quality Assurance of Higher Education Committee, convened between 2008 and 2010. The Committee produced a report entitled 'Quality Assurance Framework for University Education' which generated a wide-ranging discussion on the nature and purpose of degree-level education, involving both the higher education sector and the public.

Professor Kitahara obtained his Bachelors and Masters degrees in Physics from the University of Tokyo, and his doctorate from the Free University of Brussels. He is currently a professor in the Graduate School of Science Education, Tokyo University of Science, and is professor emeritus of Tokyo Institute of Technology and International Christian University.

Kairat Kurakbayev is an educational researcher based at the Centre for Educational Policy, Nazarbayev University, Kazakhstan. His research interests focus on higher education policy, quality and governance in the higher education sector as well as professional development (formal, informal, institutional, self-managed), reflective practice and adult education.

Before joining the Centre for Educational Policy, he served as an acting director of the Department for Strategic Planning at Gumilyov Eurasian National University, Astana. His professional experience includes developing a long-term strategy of an academic institution, applying for institutional rankings on both national and global levels, designing documents for cross-department strategic planning based on the governmental policy of higher education. He previously served as a Deputy Director of the Department for International Collaboration at Gumilyov Eurasian National University.

Kairat Kurakbayev was awarded the British Council and American Councils academic scholarships in 2004 and 2008 respectively. The former led him to graduate with an MEd degree from the University of Exeter, UK while the latter let him participate in a semester-long junior faculty development programme at the Department of Educational Leadership, Management and Policy, Seton Hall University, New Jersey, USA.

Dr Javaid R. Laghari is Chairperson and Federal Minister of the Higher Education Commission of Pakistan. Previously he was a Senator in the Pakistan Senate, and President of SZABIST, a leading multi-campus private university. He was also Professor of Electrical and Computer Engineering and served as Director of Graduate Studies and at the State University of New York (SUNY) at Buffalo, USA. Dr Laghari has published over 120 research papers, presented over 70 papers, and published three books. He has also taken part in hundreds of television and print media interviews. He attended the NATO Advanced Study Institute in the United Kingdom in 1991 and the NATO Advanced Study Institute in Italy in 1983. He was Chairman of the 1992 IEEE International Conference on High Voltage Engineering, USA, and has organised many international conferences and chaired numerous sessions and workshops. He has also served as the Chairman of the Technical Standards Committee on Radiation Effects, and is the author of the IEEE Standard 775-1993. Dr Laghari is the recipient of the Distinguished Leadership Award (1987), the IEEE Award for Leadership and Dedicated Services (1994) and the coveted national award, Tamgha-e-Imtiaz, conferred by the President of Pakistan in 1998.

Dr Jayasree Anitha Menon holds a Masters in Applied Psychology and Psychological Services from the University of Madras, India and a PhD in Health Psychology from the University of Nottingham, UK. She is Head of Psychology the Department, University of Zambia and the Chairperson for the University of Zambia Committee on HIV and AIDS. She is involved in various research and service-related projects pertaining to areas of public interest, and has written a number of peer-reviewed publications. Her research interests include: applying psychological principles in prevention and management of chronic illness with a special interest in enhancing the quality of life of HIV-positive adolescents; communication skills of health practitioners in patient care, health-related decision-making and adherence to treatment and stress management in enhancing the physical and psychological well-being of adolescents. Dr Menon has also been involved in various national and international research projects and has been the team leader for several, including a DFID-funded Development for Higher Education (DelPHE) partnership and Norad-funded Masters programme (NOMA). Dr Menon spearheaded the formulation of the University of Zambia's HIV and AIDS policy. She is the recipient of the Best Professor of Psychology award for 2012 from World Education Congress.

Professor Louise Morley AcSS is Professor of Education and Director of the Centre for Higher Education and Equity Research at the University of Sussex, UK. She has an international profile in the field of the sociology of gender in higher education studies. Her research and publication interests focus on international higher education policy, gender, equity, micropolitics, quality, leadership and power. She has given keynote presentations, undertaken research and consultancy and has been a visiting academic in almost 50 countries.

She has recently completed an ESRC/DFID funded research project on Widening Participation in Higher Education in Ghana and Tanzania, and is currently working on the knowledge exchange of this project (http://www.sussex.ac.uk/education/cheer/wphegt). She has held research grants from the Economic and Social Research Council, the UK Department for International Development, the Carnegie Corporation of New York, the Higher Education Funding Council for England, the British Council and the Leadership Foundation. She is on the editorial boards for *Studies in Higher Education, Gender and Education, Teaching in Higher Education*, and on the International Advisory Boards for *Education, Citizenship and Social Justice* and *Studies in Research: Training, Evaluation and Impact.*

Professor Morley is an Academician of the Academy of Social Sciences, a Fellow of the Society for Research into Higher Education, and a Senior Research Fellow, Centre for Gender Excellence, University of Örebro, Sweden.

Jasmina Nikolic is a Higher Education Reform Expert at the Ministry of Education, Science and Technological Development, in the Republic of Serbia. She is Project Manager for the TEMPUS REFLESS project that aims to reform foreign language studies in Serbia. She also teaches Spanish literature at the University of Belgrade, Serbia, and works as researcher in the field of orality, literacy and digitacy. She is a Bologna expert for curriculum innovation, internationalisation and collaboration between higher education institutions and enterprises. She was at the head of the first Bologna-compliant accreditation process of foreign language studies at the University of Belgrade, involved in instructional design and consulting. She is a global pioneer in transferring Agile methodologies from the world of software development into the field of higher education and instructional design. She is a Certified Scrum Master, Certified Product Owner, Open Space facilitator and agile practitioner. She worked for the Spanish Agency for International Cooperation and Development and Spanish and Catalan Ombudsman as a Serbian co-ordinator of the project Free Legal Aid in Serbia. She regularly publishes articles and research papers, and participates in relevant conferences and workshops.

Kulyanda Nurasheva is Professor and Director of the Monitoring and Quality Management Centre of M. Auezov South Kazakhstan State University. She has worked as Instructor, Associate Professor and Head of Department at the Kazakh Chemical-Technological Institute, and Dean of Faculty, Director of the Institute for Economics and Business, and Vice-President for Science and Development at MIRAS University.

In 2002 she won the Carana Corporation's Central Asian contest for her case study titled *Survival of company and factors of success.* In 2003 she received a grant from Accel Partners, EdNet for a programme titled *Visiting Professor.* She has also received grants from EdNet, AED, and CARANA for the development of a study guide titled *Business Ethics and Corruption.* In 2004 she received a grant from the US Embassy in Kazakhstan and, as a member of the Visiting International Professor programme, visited several universities and colleges there. In 2008 she won Kazakhstan's Ministry of Education and Science award for the best university instructor.

Professor Nurasheva is a graduate of the Kazakh Chemical-Technological Institute in Economy and Organization of Chemical Industry. In 1975 she defended her thesis at the Moscow Institute of Management. She is the author of over 270 published scientific works.

Dr Milton Odhiambo Obamba is a Research Fellow at the Centre for Higher Education Research at Leeds Metropolitan University, where he has been Carnegie Centenary Scholar since 2007 until he received his PhD in 2011. Dr Obamba is an Associate Lecturer in the School of Politics and Applied Global Studies at the Leeds Metropolitan University. He is also Research Associate of the John and Elnora Ferguson Centre for African Studies at the University of Bradford. Obamba received the MPhil in international education from the Norweigan Teacher Academy (Norsk Laerekademiet), Bergen in 2005 where he was recipient of NORAD Scholarship. He has served as visiting researcher at Nordic Africa Institute in Uppsala University, Sweden, as well as the African Studies Centre at Leiden University, Netherlands. Dr Obamba's current research interests focus on the interdisciplinary domains of higher education and development, including policy analysis, governance, international and comparative education, international development, and transnational research partnerships. Some of his most recent publications have appeared in various peer-reviewed arenas, including the *Higher Education Policy*, *Compare: A Journal of Comparative and International Education*, *Journal of Higher Education in Africa*, and *The Sage Handbook of International Higher Education* (2012).

Michael Peak is the Education research manager at the British Council. He trained in research methods and statistics and has experience of researching international higher education since 2005. He has been integral to the development and management of research projects covering different aspects of international education including Student Insight (a global survey of over 160,000 prospective international students), Students in Motion (a study which forecasts international student mobility), and the Global Gauge (measuring and benchmarking the internationalisation activities of different countries).

He co-authored *The Shape of Things to Come: Higher Education Global Trends and Emerging Opportunities to 2020* — a piece of research which details the impact of demographic and economic drivers on the changing higher education landscape in the next decade. Other research includes an investigation to establish the fundamental drivers for aspiring higher education hub countries, and identification of countries presenting significant potential for TNE providers.

Alejandra Ma. Vilalta y Perdomo is a senior member of the Tecnológico de Monterrey Educational System, a leading private multi-campus university in Mexico, where she is Director of Internationalization and Student Affairs at the Mexico City Metropolitan Rectory.

She served on five different campuses of the Tecnológico de Monterrey in several positions, including full-time Professor, Director of Graduate Programmes, Dean of School and Campus President.

She has been the driving force behind the creation and development of new academic projects, departments, schools, campuses as well as in negotiations and agreements with enterprises, institutions and universities in countries in America, Europe, Africa and Asia.

Her fields of academic and consulting expertise include: internationalisation, entrepreneurship, social community development, human capital, human resources, development and training, executive protocol and franchising. (She was co-author of a book on franchising development published by McGraw-Hill in 1997.) She has given lectures in Brazil, Canada, El Salvador, Finland, Mexico, The Netherlands, Spain, the United Kingdom and the United States.

She also manifested civic engagement being an active member of different community groups and associations, leading some of their boards.

She holds several different individual and team merit awards.

Professor Wendy Purcell was appointed Vice-Chancellor and Chief Executive of Plymouth University in December 2007. She was previously Deputy Vice-Chancellor at the University of Hertfordshire, and before this Dean of Applied Sciences and Pro Vice-Chancellor (Research) at the University of the West of England, Bristol. She is Professor of Biomedicine and holds a degree in Biological Sciences and a PhD in Immunopharmacology. She acted as a Special Adviser to the Department of Business, Innovation and Skills on the Postgraduate Review and is a Member of the Medical Education England Healthcare Science Board. She is current Chair of the Healthcare Science Strategic Advisory Group. Professor Purcell extended her current role with the Medical Education England Healthcare Science Programme Board to assume the role of Chair of the Healthcare Science Clinical Academic Careers Strategy Group. Professor Purcell has an international reputation in her field of biomedical research and led a number of research teams in developing cell culture models for preclinical studies. Funded by industry, medical charities, Research Councils UK and the EU, she attracted millions in research grants, published widely and had patents applications filed on her work.

Professor Dr Cameron Richards is Professor of Policy Studies based in the Perdana School of Science, Technology and Innovation Policy on the international campus of the University of Technology Malaysia. His current academic work and interests focus on policy studies and research, and ways of assisting both postgraduate students and colleagues with more effective models and practices of academic research inquiry, academic writing and general knowledge-building. As well as having worked previously at the Queensland University of Technology and the University of Western Australia, he has also worked extensively in Asia including past positions at the Singapore National Institute of Education and the Hong Kong Institute of Education.

Currently he serves as Consultant to set up a major university campus for UCLan.

Ingo Rollwagen is a Senior Analyst for Deutsche Bank Research, the think-tank of Deutsche Bank and adjunct faculty at the Berlin Institute of Technology (Technische Universität Berlin). His work consists of corporate foresight and strategic support for the board members and clients of Deutsche Bank as well as stakeholders. He monitors developments in education systems and markets, identifying emerging value-creation opportunities of different industries in the structural transition knowledge economy. Before joining Deutsche Bank Research, he worked for several years for DaimlerChrysler's Society and Technology Research Group in Berlin, on foresight and strategic projects for different business units of DaimlerChrysler and other institutions. Ingo Rollwagen has a strong background in technical studies, sociology, strategic communication, business administration, organisational design, economics and moderation techniques. He has worked as an expert for the European Commission on Global Europe in 2050, several regional and national governments and other institutions concerning education, lifelong learning, technology assessment, foresight and future technological, societal and economic developments.

Dr Aida Sagintayeva is the Director of the Centre for Educational Policy at Nazarbayev University in Kazakhstan. Before joining the Centre, Dr Sagintayeva was vice-rector for international co-operation at Eurasian National University, Astana. She has been involved in educational research projects for the Kazakhstan Ministry of Education and Science on introducing a three-tiered degree system: Bachelor — Masters — PhD. She co-ordinated the launch of PhD programmes at Eurasian National University.

Dr Sagintayeva was President of the national operator for the Bolashak International Scholarship of the President of the Republic of Kazakhstan Centre for International Programmes. She began her academic career at Taraz State University where she worked for six years after graduating.

In 2008 Dr Sagintayeva was awarded a Junior Faculty Development Programme fellowship funded by the US Department of State's Bureau of Educational and Cultural Affairs and administrated by the American Council for Collaboration in Education and Language Study.

Her teaching experience includes designing three new courses in the initial teacher education curriculum: the US Education System (as a part of courses in American studies); Media and Politics; and a Pre-Dissertation Seminar. Dr Sagintayeva's research interests include educational policy, educational administration, higher education management, internationalisation of higher education and educational leadership.

Sir Patrick Stewart is Chancellor of the University of Huddersfield. An internationally respected actor, renowned for successfully bridging the gap between the Shakespearean stage and contemporary film and television, he is best known for his roles as Captain Jean-Luc Picard in *Star Trek: The Next Generation* and as Professor Xavier in 20th Century Fox's *X-Men* movies. He has won many awards for his work in television, including nominations for the Golden Globe, Emmy and Screen Actors Guild. An Honorary Associate Artist of the Royal Shakespeare Company (he was made an Associate Artist in 1967) he has played many major Shakespeare roles to great acclaim. In 2006 he starred in *Antony and Cleopatra* and *The Tempest*, and in 2007 in *Macbeth*, for which he received the *Evening Standard* Best Actor Award and a Tony Best Actor nomination on Broadway. In 2009 he starred with Sir Ian McKellen in the sold-out production of *Waiting for Godot*. He was knighted in 2010. He takes his involvement with the University extremely seriously, spending as much time as possible with staff and students. He is Professor of Performing Arts at the University and regularly delivers sessions for drama students.

Dr Mary Stiasny is Pro-Director, Learning and International, Institute of Education, UK. She joined the Institute of Education from the British Council in July 2007, as Associate Director with responsibility for Learning and Teaching and oversight of International Strategy. She began her working life as a secondary school teacher of Social Sciences at Holland Park School. She joined Goldsmiths College in 1975 as a Lecturer in Sociology with responsibility for the Social Sciences subject specialism on the PGCE programme. In 1992 she moved within Goldsmiths to the Department of Education as Director of the Secondary PGCE, and subsequently Deputy Head of Department. She joined Oxford Brookes University as Deputy Head of School, followed by five years at the University of Greenwich as Head of the School of Education and Training (Dean equivalent). Mary Stiasny subsequently spent almost four years at the British Council as Director of Education and Training. She has written and spoken extensively about internationalism in education, taking the lead for the United Kingdom in working with the education sector recruiting overseas students, developing partnerships and enabling staff and students to develop an international outlook. She has been a member of the UK UNESCO Education Committee, and a Director of the UK UNESCO National Commission.

Professor Dame Joan K. Stringer became Principal and Vice-Chancellor of Edinburgh Napier University in January 2003, having previously served as Principal and Vice Patron of Queen Margaret University College, Edinburgh. She began her career in education in 1980 and became Head of the School of Public Administration and Law and later Assistant Principal at Robert Gordon University. Dame Joan has contributed to a number of policy initiatives through external organisations, committees and working groups, which included membership of the Scottish Committee of Dearing and UK HE Student Mobility Joint Working Group. Her current positions include: Board Member, Higher Education Statistics Agency; Board Member, Universities and Colleges Admissions Service; Board Member, National Theatre of Scotland; and Trustee of the David Hume Institute. Dame Joan's achievements have been recognised across and beyond the sector. She was recognised as the Public Sector Leader of the Year (2011) at the Scottish Leadership Awards. In 2001 Dame Joan was awarded a CBE for Services to Higher Education and an Hon. DLitt from the University of Keele for her contribution to higher education and public service. In 2009 she was awarded a DBE for services to Local and National Higher Education. Other accolades include an Honorary Citizenship of Shandong, conferred in 2007and awarded an Honorary Doctorate from University of Edinburgh in 2011.

Vangelis Tsiligiris is an economist, and for the past 10 years has been setting up, leading and managing transnational higher education partnerships between private for-profit education institutions and UK universities. Currently he is the Principal of MBS College. He has recently completed his PhD thesis at Birmingham City University, titled *Cross Border Higher Education and Quality Management: The applicability of the customer model in managing quality in transnational higher education partnerships*.

He is an academic board member of the assessment committee of EDU, and a Fellow of the Chartered Management Institute. Vangelis has conducted research on internationalization of higher education, TNE and international student mobility, student expectations and perceptions in the global context, quality management in the globalized higher education, and on the cultural influence on quality of higher education.

He is using social media to participate in the dialogue about the recent developments in international higher education and he has contributed in major media such as the *Guardian HE*, *Times Higher Education*, *University World News*, and the *ScienceGuide*.

Kevin Van-Cauter is Higher Education Adviser at the British Council. He advises on higher education policy in the United Kingdom, and specialises in the areas of transnational education (TNE) and education partnerships. He managed the higher education partnerships strand of the second Prime Minister's Initiative for International Education (PMI2) until the programme ended in March 2011. He was a member of the UK government's e-learning task force 2010–2011. Before that, Kevin Van-Cauter's roles included advising on distance learning policy and marketing UK education. He has written several articles on UK transnational education and student mobility and has presented at numerous conferences on the subject. He co-authored *Vision 2020* (published in 2003), the British Council's first attempt at forecasting international student mobility. His current work in TNE includes the development of a major piece of research on the impact and future of TNE, to be launched at Going Global in Dubai in March 2013.

Professor Dr Maurits van Rooijen is Chief Executive of the academic division of Global University Systems and Rector/CEO of the London School for Business and Finance.

Previously, Professor Dr Maurits van Rooijen FRSA was the Rector Magnificus of Nyenrode Business University. Van Rooijen is also Professor of Academic Entrepreneurship, Internationalisation and Innovation in Higher Education at Nyenrode.

Van Rooijen is an economic historian who obtained his doctorate at University of Utrecht on the theme of green urbanisation. He has held positions at several universities, including University of Leiden, Erasmus University Rotterdam and Victoria University in Melbourne. As a visiting professor, Van Rooijen has been associated with a variety of educational institutions worldwide.

Van Rooijen also holds various international administrative positions. He is Co-Chairman of the World Association for Cooperative Education, Boston, USA, which supports work-integrated learning, and President of the Compostela Group of Universities in Santiago de Compostela, Spain, an association that stimulates cooperation and dialogue in the field of higher education. Van Rooijen is also Vice-President of the London-based European Access Network, that encourages under-represented groups to participate in higher education, and was Chairman of the Managing Board of the Euro-Mediterranean University in Slovenia, an initiative of the European Parliament.

Colin Walters is Chief Executive Officer at Australian Education International (AEI). AEI is the international education arm of the Australian Government Department of Innovation, Industry, Science, Research and

Tertiary Education (DIISRTE). Colin Walters joined AEI in January 2009 from the Higher Education Group in the Department of Education Employment and Workplace Relations. His responsibilities in the Higher Education Group included policy, core funding for universities, student loan programmes and quality and accountability issues. He is a current Director of the Australian-American Fulbright Commission. He has held a number of senior appointments in government, including Group Manager of the Science Group and the Vocational Education and Training Group, Director of the National Centre for Vocational Education Research and as a member of the National Training Quality Council. Previously, Colin Walters was a member of the Senior Executive Service of the Department of Prime Minister and Cabinet where his responsibilities included the passage of the historic first Native Title Act in 1993. He spent much of his earlier career in the United Kingdom, including developing the Scientific and Technology Group for the UK Police Service as Assistant Under-Secretary of State, Home Office. He also served as Principal Private Secretary to four UK Cabinet ministers.

Dr Ian Willis is the Director of Studies for the Postgraduate Certificate in Learning and Teaching in Higher Education at the University of Liverpool. He has been involved in a number of consultancy projects to enhance learning and teaching including work in Syria, Canada, Ghana, Tanzania and Malawi. He is the University of Liverpool based Director of a collaborative project with the University of Health Sciences in Lahore to help build capacity for the development of learning and teaching in medical education in the Punjab. The three-year project is funded by the British Council and the Higher Education Commission in Pakistan. It is based on capacity building of systems and structures, staff development for learning and teaching and research and evaluation for sustainable local practice. Ian is also a course developer and tutor on the University's online professional doctorate (EdD Higher Education).